Critical Muslim 45

Transitions

Critical Muslim is published quarterly by C. Hurst & Co. (Publishers) Ltd. on behalf of and in conjunction with Critical Muslim Ltd. and the Muslim Institute, London.

All editorial correspondence to Muslim Institute, Canopi, 7-14 Great Dover Street, London, SE1 4YR
E-mail: editorial@criticalmuslim.com

C. Hurst & Co (Publishers) Ltd., New Wing, Somerset House, Strand, London, WC2R 1LA

ISBN: 9781787389571 ISSN: 2048-8475

To subscribe or place an order by credit/debit card or cheque (pounds sterling only) please contact Kathleen May at the Hurst address above or e-mail kathleen@hurstpub.co.uk

A one-year subscription, inclusive of postage (four issues), costs £50 (UK), £65 (Europe) and £75 (rest of the world), this includes full access to the *Critical Muslim* series and archive online. Digital only subscription is £3.30 per month.

A Cataloguing-in-Publication data record for this book is available from the British Library

Critical Muslim

Subscribe to Critical Muslim

Now in its twelfth year in print, *Critical Muslim* is also available online. Users can access the site for just £3.30 per month – or for those with a print subscription it is included as part of the package. In return, you'll get access to everything in the series (including our entire archive), and a clean, accessible reading experience for desktop computers and handheld devices — entirely free of advertising.

Full subscription

The print edition of *Critical Muslim* is published quarterly in January, April, July and October. As a subscriber to the print edition, you'll receive new issues directly to your door, as well as full access to our digital archive.

United Kingdom £50/year
Europe £65/year
Rest of the World £75/year

Digital Only

Immediate online access to *Critical Muslim*

Browse the full *Critical Muslim* archive

Cancel any time

£3.30 per month

www.criticalmuslim.io

CM45

WINTER 2023

CONTENTS

TRANSITIONS

Goreme National Park, Cappadocia, Türkiye. Photo taken by Ziauddin Sardar.

ARTS AND LETTERS

REVIEWS

ET CETERA

TRANSITIONS

INTRODUCTION:
ALTERATIONS AND CONVULSIONS

Samia Rahman

A track on Echo & The Bunnymen's 1997 album *Evergreen* became their first single after an almost ten-year hiatus. 'Nothing Lasts Forever' remains a lament to the misery of impermanence; the assumption that the perfect moment is an end goal, a 'happy ever after' that completes a circle, and promises to be a transformative and unchanging constant. All we need to do is seek it out, whether through hard work or good fortune; and once it is in our grasp, hold on to it and never let it go. The British post-punk band had more reason than most to be confronted with the precarity of existence. A result of the complacent and bullish belief in invincible and eternal youth.

'I want it all, I want it now.'

They were part of an explosion of synth-pop in the late 1970s that came to be known as New Wave. Post-punk guitar bands were embracing exciting technological innovations that meant they stopped thrashing chords and started playing arpeggios. Echo & The Bunnymen were among the many artists experimenting with the new kid on the block - a drum machine. It was a time when even rock bands were seizing the opportunity to utilise the latest gadgets, in order to digitally enhance their sound. In 1980, however, Pete de Freitas became the band's drummer, rendering their drum machine obsolete. The transition to technology taking place around them could take a back seat. Or so they thought. In 1989, de Freitas was killed in a motorcycle accident, a premature death at a time when cultural icons including Ian Curtis of Joy Division and Marc Bolan were dying at shockingly young ages. They seemingly had it all, until death, the ultimate transition as Hina Khalid describes in her Last Word, came calling.

'Nothing ever lasts forever.'

In death we transition to an unknown dimension. Perhaps an afterlife, perhaps reincarnation, perhaps the void of nothingness, depending on our ideological and spiritual convictions. But in life too, we are in continual transition. As Leyla Jagiella notes, tiny particles of matter that constitute our being fuse, function and power to serve the purpose of keeping us alive. Upon expiration, decay, and subsumed into the environment, they become a part of other clumps of particles whether they be human or not. It is this that Jagiella ponders while gazing upon a much-neglected plant, which has been in her possession for over two decades, a fixture in both her habitat and her biology: 'We are therefore not simply just the successful end-point of a transition. We remain in a state of transition even as human beings. The boundaries and limits of our existence as humans are not absolute because we constantly merge into other beings and they merge into us. Be it through the air that we breathe in and breathe out, be it through the other beings that we consume, cooked or uncooked. Be it through our own bodies that become nutrition for others both during our lifetimes and after death.'

Echo & the Bunnymen appeared to foreshadow this merging of sentient life with inorganic matter, problematising the separation of the two, the one providing nourishment for the other and vice versa. 'Echo' represents the drum machine, while 'the Bunnymen' were the humans playing along to the tune of the machine. Pete de Freitas stepped into the breach and metamorphosed into an echo. A music trend taking hold among musicians of his generation, rebuffed. The slow crawl to trans-humanism stuttered by a young man's desire not to be replaced by a cacophony of wires and electrics that emit inhuman sounds. Human sounds are imperfect, that is their charm; while the precision of machines is unsurpassed, clinical, impersonal. But ultimately, de Freitas too would die, too soon, too young, with the force of technology more than ready to quickly and confidently step back into the void.

Musicians who leave the earthly realm at the height of their fame leave behind a legacy they can no longer control. A body of work independent of its creator. The meaning of sounds, originally erupting out of time-specific emotions and contexts, will evolve according to the changing tastes and vogue of evolving youth culture of any given era. The creation of culture and knowledge and the ways they will be packaged and presented knows no sovereign. One generation's lauded cultural golden child is doomed to be the next generation's uncool. And that's ok. Sensitivities and attitudes should be allowed to sojourn, while at the same moment remaining constant to the subjective experience of the individual. At the same time as Echo & the Bunnymen were dealing with irreversible change and confronting the terrible toll of death, they were witness to the transformational impact of technology. Vacillating and dabbling with their human and non-human drum machine, they understood the robotic ability to detect which sounds were in vogue, or 'the next best thing' or just 'the thing'. Nothing should last forever, after all.

How can we even hope to transition into forever, if such an aspiration ignites us? After all, transitions are a natural process, deterring stagnation and inviting rebirth, stirring the spark of new energy into an existing mix. An unchanging constant isn't necessarily the panacea we might think, however appealing the comfort of a familiar state may be. A change is as good as a rest, goes the old adage; don't you ever wonder what it means to be evergreen when all around you is gradually shifting? A transition itself can be a temporary metamorphosis, a re-wilding or a re-sculpting or even a refining. Such was the case, thankfully, for Robert Hainault, who details in this issue his flirtation with right-wing New Atheism. Brought up to suppress his part-Pakistani heritage, feelings of self-loathing manifest in a passionate rejection of all that the shameful DNA, particles, atoms he harbours, represents. His mother could not bring herself to speak of her Pakistani father. The pain of finding a huge chunk of his family origins dead to him. An inability to empathise with a mother traumatised by the experience of being a white-passing, mixed-race child in a racist northern UK industrial town in the 1970s. Laden down with a dirty dark secret. *I hope they don't find out the truth about me.* This maelstrom led Hainault to fall under the spell of far-right anti-Islamists and their populist rhetoric. At last, the realisation that only by coming to terms with his identity, rather than resenting it, would he find peace, enabled Hainault to transition out of the extremist folds in which he was seeking an elusive truth:

> I was to learn that the reality of being even remotely associated with Islam in Britain, even amongst my own socially liberal generation, was far from simple, and would be asking myself how, despite being once so determined to defend

my Islamic heritage, I would end up entrenched in anti-Islam politics. Over the next few years, I would shift from being an active member of the Doncaster Socialist Workers' Party and a committed Marxist marching against the war in Iraq, to being asked to contribute material to the British wing of the French far-Right movement Generation National Identitaire.

This process of change, an ideological detour down the avenue of hate, in Hainault's case, begs the question whether transitions are an act of transformation from one self to another? Or are they the expression of a different part of what it means to form the self at any given time? Another music icon from the 1980s, Madonna, became the queen of reinvention over the following decades. While Echo & The Bunnymen grew into and within the boundaries of their New Wave-era sound, regardless of whether they used a drum machine or an actual drummer while de Freitas was alive, Madonna transitioned and mutated and contorted in every possible way to stay in the upper echelons of favoured musical trends.

In 1997, newly fascinated by Jewish mysticism and attempting to continue to ride the wave of pop music highs, Madonna worked on the *Ray of Light* album that was released the following year. With some, but not all, parallels to the journey of rebirth experienced by a new convert alluded to by amina wadud in her conversion story also in this issue, Madonna flushed away her chirpy pop star image and submerged her brand into a new-age dimension that was in keeping with the times. Emerging from the frivolity of mainstream music-lite to reveal a new introspection to her art, the move away from the artificial sounds of the 1980s, towards more authentic, real, deeper sounds, brought an explosion of fusion that illustrates the interchangeability of spirituality across a spectrum of dogmatic persuasions. Ankur Barua, who teaches at the Faculty of Divinity, University of Cambridge, recently wrote of the conjunctions in the histories of Buddhism, Hinduism and Islam, in a subversion of the popular view that they are distinctly separate with little or no theological convergence of thought. His exploration of *tawhid* and *tasawwuuf* and *bhakti* and *yoga* in devotional poetry reveals the transitioning motifs and shared allegories of love across these religious worldviews. He gives the example of the sixteenth century Indian Sufi Muslim poet Ibrahim Khan, known as Ras Khan, who became a devotee of the Hindu deity Krishna and 'recognised that this *bhakti*-shaped vision was more than malleable for Sufi hermeneutic recalibration'. Ras Khan spent much of his life creating *tasawwuuf* and *bhaktic* devotional poetry.

Of course, Islam has witnessed many movements working to inspire the masses to embrace a particular sectarian understanding of faith. The continual transitioning of what it means to be a Muslim has occurred since its origins. It was not long after Islam was revealed that a group of Muslim thinkers known as the Mu'tazilites introduced the concept of rationalism and individual free will in Islamic discourse. But rationalist thought was immediately attacked, although it managed to thrive in Islamic intellectual circles, particularly flourishing during the Islamic Golden Age and informing Shi'i thinking even today. The Ash'ari school of thought, founded by former Mu'tazalite Abu al-Hasan al-Ashari, came to dominate Sunni Islam with its emphasis on sacred scriptures and orthodoxy. Sharia is mentioned in the Qur'an only once and literally means 'the way'. Yet the zeal to establish the one and only way has caused Islam to career from one doomed sectarian epiphany to the next. However, the journey of Islamic reform continues, arguably less successfully. Renewal should be energising in the course of religious practise, but the reality is too often a return to coercive power. As Ziauddin Sardar and the late Merryl Wyn Davies write in the introduction to CM*10: Sects*, 'however much sectarian affiliation may begin with critical reason and a reformist instinct, it transforms into a complacent mindset that not only shuns genuine critique but becomes quite irrational'. Ideological transitions are regularly well-intentioned. It may seem preposterous, but the Taliban, Hizb ut Tahrir, and Salafism 'all began as dissenting reform movements seeking justice and equity'.

The desire to seek out and serve a higher purpose fuels many of the transitional ideals that motivate revolutionaries and change-makers. Cleansing a context from decay, corruption and dishonour often provides the motivation to re-configure. It was an appetite for profundity in the later 1990s that Madonna's bold new sound would lead to her being credited with not just bringing electronic dance music to the mainstream, but infusing influences drawn from as far afield as the Middle East and South Asia, surfing all the religions in-between. Ground-breaking, the queen of reinvention was applauded for her innovation and for being at the forefront of the fusion world. In-between swapping music CDs with friends and discovering raves in the industrial wastelands of London's docklands, my young self sneered at what I regarded as Madonna's flat-footed attempts to remain relevant. Perhaps this was the precocity of youth, whether or not at the cusp of middle-age, I still regard Madonna as a hot mess. It prevented me from appreciating her chameleon-like ability to transcend genres, styles and generations. Just as intolerant Wahhabis reject any practise of Islam that isn't based on the rituals and pieties of seventh century Arabia. Who doesn't remember a period in their life when they were unbearably rigid ideological purists? The late American anthropologist, David Graeber, in his posthumously published influential work, *The Dawn of Everything*, uses the term 'schismogenesis' to describe people's tendency to define themselves against one another. Subcultures offered a sense of belonging to those who cultivated an image of themselves based on what they were not. Music, attitude, cultural references, and style were the uniform of their tribe. Mods versus Rockers, Teddy Boys versus immigrants and anti-racists, pop enthusiasts versus ravers and metalheads, *Friends* versus *Seinfeld*, Sufis versus Salafis, Al Ghazali versus Ibn Rushd, mainstream versus alternative, blind faith versus rationalism.

It is Hainault's moving, confessional and raw testimony that ardently reveals the necessity of transitioning across tribes. Barua tells us the devotional poets of early South Asian history developed 'interfaces of mutual intelligibility' in stark contrast to another far-right plague, Hindutva fascism. Cheered on from the side-lines by the alt-right, and driven by its populist beacon Modi, a strain of Indian society is determined to erase Islamic culture from any and all narratives of Hindustan. To remain entrenched in a set of views or attitudes is to deny the opportunity of growth over a lifetime. Sticking to our parochial guns, the inability to value the plurality of thought, a refusal to transition out of our tunnel vision is like a form of intellectual death. Pete de Freitas died too young. We know too many cut down in their prime, taken too soon, and we feel robbed of all they still had to offer, all that they could become, all the twists and turns that life's trajectory would lead them on. But let us remind ourselves, theirs is the ultimate transition, not the final transition. And as their bodies return to the natural world, they experience transcendent growth, into new life, cells and matter that flow back into the universe, facilitating the cycle of rebirth in nature's wisdom. Life is a series of drafts, to be re-worked and reprised, as the Islamic reformers' journey seeking paradise exemplifies. An endless experimenting and transitioning into the next (no pressure to be best) version of yourself, whoever and whatever it is you are.

Death is destructive but an inevitable part of the cycle of life. But what of the transitions upon which nature, crucial to the sustenance of life, depends? The stability of our climate and the predictability of distinctly changing seasons form the foundation of our world systems. Winter is Winter because it is not Summer. Spring in the UK signals an emergence from the dormancy of long, cold, dark months. A sign for nature to wake from its cosy slumber and busily create new life in the form of plants, flora, fauna, animals and crops. Spring brings new shoots, Summer a modicum of sun, and Autumn an abundance that is harvested to sustain us through the harshness of winter. In her poignant essay, Naomi Foyle laments our trashing of our environment that has lead to an unwieldly transitioning natural cycle and subsequent climate collapse. With climate chaos comes food and energy insecurity, triggering the loss of livelihoods, poverty, wars competing for scarce resources, and more death, more destruction. But before the ultimate, but not final, transition comes, we can either be defeated by this terrifying apocalyptic passage, or devoted to affecting change. Foyle has chosen the latter:

> With the years left to me, I intend to be involved in co-creating, connecting and protecting safe havens in the storms to come: places and communities that will act as seed banks of human gifts, greenhouses for regenerative, pluralist visions of how human beings could live equitably and sustainably on the planet we evolved to inhabit. In my experience the Muslim Institute is one such powerful hothouse and I am always grateful for an invitation to join its conversations.

Foyle's words resonate as a well of emotion tumbles from her words. Organisations and intellectual movements that champion plurality of thought, which are unafraid to carve out spaces welcoming critical thinkers turfed out and shunned by the mainstream, bringing into their fold enquiring minds that have been pushed to the fringes by a self-appointed centre, seeking place, belonging and sanctuary. These 'hothouses' should be at the forefront of courageous and pioneering conversations of reform and renewal. They must embrace the tumult that comes with transitioning away from old models and patterns of organising that perpetuate entitlement, patriarchy, nepotism, and stagnation. Injecting fresh new energy into a well-oiled machine is the secret to remaining relevant and avoiding decay. Synergy and the exchange of ideas, just like the inhalation and expiration of molecules during and after the expanse of a life, expelled into the ether to form the building blocks of the future of all that is around. Trying to hang on to the ghosts of the past, without learning from them, is a fatal mistake. After all, nothing lasts forever, not in any guise.

Who occupies the centre anyway, if wherever we locate the core of a community, an axis of power, a global order, a body of thought, is in constant transition? The Iranian philosopher Seyyed Hossein Nasr described the West's construct of globalisation as based on a culture of waste and the inhumanity of brutal competition; something the sadly departed David Graeber, gone too soon, as the best of us are, would strongly agree with. Globalisation and its partner in crime, neoliberalism, have trashed the natural world and exploited it mercilessly, much to Foyle's anguish. Inspired by modernity and its dethroned younger sibling postmodernism, the impact was not uplift and newness, but a descent into a dystopian simulacrum. Modernist theories promised to benefit humankind by embracing reason, knowledge and progress. Postmodernism went further, declaring the hollow shell of subjective existence to be devoid of truth. Each contributed to the globalisation project that rejected a theocentric view of reality. By removing God and putting man at its centre we transitioned into a society of consumers. How apt was Madonna's synth-pop *Material Girl* of the 1980s. Globalisation, modernity and postmodernism were so well-intentioned, yet wreaked their havoc, and extracted and mistreated our natural world. Nothing lasts forever, even nature's patience and fortitude in the face of sustained attack.

Nature is transitioning to a slow potential death, and if it is to gasp its final breath, will take us, the perpetrators of the crime, down with it. The statistics and research are unmistakable, despite the ostrich-headed assertions of deniers such as Saudi Arabia and the Emirates, the oil giants and corporations, and legions of Trump supporters, Brexiteers, and conspiracy theorists. Where do we go from here? Boaventura de Sousa Santos is unequivocal. We are (finally?) transitioning away from the status quo augmented in the twentieth century: 'the Eurocentric Western cultural universe comes from a long trajectory of historical victories that seems to have come to an end. Europe spent five centuries dominating and teaching the non-European world and finds itself today increasingly in the condition of no longer being able to dominate nor having anything to teach.' As we see in Rehan Jamil and Asyia Iftikhar's photo essay of British Pakistanis contemplating 75 years since Pakistan declared independence from the British Empire, the repercussions of all that Santos describes, still resound. More than once I've heard it said; *We are here because you were over there.* And how has Pakistan navigated the transition to independence? Dare I even ask? India descends into fascism yet at least Bangladesh, once designated East Pakistan, is relatively less economically destitute. Or is it? Let's look a little closer, at the Land of Rivers. Utterly at the mercy of climate mayhem, rising seas, incessant and destructive floods and the reclaiming of the land by oceans. Life is cheap in the face of the globalists' grand game. How do we persuade the elites they will soon run out of resources, and end up without even a habitable corner of the earth they can claim for themselves? As globalisation, and its consequential reaction deglobalisation, accelerates the transition out of the Anthropocene epoch to a post-human future, we are facing deep uncertainty. Ziauddin Sardar and his colleagues have described our current period as postnormal times, an in-between period of contradiction, complexity and chaos. Santos uses the term interregnum as 'a temporal metaphor that points to an ambiguous temporality in which the new society is not yet fully born and the old one has not yet definitively died. It is a time of monsters.'

A transition to a green economy is a solution. But the resistance to a vision and practise that aims to concentrate and nurture power away from an extractive economy to a regenerative one is immense. Tick-box compliance, otherwise known as greenwashing, enables profiteering and exploitative multinational companies to claim a clean, green conscience. They do this while simultaneously absolving themselves of any meaningful action to mitigate climate catastrophe and continuing to pollute and bypass nature's concerns while prostrating at the altar of capitalism. A just transition, which is what Foyle is likely dedicating herself to, will ensure that profit-driven industrial economies rooted in modernity will be dismantled and resources redistributed to local economies striving for ecosystem restoration. The wealth of the global north was built on the horrors of colonialism. Reparations for the global south who continue to suffer from this economic and emotional trauma, bearing the brunt of climate transition, will be an opportunity to heal the monsters of the past.

But these monsters are indeed in denial. The first generation of Pakistanis, whose children, and grandchildren and great-grandchildren Iftikhar and Jamil spoke to and photographed, were greeted with this denial when they packed up their lives in the hope of something better. Those who transition across borders in planes, boats, trains and on foot are slapped in the face with denial. They are scorned for daring to encroach the shores from whence they didn't come. From the land of a mother tongue to alien intonations and script. Migration, increasingly caused by planetary chaos, erratic climate, food insecurity, loss of livelihood, is a transition of hope, tragedy and the yearning for something better. Raha Rafii uprooted her life in the pursuit of a career in academia but found nothing but those same monsters in denial. 'Instead of answers, I found Orientalism at every turn— repackaged, renamed, and rehabilitated, but still recognisable—sculpted into garish, four-cornered texts, with Europe as its centre. These disciplines, these studies, were nothing but a folly, a white man's vanity project, alone and crumbling on a green hill overlooking a murderous shore.'

As Pakistan celebrates 75 years of independence, its transition from a colonised satellite into a flourishing democracy has choked. The country's 2022 floods, a direct result of the injustice of climate change and the disproportionate impact upon the poorest, who are least responsible for causing this planetary aberration, is one more example of these monsters in denial. All this while the tentacles of Islamism transition society to a more radicalised persuasion. Climate deniers scoff that those campaigning for climate justice through reparations and equity are prophets of doom but the death they are really afraid of is the death of the privileged lifestyle of those in the global north. Hainault may have noticed that far-right populists, climate deniers, and forces of oppression, are not only all monsters in denial, but are nauseating bedfellows. What ugly folly. How long can this interregnum that punishes the global south for the greed of those who pushed globalisation upon the world last? The reckoning will come.

It will come but it won't be with ease. Those whose existence is cushioned by the brutality of colonialism and the slave trade will resist any attempt to change their circumstance. Even if it is to redistribute wealth more equitably and make the poor less poor. Who doesn't fear forcible and seemingly detrimental transitions in our material and emotional lives? The profiteering oil and gas and banking industries are major employers, as Yassmin Abdel-Magied's essay *On The Rigs* illustrates. These powerful actors will not hesitate to generate unease and insecurity in those reliant on the opportunities they bring. The rise of right-wing populism leaves us in no doubt how easy it is to distract a tremulous population from the real causes of their problems.

Against all these odds, a just transition is gaining ground in some parts of the world and may well become inevitable. Employment trends are altering as industries respond to societal changes and innovations in working practise. In the same way that agriculture made way for the industrial revolution, and manufacturing was decimated by the service industry, the service industry, which fuelled consumption lifestyles, is now wavering to the power of tech. The transformative impact of technology is being felt all around the world. With economies impacted, it follows that social, cultural and religious spaces become sites of change too and the final frontier is political transition. Much has been made of the impact of technology on our lives. Synth pop, drum machines and the death of imperfect sounds were touted as the future. Pete de Freitas navigated his own encounter with trans-humanism before succumbing to nature's volition. Is it true that nothing lasts forever? Or will a dystopian horizon inadvertently help to herald a just and green transition that saves future civilisation on earth from both an ultimate and, indeed, a final transition?

TURNING TOWARDS THE SOUTH

Boaventura de Sousa Santos

It is hard to imagine that we share the journey with someone coming in the opposite direction. Nevertheless, I think that this strange sharing is perhaps what best characterises our time. Coming from very different trajectories and histories, from the accumulation of multi-secular defeats or victories, different cultural (philosophical, aesthetic, political, ontological, epistemological and ethical) universes seem today more exposed than ever to the presence of and competition with rival universes in conditions that do not allow unilateral movements, be they of assimilation or of conquest. The inequalities of power among them exist and are historically sedimented, but they are increasingly relative and unequally distributed among the different areas of collective life or the different regions of the world. The opposite trajectories converge in a field of maximum uncertainty that produces restlessness and instability. The sharing of uncertainty is bound to result in the uncertainty of sharing.

The Eurocentric Western cultural universe comes from a long trajectory of historical victories that seems to have come to an end. Europe spent five centuries dominating and teaching the non-European world and finds itself today increasingly in the condition of no longer being able to dominate nor having anything to teach. The drama of the cultural universe that considers itself historically victorious is that it does not want to learn from the cultural universes it has become accustomed to defeat and to teach. In turn, the non-Western cultural universes, be they Eastern (Chinese or Indian), Islamic, African and indigenous or first nations people of the Americas and Oceania, come from trajectories of historical defeats by the Western universe, defeats which, however, varied greatly in time and extent. They have gone through different processes of destruction, disfiguration, acculturation (or more accurately, inculturation or deculturation), but they have survived and today they take on a new confidence, self-esteem, and forward-looking stance from which stems the perception that the defeat is over. What kind of sharing can be expected from these trajectories progressing in opposite direction? Are they meeting and converging in some way or are they missing the possibility of the encounter and heading for confrontations of unknown contours?

Mismatches and conflicts can be as potentially destructive as encounters and convergences can be potentially and mutually enriching. The deep uncertainty this creates stems from four epochal conditions: interregnum, interruption, transmigration, reflexivity. Drawing upon the thought of the Italian philosopher Antonio Gramsci, the term *interregnum* is a temporal metaphor that points to an ambiguous temporality in which the new society is not yet fully born and the old one has not yet definitively died. It is a time of monsters. The unstable oscillation between strengthening the new and rescuing the old is characteristic of the interregnum. *Interruption* is a spatial metaphor that suggests the insertion of a rupture or break in the established order that provokes a suspension, be it political, legal or philosophical. Such suspension can be more or less vast and more or less lasting. It is a time of crossroads. *Transmigration* is a metaphor of an outward-looking movement that evokes the transitoriness of social relations, of contrasts, of identities and of the constant disturbance of linear movements. It is a time of transculturation, to use a concept developed by the Cuban sociologist Fernando Ortiz. Finally, deep *reflexivity* is a metaphor for an inward-looking movement that involves revisiting and revising history. It is a time of roots turning into options and of options turning into roots.

Interregnum, interruption, transmigration and deep reflexivity make possible new types of conflicts as much as new types of encounters, generating unmapped and surprising contingencies and hybridisations. Two main features account for the specificity of the contemporary zeitgeist. The first one is the apocalyptic character of possible conflicts (e.g., unprecedented social inequality, nuclear war, imminent ecological catastrophe) and the exhilarating nature of possible encounters and convergences (e.g., the World Social Forum, intercultural conversations, religious ecumenisms). The same social and cultural transformations of the last decades that have caused vast conflicts, mismatches and resistances have also generated conditions and opportunities for encounters and

convergences of a new type. The second feature lies in a specific
questioning of the past that consists in revisiting and revaluating the
intellectual heritage before the modern period – more specifically, before
modern colonialism and the hierarchies and conflicts among cultural
universes it generated. Modern colonialism, starting with its European
expansion in the fifteenth century, can thus be viewed as a crucial historical
process causing deep wounds upon the defeated and subjugated cultures
and populations that last until today. Understandably, revisiting and
reevaluating the premodern or early modern pasts occurs mostly in the
cultural universes that were defeated or humiliated by Eurocentric
modernity, but it is equally visible inside the Eurocentric cultural universe.
However, in very different ways, colonialism transformed European
cultural traditions as much as it transformed the cultural universes it
subjugated or sought to subjugate. As underlined by the Tunisian scholar
Albert Memmi:

> Colonization distorts relationships, destroys or petrifies institutions, and cor-
> rupts men, both colonizers and colonized. To live, the colonized needs to do
> away with colonization. To become a man, he must do away with the colonized
> being that he has become. If the European must annihilate the colonizer within
> himself, the colonized must rise above his colonized being.... For the colo-
> nized just as for the colonizer, there is no way out other than a complete end
> to colonization. The refusal of the colonized cannot be anything but absolute,
> that is, not only revolt, but a revolution.

Without losing sight of the existence of oppressors and oppressed, and
perpetrators and victims, identifying, confronting and healing the colonial
wound in all its vastness and depth involves some kind of reciprocal
movements. Without the latter, the possibility of sharing and encounter
among cultural universes transiting in opposite directions in the same
space-time will be missed.

In this essay, I focus on the conditions that might propitiate sharing and
encounter. I start from the idea that the global social injustice caused by
modern colonialism, together with modern capitalism and modern
patriarchy, was grounded in a cultural, ontological and epistemological
universe that exerted itself systematically and arrogantly, ignoring other
cultures, ways of being and ways of knowing, ontologies and epistemologies.

This led to a massive loss and waste of social experiences and justified the subjugation and elimination of the populations that lived by such cultures and social experiences. Global social injustice was therefore the other side of global cognitive justice. I designate this systematic ignorance by the Western-centric cultural universe as ignorant ignorance to convey the idea that in most cases such ignorance was not aware of itself. It was simply assumed that there was nothing worth knowing beyond what the Eurocentric universe knew, pretended to know or allowed to be known. In light of this, I will defend that there is no global social justice without global cognitive justice. In order to move in the direction of cognitive justice I will not engage in any kind of project for a global, complete, universal or unified knowledge. Inspired by the fifteenth century philosopher Nicholas of Cusa, I will rather defend the idea of a learned ignorance (Santos, 2009: 103-125). I will start by briefly identifying the roots of modern cognitive injustice. I will then describe the main dimensions of modern ignorant ignorance and finally expound the outlines of learned ignorance conceived of as a tool to maximise the possibility of sharing and of mutually enriching and transformative encounters.

Abyssal thinking and monocultures

In my body of work, I have proposed the epistemologies of the South as a set of alternatives to Western-centric dominant epistemologies. The epistemologies of the South belong to a vast family of postcolonial and decolonial studies. They concern the production and validation of knowledges anchored in the experiences of resistance of all those social groups that have systematically suffered injustice, oppression, and destruction caused by modern capitalism, colonialism, and patriarchy. The vast and vastly diversified field of such experiences I designate as the anti-imperial South. It is an epistemological, non-geographical South, composed of many epistemological souths having in common the fact that they are all knowledges born in struggles against modern domination. They are produced wherever such struggles occur, both in the geographical North and the geographical South. The objective of the epistemologies of the South is to allow the oppressed social groups to represent the world as their own and in their own terms, for only thus will they be able to change it according to their own aspirations. The epistemologies of the South are in the antipodes of the epistemologies of the North, but we must be careful not to caricature these as merely mirror images of each other.

We can describe dominant modern Western thinking as abyssal thinking. It is characterised a radical and radically invisible line that separates the realm of full humanity (what I refer to as the metropolitan zone) from the realm of sub-humanity (what I call the colonial zone and Franz Fanon called the zone of non-being). It is therefore constituted both by an epistemology (how we know what we know) and an ontology (the nature of being). This abyssal line operates by negating the validity, relevance or even existence of the social, epistemic, and cultural experience taking place 'on the other side of the line'. It has thereby created a massive sociology of absences that encompasses both vast populations and vast bodies of cultures, ways of knowing, and ways of being. The other side of the destruction of populations (genocide) has been the negation of their knowledges, what I have designated as epistemicide. The sociology of absences consists in unilaterally defining what is worth knowing or experiencing. The monopoly of knowledge entails the monopoly of whatever is knowable by the tools of the epistemologies of the North. Beyond the limits of the North's horizon of knowledge and existence, whatever is unknown is defined as irrelevant or dangerous, or even as non-existent. The ignorance thus produced is an ignorant ignorance because it is inherently deprived of the consciousness of what it ignores. Such an ignorance takes five main forms of what I refer to as monocultures.

First, *the monoculture of knowledge* and of the rigour of knowledge. This monoculture is the most powerful of all because it helps sustain all the other monocultures. It consists in turning modern science and high culture into the sole criteria for truth and aesthetic quality. Everything that is not recognised or legitimised by the epistemic or aesthetic canon is declared non-existent or irrelevant. This is why hip hop is not philosophy, village sages are not philosophers, slam poetry is not poetry, orature is not attributed the same value as literature, and home-grown sociologists, the organic intellectuals in the poor peripheries of large cities, are not considered to be engaged in 'proper' sociology. These forms of aesthetic or philosophical expression are not respected for their intrinsic value and such lack of respect is extended to the social groups that practice them.

The terms that define the *modus operandi* of this monoculture include ignorance, illiteracy, handicrafts, superstition, tradition, primitivism, provincialism, obscurantism, brutality, naïveté, and subjective opinion.

Second, *the monoculture of linear time* rests on the idea that history has a unique and widely accepted meaning and direction. This meaning and direction have been formulated in different ways over the last two hundred years: progress, revolution, modernisation, development, growth, and globalisation. Common to all these formulations is the idea of a centre, the North Atlantic, and the idea that the core countries of the world system are at the cutting edge of time, together with the dominant knowledges, institutions and forms of sociability typical of the core countries. This logic produces non-existence by describing whatever is asymmetrical as backward, according to the temporal norm, vis-à-vis whatever is declared advanced. It is through this logic that Western modernity produces the non-contemporaneity of the contemporaneous. Anything that diverges or differs from the normative present does not belong to the same historical time. The Latin American indigenous woman who appears in court wearing her *pollera* is a doubly strange body, because of what she is and of what she is wearing. The peasant or indigenous person's non-existence takes the form of backwardness, a residuum, something outside of time and space. The production of non-existence or irrelevance has assumed many names over the past two hundred years, the first being the primitive, closely followed by the traditional, the premodern, the simple, the obsolete, the local, and the underdeveloped.

Third, *the monoculture of* ex natura *social classification* is based on the naturalisation of differences. It consists in distributing populations according to categories that regard hierarchies as natural. Social classification produces non-existence in the shape of inferiority – insuperable inferiority, because it is natural. The inferior, because insuperably inferior, cannot be a credible alternative to the superior. Racial, sexual, and ableist classifications are among the most salient manifestations of this logic, although a dominant religion or the caste system can also operate as *ex natura* classifiers. Unlike the relation between capital and labour, social classification is based on attributes that negate the intentionality of social hierarchy. The relation of domination is seen as the consequence, rather than the cause, of this hierarchy, and it may even be considered to impose an obligation on whoever is classified as superior – for example, Kipling's description of imperialism's civilising mission as the 'white man's burden' or the categorisation of the man as the 'breadwinner'. Among the different forms of *ex natura* classification, race (along with tribal/ethnic and caste-based classifications) and sex have been decisive in enabling the relation between capital and labour to stabilise and spread globally.

Fourth, *the monoculture of the dominant scale* operates by adopting a given scale which is then used to disqualify the relevance of all other possible scales. In capitalist, colonialist, and patriarchal modernity, the dominant scale appears in two different forms: the universal and the global. Abstract universalism is the scale of the entities or realities that prevail regardless of specific contexts. In this monoculture, universal entities take precedence over all other realities that depend on contexts and are therefore considered particular or vernacular. The Universal Declaration of Human Rights was generated in an instance of abstract universalism. Globalisation is the scale that has acquired unprecedented relevance in various social fields since the 1980s. It is the scale of the entities or realities that extend their scope to the whole globe, thus earning the privilege to designate rival entities or realities as 'local' or 'particular'. For example, as the hamburger or pizza became globalised, *feijoada*, *bolos de bacalhau*, *acarajé*, *moamba*, *paçoca* or *cachupa* were gradually reduced to local specificities and have no place in global food chains. The entities or realities defined as particular or local are captured in scales that render them incapable of being credible alternatives to what exists globally and universally.

Fifth, *the monoculture of capitalist productivism* holds that infinite economic growth is an unquestionable rational objective which applies both to nature and to human labour. Productive capitalist nature is nature at its maximum fertility in a given production cycle, whereas productive labour is labour that likewise maximises the generation of profit in a given production cycle. According to this logic, when applied to nature non-existence is named as non-productiveness, infertility and sterility; when applied to labour, as sloth, inefficiency, idleness, and domesticity.

These five modes of ignorant ignorance create five forms of non-existence because the realities to which they give shape are present only as obstacles to the realities deemed relevant – scientific, advanced, superior, global or productive realities. They are therefore disqualified parts of totalities which are only ever seen as homogeneous. They are what exists, albeit irretrievably, under disqualified forms of existence.

The epistemologies of the South start by denouncing the existence of the abyssal line and the epistemic and ontological degradation that it involves. It is the precondition to acknowledge the ways of being and the ways of knowing existing on the other side of the line, in the colonial zone. The epistemologies of the South therefore make possible the sociology of emergences. But rather than aiming at any goal claiming complete knowledge – indeed, a most Western-centric modern utopia – the epistemologies of the South seek to deepen the consciousness of the incompleteness of human knowledge. They assume that the epistemic diversity of the world is infinite. Developing the consciousness of such diversity means transitioning from ignorant ignorance to learned ignorance.

Learned ignorance...

My suggestion of the concept of learned ignorance is inspired by the fifteenth century philosopher Nicholas of Cusa. More than a concept, it is an epistemic and ethical stance or disposition to assume ignorance, that is to say, to develop the consciousness of not knowing. In 1440, Nicholas of Cusa published *De Docta Ignorantia* (1985). In this and in the books that followed, particularly in *Apologia doctae ignorantiae* (1988), *Idiota de Mente* and *Idiota de Sapienta* (1996), Nicholas set the task of showing that 'to know is to ignore'. The consciousness of ignorance grows as the finitude of human knowledge confronts the incomprehensibility of the infinite. The infinite, be it God, the 'maximum absolute', according to Nicholas, or the universe, 'maximum contracted', is beyond human comprehension. This, however, does not lead to frustration, since the desire of ignorance is nourished by the infinite search for truth, i.e., for knowledge.

While absolute truth is not accessible to humans, the infinite search for truth is what best characterises our humanity. The process of knowing is forever incomplete. Only by deepening and expanding knowledge can humans grasp a more precise idea of the inaccessibility and incomprehensibility of absolute truth, thus becoming learnedly ignorant: 'Therefore, the quiddity of things, which is the truth of beings, is unattainable in its purity; though it is sought by all philosophers, it is found by no one as it is. And the more deeply we are instructed in this ignorance, the closer we approach to truth.'

Nicholas of Cusa used the metaphor of the polygon and circle to show the possibilities and limits of human knowledge. The more sides and angles we add to the polygon, the closer it becomes to the circle. If the addition were infinite, the polygon would cease to exist as a polygon. It would become a circle, the negation of the self. In Nicholas's words:

> For the intellect is to truth as [an inscribed] polygon is to [the inscribing] circle. The more angles the inscribed polygon has the more similar it is to the circle. However, even if the number of its angles is increased *ad infinitum,* the polygon never becomes equal [to the circle], unless it is resolved into an identity with the circle. Hence, regarding truth, it is evident that we do not know anything other than the following: that we know truth not to be precisely comprehensible as it is. For truth may be likened unto the most absolute necessity (which cannot be either something more or something less than it is), and our intellect may be likened unto possibility.

In his four dialogues, Nicholas chooses as interlocutors the philosopher (orator) and the layman (*idiota* in Latin), an artisan. The dialogues take place in public squares and markets, not in universities or monasteries. The dialogues constitute a devastating critique of scholastic philosophy and its pretension to having an answer for all possible questions and finding them in the books of erudite tradition. Nicholas uses the layman as the spokesperson of his own ideas. Addressing the philosopher (the orator), the layman says:

> This is what I was saying – that you are being led by authority and are deceived. Someone has written the word that you believe. But I tell you that wisdom proclaims [itself] openly in the streets; and its proclamation is that it dwells in the highest places… Perhaps the difference between you and me is the following: you think that you are someone knowledgeable, although you are not; hence, you are haughty. By contrast, I know that I am a layman; hence, I am quite humble. In this respect, perhaps, I am more learned [than you].

Contrary to ignorant ignorance, learned ignorance is an active and demanding exercise that consists in conceiving the unknown not as the opposite of what one knows but as an integral part of what one knows. Knowledge is a human task that only makes sense because there is the unknown. There is no proportionality between the finite human knowledge and the infinite unknown but, as human knowledge advances, the idea of the unknowable – the incomprehensible and ungraspable – becomes more intense in its opacity. In this sense, the more we know the more we know that we don't know. This consciousness of what is ignored is what most distinctly unites human beings. Different ways of knowing permit us to know differently different areas or dimensions of reality, but all of them are bounded by the unknown that constitutes them. Humans are united not by what they know but by the fact that, no matter how diverse whatever they know, they always face the same limit, the same darkness, the same opacity, the same silence of the incomprehensible unknown. The more they know, the more precise the idea of such incomprehensibility.

Nicholas of Cusa also illustrates how, prior to modern capitalism and colonialism, in the transition from the medieval to the modern period, Western thinking was engaged with other philosophical and cultural traditions in a horizontal fashion as equal partners in a conversation of humankind. Reading Muslim thinkers such as Ibn Sina, Ibn Rushd, Al-Ghazali, or even Ibn Khaldun, one experiences the same sense of cosmopolitan attitude I suspect that in a zeitgeist characterised by different systems of knowledge and cultures transiting in opposite historical paths but sharing the same search for a new equation between roots and options, epistemicides were not committed on the same scale and with the same unilateral cognitive despotism that characterises Western modernity in the period after the European colonial expansion.

In the *Apologia Doctae Ignorantiae* – a response to a vicious critique of *De Docta Ignorantia* by John Wenck in *De Ignota Litteratura* – Nicholas draws upon Al-Ghazali to defend learned ignorance. Citing approvingly and praising the elegance of the formulation, Nicholas quotes Al-Ghazali's reference to God in *Metaphysics*:

> 'If anyone knows demonstratively the necessary impossibility of his apprehend-
> ing Him, then he is a knower and an apprehender; for he comes to know that
> God cannot be grasped by anyone. But if anyone cannot apprehend, and does
> not know (on the basis of the aforementioned demonstration) that it is neces-
> sarily impossible to apprehend God, then he does not know God. And all men
> are thus ignorant, except for the worthy, the wise, and the prophets – all of
> whom have profound wisdom.' Al-Ghazali [said] these things.

Later in the book he praises Al-Ghazali for his defence of logic as the 'power of reasoning. Al-Ghazali is thus cited side by side with Socrates, Augustine, and Pseudo-Dionysius. The range of the philosophical dialogues entertained by Nicholas of Cusa is in itself a masterful exercise in learned ignorance.

...and the epistemologies of the South

For the epistemologies of the South, the infinite is the epistemic diversity of the world, and the different, constituent human ways of knowing share the same condition of being finite. Herein lies the dialectical bond between unity and diversity in the domain of human knowledge: infinite diversity is incommensurable with what we can know about it. What unites humankind is the inaccessibility of the full epistemic constitution of the world. According to Carl Jung, this unity is primordial – the *unus mundus* of the alchemy – and it is traceable in ancestral time from where archetypes emerge.

The ancestral is the configuration of the common from which diversity developed or unfolded. No system of knowledge can thus claim the monopoly of truth. To claim the monopoly of truth is the utmost exercise in ignorant ignorance as it can only be based on extra-epistemic (political, military, ideological) power. The tragic consequences on this monopoly of truth have thus been both epistemic and political – epistemicide and genocide as the two sides of the same coin. The claim of the monopoly of truth served to legitimise modern capitalism, colonialism, and patriarchy.

If societies or social groups are divided as to what truth is, they are united in the search for truth. From the perspective of the epistemologies of the South, such commonality is what grounds the struggles against modern domination. Such struggles often combine different knowledges and ways of knowing. Hence the need for ecologies of knowledges. Knowledges developed by the epistemologies of the North can be a valuable contribution to such ecologies, provided that they forsake the claim of exclusive truth and combine with other knowledges and ways of knowing with the common purpose of strengthening social struggles against oppression and domination. The epistemologies of the South are an epistemic, political, and ethical proposal geared to promote and legitimise the movement or transition from monocultures to ecologies, with the objective of making possible global cognitive justice. The ecologies of knowledges are a precondition for building all the other ecologies. Counter-posed to the five Western-centric monocultures, the five ecologies – of knowledge, time, classification, scale, and production – make up the sociology of emergences and progress through learned ignorance. In light of the epistemic diversity of the world, intercultural translation is often required to facilitate the transition from monocultures to ecologies.

Ecologies of knowledges and intercultural translation

The grounding principle of intercultural translation is that there is no proportionality between any single system of knowledge and the infinite epistemic diversity of the world. This means that no single way of knowing can claim to be closer to the infinite epistemic diversity of the world than any other way of knowing. There may be claims of more advanced knowledge in a given area and others may claim to be more advanced in other areas. There is no absolute criterion to determine the epistemic advancement of a given system of knowledge except by evaluating it in the context of the areas of collective and interpersonal life most cherished or privileged by the specific knowing community. Indeed, all systems of knowledge are incomplete, but not all of them in the same sense. Some will know more about spirituality, others about physicality; some more about time, others about space; some look backwards to imagine the future while others look forward to imagine the future.

In our vastly interdependent era, most transformative collective actions require intercultural translation. Intercultural translation progresses as the participants coming from different cultures and ways of knowing intensify the consciousness of their own ignorance about other cultures and ways of knowing. And since intercultural translation involves contrasting and comparing among different ways of knowing, the specific way of knowing one is most familiar with is likely to emerge from such comparisons and contrasts in a new and surprising light. Hereby learned ignorance about one's own system of knowledge will emerge. This means that the ecologies of knowledges aimed at by the intercultural translation are also ecologies of learned ignorances. To view them as learned ignorances emphasises self-reflexiveness, while to view them as learned knowledges emphasises their transformative capabilities in the outside world.

Epistemologies of the South are political and ethical – that is, oriented to promote and strengthen liberating activism against modern modes of domination. Oppressed social groups and their epistemologies are subjugated differently by different monocultures. If resistance occurs in isolation – be it epistemic or political isolation – it is bound to fail, given the historical asymmetry between the combination of the different modes of domination and the fragmentation of the resistance against it. Epistemic cooperation (through ecologies of knowledges and intercultural translation) is the precondition for political cooperation (through artisanship of liberating practices). The more angles on the unknown, the more credible and potent the concretely known. The greater the combination of social struggles, the more effective and potentially transformative the resistance. In sum, the ideas grounding the transition from monocultures to ecologies through learned ignorance are as follows:

1. The epistemic diversity of humankind is infinite; as a consequence, the understanding of the world by far exceeds the Eurocentric understanding of the world.

2. Knowing that such diversity, being infinite, is ungraspable, means that the range and depth of our ignorance increases with the range and depth of our knowing. The greater the consciousness of the breath and the depth of our ignorance, the richer the understanding of the epistemic diversity of the world and of the impossibility of grasping its totality with any kind of totalising knowledge.

3. Our will to know is measured by our will to ignore by further knowing.

4. Striving for knowing the maximum incompleteness of our knowledge is the same as striving for grasping the maximum epistemic diversity of the world.

5. Such knowledge cannot but be partial and conjectural, but the more it is led by learned ignorance the more credible and reliable it becomes.

6. Guided by learned ignorance, the conversation of humankind will
    not fall on either relativism or dogmatism; it will rather progress
    in inclusiveness by changing the criteria of inclusion as more
    participants enter the conversation and engage in the struggles against
    oppression and domination.

7. Supported by learned ignorance, critical and transformative ways of
    thinking will build rear-guard theories of social transformation rather
    than vanguard theories; such theories, emerging from the sociology
    of emergences, are the not yets symptomatically signalled in the
    practices of social groups resisting against oppression, and hence
    against epistemicide.

Paths toward learned ignorance

As a positive stance consisting in the consciousness of not knowing,
learned ignorance is both an epistemic and a methodological stance which
can be enumerated in some of its key moments or dimensions.

The unknown as God and as the infinite epistemic diversity of the world

For Nicholas of Cusa, God is the apex of the unknown, the absolute
maximum; learned ignorance finds in the incomprehensibility of God the
most convincing demonstration of its epistemic and ethical correctness.
But any entity endowed with infinitude, be it the universe or truth, is
equally the domain of the unknown, thus requiring the same learned
ignorance. For the epistemologies of the South, the unknown is the infinite
epistemic diversity of the world. God and the epistemic diversity of the
world point to different conceptions of the unknown – two different
experiences of incomprehensibility, opacity and silence. Different
metaphors will be guiding the path of learned ignorance.

Concerning the unknown as a monotheist God, the metaphor of ascent
fits the task of learned ignorance. The early Christians used the idea of the
ladder to express their mystic path toward the extreme light (and deep
darkness) of God, as in John Climacus's *The Ladder of Divine Ascent* in the
sixth century. The same is true of Islamic theologians and mystics, most

notably in the case of Sufism and of Al-Ghazali's conception of the wise reason ascending to the loving reason. Similarly, Ibn Khaldun, while analysing the 'science of Sufism', considers the 'stations' of Sufi mysticism as forming 'an ascending order'.

Concerning the infinite epistemic diversity of the world, the most adequate metaphor to express the progress of learned ignorance is probably the metaphor of the road. While the ladder conveys a vertical movement, the road conveys a horizontal one. Both imply openness, incompleteness, and transcending, but invite different discursive and cooperative practices. Only through intercultural translation will it be possible to address such differences and to identify possible convergences in political and social activism.

Adding in complexity, the path of learned ignorance concerning the unknown God will be different in different religious and cultural universes. For instance, the process of secularisation that characterised Christianity in the Western cultural universe from the seventeenth century onwards is not present (at least, not in the same way) in other cultures. Any exercise of intercultural translation and ecologies of knowledge concerning the role of religious experience in social struggles against domination must bear this in mind. For instance, in the absence of secularisation, the path of learned ignorance concerning an unknown God will not be different (or totally different) from the one concerning the infinite epistemic (ontological and ethical) diversity of the world. Finding commonality or complementarity between the ladder and the road will be a task for intercultural translators.

Enigma, dispersion and bond

Learned ignorance starts from a primordial enigma. It consists in the undecidability concerning two opposing perceptions: it is as plausible to view life (including human life) as a *unity* as it is to view it as a *diversity*. Yet the unity of life manifests itself in diversity and diversity signals an underlying unity. The enigma is present at the epistemological, ontological, and ethical level. Different cultures, societies or eras may privilege one of the options but the other will always linger on the margins or underneath, thus showing that, in the end, the option is arbitrary and the issue remains as undecidable as ever. The enigma is how the infinite epistemic diversity of the world manifests its incomprehensibility and ungraspability in regard to any way of knowing.

Learned ignorance starts from this enigma to expand and deepen the consciousness of the diversity of ways of knowing, born in struggle against domination or susceptible to being used in struggle. *Dispersion* expresses the moment or stage in which such partial diversity is grasped. In the last instance, such dispersion is responsible for the fragmentation of the liberating struggles.

Because the epistemologies of the South are political and aim at strengthening the struggles against domination, learned ignorance is the privileged method to build ecologies of knowledges by exploring what unites the different ways of knowing and the complementarities and convergences that can be found in them so that more effective and potentially more successful combinations of liberating struggles can be designed. This is the epistemic and political movement which signals the transition from *dispersion* to *bond*. The bond is the glue that combines diversity with unity and provides direction and meaning to such combinations. The bond is both reasoned and mythical, a kind of 'warm reason' that excels in strengthening the will and potential to resist against subjugation, humiliation, and oppression. Evoking Al-Ghazali, it may be said that the bond expresses the movement from wise reason to loving reason, having in mind that love now is directed to all comrades, *compañeros*, *compagnons*, *camaradas*, *tovarisch* that are on the same side of the struggle against domination, and more than willing to join the struggle. The bond is risk, sacrifice, and celebration, existential experiences that presuppose the warm reason or the *sentir-pensar* of Orlando Fals Borda (2009) or still the *corazonar* of Patricio Guerrero Arias (2016).

Recognition before cognition

Recognition in the sense used here is the specific way learned ignorance transits from enigma to dispersion and to bond. It is an existential and normative pre-understanding of other human beings or human collectives as bearers of knowledge worth knowing as they may enrich the liberating struggles in their own specific ways, including in defining what counts as struggle and as liberation.

Paradoxically, recognition precedes cognition. Recognition means co-presence before meaning. It has epistemic, ethical, and ontological dimensions. Modern Western domination, especially when exercised by violence and appropriation, has yielded – over the centuries, generation after generation – an unfathomable field of dead and suffering bodies. But it has also given rise to a history of struggles, and of strong utopian will, offering resistance to such unjust destruction and suffering. This historical fate calls for immediate care, including care for the families and social groups most severely affected by the violence against bodies. The immediate and unconditional care for those in need comes first and before any judgment about the political or ethical evaluation of the occurrence. This is another reason why recognition comes before cognition.

Conjecture and the intensification of intersubjectivity

Learned ignorance progresses by deepening the understanding that, as absolute truth is unattainable, human knowledge is conjectural. The conjecture is the epistemic quality of something which, while not claiming the truth, is not a lie. The conjecture can only exist in community. As João Maria André emphasises, 'to conjecture is not to objectivise, and the difference can be traced in the distinction between the prefix *ob* in ob-jectivise and the prefix *cum* in con-jecture'. The communitarian and participatory character of conjectural knowledge progresses by expanding the circle of participant subjects rather than by transforming them into objects of someone else's knowledge. In this sense, it intensifies intersubjectivity, a precondition for the aggregation and combination of wills in any complex struggle against oppression. Learning is therefore co-learning, just as acting is co-acting. Learned ignorance informing conjectural knowledge is at the antipodes of any central religious or secular command.

Learned ignorance and the shadow

The ideas of light and darkness and the dialectical relations between them are a constant leitmotif in different cultural universes. In both Western and Islamic philosophical tradition light and darkness are the privileged metaphors to express the progress and the limits of human knowledge and understanding. For Nicholas of Cusa, darkness is both the absence of light and the excess of light, and human vision (knowledge) is possible along a continuum without, however, reaching the extreme. As much as the divine unknown must be comprehended as incomprehensible, the full light is only 'visible' as darkness, as an invisible light. Similarly, in Islam the parables of light and darkness are abundantly present in the Quran. Al-Ghazali and other Islamic scholars have dealt with the enigma of light both as a scientific phenomenon and as a metaphor for the cognitive and mystic experience. Light is indeed one of the names of God, as well as a term associated with guidance.

Focusing on the epistemic variant of the light/darkness dialectics, let us consider the Italian philosopher Giordano Bruno's elaborations on the concept of the shadow, one of the most exhilarating creations of the early Western tradition. It is, indeed, another instance, like Nicholas of Cusa and, later on, Baruch Spinoza, of the wayward nature of philosophising in the early period of Western philosophy that faded away in the following centuries. Of course, disobedience, however possible, was exercised at great personal cost. Giordano Bruno was sentenced to death by the Inquisition and burnt at the stake in 1600. In 1582 his *De Umbris idearum* [*On the Shadow of Ideas*] was published in Paris. In *intentio secunda*, he writes:

> The shadows are not darkness. They are rather traces of darkness in the light or traces of light in the darkness. Or they partake of light and darkness. Or they are composed of light and darkness. Or they are a mixture of light and darkness. Or they are indifferent vis-à-vis light and darkness or alien both to light and to darkness. This is due to the fact that truth is not all light or that light may be false or perhaps neither true nor false. It is just a trace of what is true or false. In any case, in our exposition, the shadow is to be considered a trace of light: it partakes of light though not full light.

In my view, this is the most encompassing and creative formulation of the idea of learned ignorance.

From fragmented to combined resistance

The specificity of modern domination lies in this: while it is possible to imagine a non-capitalist society with some form of colonialism and patriarchy (indeed, it has existed as an historical fact), it is not possible to imagine a capitalist society free of modern colonialism and modern patriarchy. Therefore, there is no way of overcoming domination without overcoming the fragmentation of the resistance it causes.

Overcoming fragmentation is one of the central objectives of the epistemologies of the South. However global, the three main modes of modern domination operate differently across time and space and are experienced at the existential level very differently by different social groups. For instance, the experience of colonised African people was and is different from that of indigenous people in the Americas, as much as the experience of colonised Muslim peoples in the Middle East was and is different from that of colonised Muslims in Europe. The same is true of capitalist and patriarchal domination.

Moreover, a given population may experience all main modes of modern domination or only one or two of them. It may experience them with different intensities. Indeed, some of its members may be oppressors concerning a given mode of domination yet be oppressed in relation to other modes. For the epistemologies of the South, even if the three main modes of domination are equally important, it may be that in a given space-time context resisting one of them may be more urgent than resisting others. It may also be the case that other modes of domination, such as political, religion, and caste, intervene in conjunction with the three main modes of domination. Under these circumstances, it is not always easy to determine who is on the same side of a given struggle, assuming that a specific struggle is easily identifiable.

Overcoming fragmentation is thus a very demanding task, which, except in the case of extreme social turbulence, tends to be partial and not lasting. Guided by learned ignorance, ecologies of knowledges and intercultural translation are the key tools to maximise the possibility of aggregation and combination of social struggles (or an artisanship of practices, as I explain below).

Any secular or religious central command, deciding in a top-down fashion about the struggles to be fought and how they are to be fought, will always be grounded on ignorant ignorance and are bound to end up in totalitarianisms of different types. This is at the antipodes of the learned ignorance that is the hallmark of the epistemologies of the South.

Artisanship of liberating practices

The artisanship of practices consists of designing and validating the practices of struggle and resistance carried out according to the premises of the epistemologies of the South. Given the unequal and interlinked ways in which modern modes of domination are articulated, no social struggle, however strong, can succeed if it concentrates only on isolated modes of domination. It is therefore imperative to build combinations between all the different kinds of struggles and resistances.

The particular way in which they actually occur in practice requires a kind of political work that is similar to artisanal work and artisanship. The artisan does not work with standardised models and never produces two pieces exactly alike. The logic of artisanal construction is not mechanical — it is, rather, repetition-as-creation. Processes, tools, and materials impose some conditions, but they leave leeway for a significant margin of freedom and creativity. The political work underlying the combinations between struggles has many affinities with artisanal work.

Curiously enough, the layman (the *idiota*) that Nicholas of Cusa uses to convey his own ideas about knowledge, wisdom and learned ignorance is an artisan whose craft is spoon-making — wooden spoons that he sells in the market.

Transition to a real utopia

The epistemic differences between the epistemologies of the North and the epistemologies of the South are as decisive as the social, political, and cultural blueprints they make possible. While the epistemologies of the North progress through ignorant ignorance and have tended, in general, to service the interests and powers of modern capitalism, colonialism, and patriarchy throughout modern history, the epistemologies of the South progress through learned ignorance. The epistemologies of the South are born in the struggles against capitalism, colonialism, and patriarchy by those social groups that have suffered most from the systemic injustices caused by these modes of domination.

The epistemologies of the North were foundational in defending the idea that the new is to be built *against* the ruins of the old and on the top of them. Epistemicide was the other side of modern innovation. For the epistemologies of the South, on the contrary, the new is always built *with* the ruins of the old. The old of the modern period is the current combination of the three main modes of domination – capitalism, colonialism, and patriarchy – and the fragmentation of the struggles resisting against them. The epistemologies of the North and the constructs they gave rise to (such as, modern science, modern state, and modern law) made possible both the combination among modes of domination and the fragmentation of the resistance against them. This explains why the epistemologies of the South, while opposing the epistemologies of the North, do not reject in principle all the cognitive advancements they made possible. On the contrary, they use them selectively and to the extent that such advancements contribute to the five main ecologies.

Only through learned ignorance will it be possible to transition to new ways of thinking and only by means of these will combinations among struggles against capitalism, colonialism, and patriarchy be attainable. In such combinations lie the hopes for effective liberation. They are the real utopia of our time.

For all bibliographical references please see the citations list beginning on page 245.

ETERNITY'S SUNRISE

Naomi Foyle

He who binds to himself a joy

Does the winged life destroy

He who kisses the joy as it flies

Lives in eternity's sunrise

'Eternity' by William Blake

'If the final hour comes and you have a seed in your hand, plant it.'
From Imam Bukhari, *Al-Adab Al-Mufrad*, book 27, Hadith no 479 (English
translation)

From my vantage point in Brighton, UK, it's a strange time on Planet
Earth – for all the sound and fury, social media meltdowns, strikes and
protests, it has felt to me this autumn of 2022 as though we are just
miming political action, that in fact we have silently slipped over an
indelible threshold beyond which nothing can help us: that we are now
powerless to avert the coming global cataclysm – an unimaginable future
of terminal chaos, writ large on the wall in charcoal from the fires in
Australia and stains from the floods in Pakistan. I am writing in the
immediate aftermath of COP27, the UN climate change talks in Egypt
which, although it achieved a historical victory for developing nations in
the form of a loss and damage fund, again failed to make solid
commitments to measures that would limit global temperature to 1.5°C
above pre-industrial levels. Though extreme weather events and their
associated effects of famine, floods, disease, refugee crisis and war would
still intensify at that limit, there would remain a chance of reversing some
of the most disastrous environmental changes. Beyond 1.5° we hit

planetary tipping points which would take us into wholly uncharted territory and are likely to bring about global civilisational collapse.

Perhaps the flame of hope is still just trembling: Alok Sharma, president of COP26 in 2021 in Glasgow, addressing the closing day of the conference in Egypt, declared that 1.5°, as a goal, 'unfortunately remains on life-support'. Given, however, the chronic refusal of world leaders to remove the fossil fuel IV tubing and robustly revive the patient, we are still driving hard toward a largely unliveable planet. The vital question then, as we transition into a radically uncertain future, is how do we, as a species, prepare for the trauma, loss and, I believe, radical opportunities to come? For the lights aren't going to go out all at once: human beings are numerous, intelligent and adaptable and even on a hot and largely barren planet some of us will most likely survive. How exactly we do that is up to us, and very much dependent on the stories we tell about ourselves and our times.

For, apocalyptic as my language is here, I see our current existential crisis as a crucible in which our future is held in a volatile cosmic balance, an archetypal roiling of destructive and creative forces that could boil over uncontrollably or result in powerful alchemical change. It could well be that we are, ultimately, a rogue species, a parasite that kills its host, and the Earth and all its living creatures would be better off without us. But at the same time, there are so many good people on the planet, bubbling away with brilliant ideas and positive actions – it may well be that the violent upending of our toxic world order smashes the suffocating lids of neoliberalism and totalitarianism and energises a human eco-liberation project on a scale the likes of which the world has never seen before. I'm fifty-five and unlikely to see that transpire, but I want to try and enable it. With the years left to me, I intend to be involved in co-creating, connecting and protecting safe havens in the storms to come: places and communities that will act as seed banks of human gifts, greenhouses for regenerative, pluralist visions of how human beings could live equitably and sustainably on the planet we evolved to inhabit. In my experience the Muslim Institute is one such powerful hothouse and I am always grateful for an invitation to join its conversations. Drawing on my recent work in theatre I would like to reflect here on the ways I am currently trying, as an artist-activist, to carve out and interconnect other such transformative spaces in our imperilled world.

Moving through despair

Much as I appreciate a cogent argument, as a poet and novelist a key part of my job is to explore human emotions. To do that effectively, I must honestly acknowledge my own. Between losing two friends to cancer and knowing in advance that COP27 was highly unlikely to succeed, I have felt overcome at times this autumn by a profound sense of pointlessness, physically experienced as an empty stomach and hollow heart. I knew I was grieving my friends, and expected to cry, which I did, but the knowledge that 1.5° was now pretty much impossible triggered something deeper than sorrow – a sense of futility that threatened to render all my plans and goals obsolete in advance. I didn't take to my bed: I showed up everywhere I was supposed to, but with an eerie sense of being my own ghost, drifting, tangential, purposeless. The only thing that helped me was being with other people. I felt animated and involved in the classroom, enjoyed the 2022 Muslim Institute Winter Gathering, and honouring my late friends on social media and at live events was a balm. But on my own, I have felt detached, not exactly void of self-belief, but misplaced, ineffectual, stuck on repeat, unable to grasp what I should be doing in response to this irrevocably altered world. Nothing I was doing with my life – nothing anyone anywhere was doing – had helped to prevent a near inevitable future of runaway global warming, so why were we bothering doing anything at all? Essentially, I have been experiencing a feeling of terrible powerlessness.

I still feel drained and unsure, but writing about it now, I can say that's okay. Despair is a valid emotional response to climate catastrophe and mass extinction, and it would be unhealthy to repress it. Returning for inspiration to *The Transition Timeline for a local, resilient future* (2009) by Shaun Chamberlain – a co-founder of the global Transition Network, which aims to 'shift our cultural assumptions to fit our circumstances and move into a more fulfilling, lower-energy world' – I took solace in the words of Buddhist scholar and deep ecologist Joanna Macy:

> The suppression of despair, like that of any deep recurring response, contributes to the numbing of the psyche … Of all the dangers we face, from climate chaos to permanent war, none is so great as the deadening of our response. For psychic numbing impedes our capacity to process and respond to information.

The energy expended in pushing down despair is diverted from more crucial uses, depleting the resilience and imagination needed for fresh visions and strategies.

It is good to realise that falling apart is not such a bad thing. Indeed it is as essential to transformation as the cracking of outgrown shells.

Macy's conclusion, although not a new insight, also resonated with me. I don't mean to be facetious – it seems morally abhorrent to equate eco-apocalypse with the making of breakfast – but faced with the failure of COP27, twelve years of Tory rule, the cost-of-living crisis throwing millions into abject poverty, even the war in Ukraine, the only way I can cope is to embrace what Chamberlain calls 'dark optimism' – another movement he co-founded that responds to our various existential challenges 'with an indomitable belief in the potential of humankind'. It's a view I've long shared, though I have to say COP27 has given it a beating. The way we live in the industrialised world is both unsustainable and unhealthy, so the fact that it must end will force new forms of social organisation to arise. The rise of repressive governments is an inevitable part of this process, as vested interests strive to shore up their wealth and power – here in the UK, the Conservatives are aiming to effectively outlaw protest: the proposed Public Order Bill, at time of writing, aims to turn noise-making on a demonstration into grounds for arrest in Britain, as well as 'inciting' other people to protest. But the victory of fascism is not a foregone conclusion. The strikes and protests erupting all over Britain this year are a hugely positive sign: hammers on an outgrown shell. And, I am relieved to report as I proofread this essay, as of Feb 2023, the House of Lords has inflicted heavy defeat on key aspects of the Public Order Bill, leaving its future at the mercy of a fierce game of parliamentary ping-pong.

What's essential in the fightback is to avoid getting sucked into the politics of fear and hatred. I don't mean to be contradictory here: as Macy puts it, we must avoid at all costs going numb, and it is right to be angry at injustice and afraid of catastrophe. But as William Blake wrote, 'The deeper the sorrow, the greater the joy' – a sentiment akin to the Sufi aphorism 'When the heart weeps for what it has lost, the spirit laughs for what it has found'. What these declarations mean, I think, is that painful emotions carve out channels within us through which light can also penetrate our hearts. That may not be a steady light, but even a single ray reminds us how good it is to be alive. When we are able to let that light shine forth from us, we are capable of meeting other people within it, creating a politics of love, joy, wonder and laughter: a politics of solidarity in defence of our shared home. Solidarity is by no means guaranteed to stave off environmental disaster, but it will be even more necessary if and when social structures disintegrate. It's widely assumed that at this point chaos will overwhelm us, and the world will end up being ruled by warlords and cannibals. But is that true?

In fact, crises often bring out the best in human beings: journalist Sebastian Junger, in his book *Tribe* (2016), reports on many such cases, including the London Blitz, the siege of Sarajevo and a volcanic eruption in Peru that caused an ash-cloud emergency services could not penetrate for three days, during which people voluntarily risked their own lives to help strangers, regardless of social class. Under long-term conditions of desperate food scarcity, of course, people might well revert to strongman survivalism. It's more likely, though, that governments, with their armies and police forces, will take control of at least some areas – and so it's crucially important to start electing accountable politicians with a social conscience. But even if nuclear war destroys every centre of political power in the world, if enough people, trained in self-defence and negotiating skills, commit themselves to working together for the collective good, it will be much harder for bandits to rule a postapocalyptic world.

Also, we still have time to avert global famine. Everywhere scientists are closely considering the material transitions we need to make to live sustainably on an overheating planet and drafting realistic proposals to achieve them. COP27 saw, for example, the launch of the 'Rebooting Food' movement, which, as proponent George Monbiot explains, urges the replacement of livestock farming with precision fermentation, a microbial brewing method based on hydrogen, methanol and water. Powered by renewable energy sources, precision fermentation can deliver vegan food with a high protein and healthy fat content and an incredibly low land, water, energy and carbon footprint. This is not a Soylent Green future of highly processed 'wafers' or mush: I haven't tasted them, but PF products already available or in development look delicious – ice cream, meltable cheese, macaroons made from PF egg whites and, for anyone who misses meat, PF steaks and burgers that 'bleed'. Sushi is also possible! The technology, Monbiot points out, would not only improve many people's diets, but liberate vast swathes of land for rewilding, thus acting as carbon sinks and biodiversity havens; and also preserve developing countries from the insecurity of importing food in a volatile world market. Agriculture would still exist: we would still grow fruit, vegetables, nuts and grains, and farming could return to being an emotionally rewarding occupation.

It's a heartening, even joyful vision, in perfect alignment with the Transition Network philosophy of creating a low-energy world that prioritises human happiness. The close relationship between access to nature and psychological well-being is well-established now and I love the thought that we could rewild much of Britain, creating safe havens not just for plants and animals, but also for people. In the absence of airflight, most of us would holiday in our own national parks, walking and camping in forests, swimming in rivers. Being in nature would be a common experience, uniting us in appreciation of the beauty of the Earth: glimpsing otters and beavers, watching the summer asteroid showers from woodland glades, telling stories and playing music around firepits, we would understand ourselves anew as part of the great web of life, and, if we have faith, thank God for our place in it. It's a transformative vision that inspires me to work on rewilding projects – though, frustratingly, the whole point of rewilding is for people to get out of the way.

Reassuring as it is, though, to know that this technology exists, as Monbiot points out, making a purely material transition is not enough to save us from ourselves. To ensure that – in a best-case scenario – financial and material gains are shared equitably in a functioning new world order, and, at worst, that the mega-rich or other armed gangs are not permitted to starve or enslave the rest of us, we need a green social revolution. All around the world, countless people are deeply committed to such a vision, making their voices heard in institutions, workplaces, governments and on the streets, in many cases risking their lives to do so. Everywhere, in short, people are rethinking everything, and increasingly centring social justice and well-being in their demands for a truly liveable future. Chamberlain writing in 2009 on the Transition Vision, imagined a Britain in which by 2027 'values like contentment, good-naturedness and humility became far more highly prized, and indeed conspicuous consumption of material goods became seen as rather unacceptable at a time when everyone was pulling together to address the sustainability emergency'.

But part of my despair this autumn has stemmed from a sense that we are not all pulling together, that even all this progressive activity is not adding up as it should. Here in Britain, it seems to me, we are lacking a widespread understanding of the interconnected nature of the crises we face. What follows is a reflection on this problem as I see it, and how I have tried to react to it in my work.

Building pluralism

I said at the outset that my aim as an artist and writer is to help create hothouses for regenerative, pluralist visions of how we might co-exist with each other and all living beings on a healthy planet Earth. Pluralism, as Ziauddin Sardar and Merryl Wyn Davies discuss in *Distorted Imagination: Lessons from the Rushdie Affair* (1990) — a book that bears reading or re-reading in light of the violent attack on Salman Rushdie in the summer of 2022 — is not identical with diversity. The latter is simply the human condition, while pluralism is a political value and infrastructure, suggesting 'the participation of equally valid and respected systems of thought and belief in the mutual activity of constructing a society'. Britain, Sardar and Davies argue, is a country which, despite its diverse population, culturally and politically lacks pluralist frameworks which would enable people to listen to and learn from each other, and work together to effectively resist common oppression.

For the benefit of those who have not read the book, it must be said that Sardar and Davies reject the Ayatollah Khomeini's fatwa against Rushdie, stressing that there is no Quranic basis for the execution of apostates, and even if there was, such a sentence would have to be carried out formally by sharia courts, not global bounty hunters. They also note that ninety percent of Muslims at the time rejected the fatwa, pointing out that Sunni Muslims embrace the politics of consensus and consultation; and that not even all Shiites supported the fatwa. In closely argued and contextualised chapters, they also, however, comprehensively demonstrate that *The Satanic Verses* is an epic and malicious misrepresentation of Islam and the Prophet Muhammad, hugely offensive to most believers, and the very fact that it saw print is proof that Muslims are not respected in Britain, or indeed the non-Muslim world. The British mainstream media's reaction to the demonstrations in Bradford served only to further belittle and demonise Muslims: the media gave far more airtime to Rushdie's defenders than Muslims keen and able to analyse the protests from the standpoint of believers. Rushdie's brutal stabbing this summer was a criminal act – no writer deserves to be maimed or slaughtered for their work – but I found it disturbing that in the wake of it, discussion of the book's blatant Islamophobia was taboo. Mainstream Western media framed the assault as an attack on free speech, not just preserving the book from criticism, but cementing it into place as an icon of creative expression. I'm not saying the book should be burned or pulped or even retracted, but the fact that it caused such grave offense among ordinary Muslims should be taken seriously, as is increasingly the norm in regard to racism in British publishing.

I'm hard pressed to present in contrast an example of a truly pluralist society, but some countries do offer examples of a more mutually respectful approach to potentially conflicting values and interests: the triangular negotiations that exist as a matter of course between German trade unions, businesses and government are a healthier model of labour relations than the 'smash the union' policies of British governments. In democracies with a form of proportional representation (PR), where more governments are forced to govern in coalitions, pluralism gains a foothold. Here in Britain, the Transition Network – which operates globally according to eight key principles, including promoting inclusivity and social justice, and freely sharing ideas and power – often creates spaces where diverse communities can come together and share knowledge. Transition Chichester, for example, has won funding from church charities to support a 'Food for Friends' initiative, a befriending project whereby refugees are invited to meet with other Chichester residents to prep, cook and eat food from their home countries.

But the Transition Network is very much under the radar in the UK, in a nascent stage with a deliberately local focus that hasn't yet translated into a national vision. The Labour Party has, until its last conference, resisted PR, somehow believing they could win a general election all on their own. While it is hopeful that Labour might have changed their minds on this issue, the British left still does not effectively interconnect issues and communities. Despite the multiple rolling strikes occurring now in the UK — at last count, railway workers, post office workers, nurses, further education and university staff, and Border Force staff — a mechanism to call a General Strike seems entirely lacking. Many are pursuing their own limited (if entirely worthy) agendas. Even if British trade unions wanted to combine forces, thanks to restrictive legislation, it is difficult for them to do so: secondary pickets, striking for political reasons, and calling a General Strike are all illegal now in the UK. The simultaneous strikes on 1 February 2023, a 'protect the right to strike day' called by the Trades Union Congress, marked a welcome move by the TUC to revive its three decades dormant coordinating function; but given the dramatic fall in union membership since the seventies, even if a de facto General Strike occurred, it would not, according to Labour peer and leading labour lawyer John Hendy KC, 'be terribly effective'. Coalition groups are emerging at the grassroots level, but while Enough is Enough makes five strong demands — 1. A Real Pay Rise. 2. Slash Energy Bills. 3. End Food Poverty. 4. Decent Homes for All. 5. Tax the Rich — delivering a green economy is not among them. And despite both coalition groups demonstrating in London on 1 May 2022 (I was there), Just Stop Oil and Enough is Enough failed to join forces at Parliament Square. Meanwhile, unlike Extinction Rebellion US, XR UK has still not adopted the 'Fourth Demand', effectively declaring solidarity with Black Lives Matter:

> We demand a just transition that prioritizes the most vulnerable people and indigenous sovereignty; establishes reparations and remediation led by and for Black people, Indigenous people, people of color and poor communities for years of environmental injustice, establishes legal rights for ecosystems to thrive and regenerate in perpetuity, and repairs the effects of ongoing ecocide to prevent extinction of human and all species, in order to maintain a liveable, just planet for all.

I fail to understand the problem with this demand, and not adopting it only alienates people who are not only historically and socioeconomically the most vulnerable to climate crisis, but in many cases are highly experienced activists.

Against this great British fragmentation, the two main parties are looking increasingly similar — Keir Starmer has been notably quiet on the

Public Order Bill, choosing instead to spout dog-whistle rhetoric on immigration, ban his front bench from appearing on picket lines, and continue to eject anti-Zionists from the Labour Party. As a result, many thoughtful British people feel politically homeless. I don't – I belong to the Green Party. I also attend various grassroots political meetings and demonstrations when I can, and report on them on social media. But though I feel uplifted by marches, in recent years I have decided that my time and skills are best deployed in my roles as writer, educator and editor. This is partly due to my autism – I am happiest and feel most empowered when focused on my work; I am good at lecturing and performing, less comfortable in group meetings where I find it hard to know when to speak and for how long. But it's also because between those three roles I simply don't have the time to make a proper commitment to a campaigning group. I currently work pro bono for Waterloo Press, which takes up a considerable amount of time, and given the press's commitment to publishing marginalised voices, I consider this a political activity. Having researched Transition Towns for this essay, I am motivated to give some time to Food for Friends in Chichester and check out the Brighton group, People into Permaculture, which aims to make the holistic principles of permaculture accessible for people of all backgrounds and abilities. I am an active member of my union, UCU, and committed to our current industrial action. But my priority right now is to work as an artist to create politically charged shared spaces; a goal which has led me back to an enthusiastic engagement with theatre.

Creating cultural political spaces

As a novelist, sometime playwright, and sometimes as a poet, I am a storyteller. Storytelling, as Shaun Chamberlain says, is key to the transition we need to make to a sustainable society: to act differently, we need to think differently. We need to challenge myths about our dominant culture – that Western civilisation is the most advanced the world has ever seen; that governments should be elite bodies composed mainly of white, able-bodied and expensively educated men; and that endless economic progress is both necessary and attainable. We need to replace these dangerous myths with truer tales: that Western colonial extractivism has brought us to the brink of global collapse; that in human diversity lies our strength as a species; that Indigenous cultures and world religions hold knowledge and wisdom from which Christian nations can and should learn a great deal. These are all stories I tell in my eco-SF quartet *The Gaia Chronicles* (Jo Fletcher Books), a work of 'Silk Road Science Fantasy' which I have written about before in *Critical Muslim 15*. In 2022, thanks to grants from Arts Council England and the University of Chichester, I worked with director, designer and child protection activist Raven Kaliana to bring *The Gaia Chronicles* to the stage as ASTRA: a multimedia theatre production that won the Brighton Fringe ONCA Green Curtain Award 2022 for shows that engage artists and audiences with social and environmental challenges. Writing and producing ASTRA was a revelatory experience that showed me the powerful potential of art to bring people together to collectively imagine a better world.

Set in a post-fossil fuel Mesopotamia, *The Gaia Chronicles* explores the spiritual and political coming-of-age of its heroine, young Astra Ordott. Astra's people, the vegan, science-oriented Gaians, snatched a green homeland from the chaos of global eco-collapse – but after a family tragedy, Astra learns the costs others, including her own brother, have incurred for her security. Determined to seek the truth, she embarks on a journey of discovery that takes her into the heart of an uprising of disabled young refugees and introduces her to societies run on principles of co-existence, restorative justice and participatory democracy – complex political relationships explored in detail in the books and rendered in the theatre piece in scenes of a courtroom trial and street protests.

Given the show's narrative journey toward environmental justice, inclusivity and accessibility were values at the very heart of ASTRA, not 'bolt-ons' or tick box exercises. The 70-minute research and development show was neurodivergent-led, by me as producer, with a creative team including dramaturg Hassan Mahamdallie (not just a leading light in the Muslim Institute, but also a playwright, cultural critic and author of *The Creative Case for Diversity*), British Sign Language interpreter/performer Sumayya Si-Tayeb, access consultants Hannah Thompson (Disability Studies scholar at Royal Holloway University, and author of the influential *Blind Spot* blog) and Troi Lee (co-founder and director of cultural arts organisation Deaf Rave). The show featured an innovative blend of projections, tabletop and shadow puppetry designed and built by Raven Kaliana, and a cast of mainly young people of diverse backgrounds, including two puppeteers of, respectively Hong Kongese and Afro-Portuguese heritage, and voice actors who brought a multiplicity of international accents to the story. The creative/integrated use of BSL interpretation and audio description ensured that access elements added meaning for all members of the audience: many people, for example, commented on the mesmerising nature of Sumayya Si-Tayeb's performance, whose signing and facial expressions brought human emotion to the show in a way that the puppets could not provide. The soundtrack combined field recordings from Zaatari refugee camp (Jordan), and music composed by asylum-seeking unaccompanied minors working with the Crawley-based charity Play for Progress, curated and mixed by London-based Palestinian music and theatre artist Mo'min Swaitat of the Majazz Project. The ASTRA team also involved local organisations, including project logistics support from jenni lewin-turner of Brighton-based cultural organisation Urbanflo, and community outreach work from Ümit Öztürk (founder and coordinator of Brighton-based cultural activism organisation Euro-Mediterranean Resources Network) and Rachel Searle (director of BlakeFest, Bognor Regis).

Performed live at Brighton Fringe, Chichester Fringe, and a neighbourhood sharing in Brighton, ASTRA was followed by food sharing and Q&A sessions with paid audience members and invited guests from community groups and disadvantaged neighbourhoods, all of whom were invited to respond to the show's challenging themes of racism, child abuse, ablism and climate crisis, by 'having a say', networking and problem-solving. The food was a sumptuous Mediterranean buffet provided by Ümit Öztürk, and leftovers went to local people in need. I suspect it was in large part due to the after-show forums that ASTRA won the ONCA Green Curtain Award. It was clear from people's reactions that the Mesopotamian setting was no barrier to a general audience engagement in the characters and stories, which were felt to reflect our global situation: a man from Hong Kong (no relation to the puppeteer) who had only been in the UK for a month, broke down in tears when speaking about how deeply he related to Astra's journey. Neither – probably because the production included and foregrounded people from the MENA region – were Raven and I accused of cultural appropriation. Conversations instead focused on human rights, protest, freedom of speech, the representation of disabled people, the challenge of depicting racism and racist violence sensitively, and the power of puppets to engage the inner child and win our hearts.

The whole experience reignited my passion for theatre, where my writing career began in Canada in the early nineties as a chamber opera librettist. Some argue that in the age of film and TV, theatre is a redundant and middle-class art form, but I vehemently disagree. It seems to me that in our post-lockdown, social media-riven world, the opportunity to come together at live events and discuss issues in person is needed more than ever. And, from the stories we tell, to the people we tell them to, there are many ways to invigorate and radicalise theatre conventions: practices like inclusive casting and creative/integrated access are attracting new audiences to this ancient art form. For myself, as I said from the stage in Brighton, theatre attracts me as a collaborative medium with the power to create a microcosm of the world as it could and should be. On ASTRA I was fortunate to work again with the renowned director and playwright Peter Hinton-Davis, Order of Canada, who served as the project's international theatre consultant. A pioneer in queer theatre and long-term supporter of Indigenous Canadian theatre, he gave us invaluable insights into the First Nations practices of land acknowledgement – which makes explicit the original ownership history of the land on which cultural venues sit, and the long table – in which after-show intellectual analysis of a piece of theatre is replaced by an invitation to eat and simply share an emotional response to the work. These are practices that could be adapted for a British context, but thanks to our audience feedback, I am confident that ASTRA, with its pluralist vision, succeeded in making its artists and audiences aware of each other's differing experiences, and the threats to the planet we live on. The enthusiastic response has generated momentum toward upscaled productions: Raven and I are currently working on a 100-minute two-act revision of the show for a national tour, while Peter Hinton-Davis and I are in discussion about mounting an epic non-puppet version of the show.

Conclusion: Transitioning into eternity

Perhaps, after the excitement and hard work of the ASTRA marathon, exhaustion and a sense of anti-climax have played a role in my brush with despair this autumn. The failure of COP27 though, is a watershed moment that courses through us all, and I know I'm not the only person who has felt badly shaken by it. The greatest shock it caused me was the chilling sense that eternity no longer existed. That is, a human eternity, the sense of a 'world without end' we all need to believe in to give our actions meaning. William Blake's poem 'Eternity', which meant a lot to me in the aftermath of my friends' deaths, suggests that we should not fight to hold on to the things we love: if instead we cultivate gratitude for their ephemeral presence, then we are able to experience a deep sense of oneness with the timeless cycles of life. That makes sense in relation to bereavement, but does it apply to the biosphere?

Perhaps so. At the 2022 Winter Gathering of the Muslim Institute, I told several people about a saying my late mother often quoted: 'If I knew the world would end tomorrow, I would still plant my garden today.' In recent years I had heard it mentioned that the saying is a hadith, which my friends at the Gathering, and later Ziauddin Sardar confirmed. I've also seen a version involving an apple tree attributed to Martin Luther, and online arguments about whether Luther said it too or the German Confessional Church attributed it to him to build morale in the resistance under Hitler. Perhaps it is another unacknowledged contribution Islam has made to the world, but in any case it makes sense to me that it has become a pan-religious aphorism: as an adolescent, I used to secretly scoff at what I considered my mother's ludicrous work ethic, but over the last decade or so I have understood the prophetic wisdom of the saying: as the storm clouds gather and the ice caps melt, not only must we literally plant trees and gardens, but we must cultivate our inner gardens of love, peace and joy. As in every case of illness or violent threat, even if we physically perish, our aim must be to do so in a way that expresses the best of who we are. That means finding more ways to find common ground with each other, not just politically, but spiritually and psychologically. One of the friends I have been grieving is Niall McDevitt, the London Irish poet, Blakean scholar and psychogeographer, my time twin — we were born on the same day and year – and friend of sixteen years. Of my many treasured memories of Niall, in the days after the unexpected news of his death, I kept returning to his interest in the perennial philosophy, which he used to speak about on his literary walking tours of London. My interest had been piqued at the time, but I'd never followed up on it; now the phrase resonated like a bell. It's not a topic people bring up often, and one of the many synchronicities I experienced in the wake of Niall's final transition, was the mention of the perennial philosophy at the Winter Gathering in a talk by H.A. Hellyer – who does not ascribe to the philosophy, but touched on it, as I recall, in relation to French metaphysician René Guénon [Abdalwâhid Yahiâ]. Back home, I acquired the book by Aldous Huxley and learned that, originally ascribed to Leibniz, the perennial philosophy is:

> a metaphysic that recognises a divine Reality substantial to the world of things and lives and minds; the psychology that finds in the soul something similar to, or even identical with, divine Reality; the ethic that places man's final ending in the knowledge of the immanent and transcendent Ground of all being – the thing is immemorial and universal.

Huxley's book is a compendium of mystic revelations from various world religions demonstrating this universal claim with a long commentary analysing its significance. The sources are mainly Christian and Hindu, it must be said – Islam is not listed in the index, Huxley barely mentions Muhammad, and perpetuates harmful stereotypes about Islam as a 'violent' faith (though to be fair he thinks Christianity is as well). So I could well understand why an Islamic scholar was not an adherent of Huxley's 'faith of faiths'. But alongside Jewish and Buddhist sages, the book cites Sufi saints and poets including Rumi, Bayazid of Bistun, Rabi'a, Al-Ghazali and Kabir, revered by Muslims, Hindus and Sikhs, and I don't think it is totally without interest or insight for Muslims. One can, of course, critique a 'pick and mix' attitude to religion, or argue that attempts to dig for universal truths will only unearth platitudes. I don't believe that all religions are identical beneath their culturally specific window dressings. But different temples can be built on the same ground, and I found that Huxley's chosen quotes and his commentaries felt relevant to our global predicament.

First, the historic quotes demonstrate that wise voices down the ages have always been raised in defence of care and co-existence. As Rumi says: 'the astrolabe of the mysteries of God is love', while Kabir, with his experience of migrating faiths, declares: 'Benares is to the East, Mecca to the West; but explore your own heart, for there are both Rama and Allah'. Second, Huxley distinguishes sharply between the pseudo-religions of fascism, populism and nationalism, in which the individual is suppressed in the name of a false, material unity; and the spiritual unity of right relationship with the Divine, in which the individual finds liberation. And finally, I found his discourse on the nature of time consoling and, well, timely.

For Huxley, the present moment is the Ground of all being and as such the only earthly portal into eternity: we cannot achieve heaven in the future, or resurrect it from the past, and a fixation on trying to do so only results in conflicts and aggression. In this argument, again, Huxley draws on Rumi:

Past and future veil God from our sight;
Burn up both of them with fire. How long
Wilt thou be partitioned by these segments, like a reed?
So long as a reed is partitioned, it is not privy to secrets,
Nor is it vocal in response to lip and breathing.
Rumi (translated by E.H. Whinfield)

Huxley distinguishes between what he calls time-philosophers – revolutionaries who seek to enforce change, or conservatives to seek to prevent it – and eternity-philosophers, such as the Quakers, Sufis and William Blake, who seek to be filled with the music of God in the here and now. For time-philosophers the present is just a step on the way to a future goal, and the ends therefore always justifies the means; but, just as the Quakers upheld peace and justice but are openly taking steps to correct their own historical complicity in the transatlantic slave trade (even whilst they supported its abolition), eternity-philosophers respect the divine nature of all other human beings and the sanctity of the present moment, and therefore – while actively opposing wrong-doing – are pacifists and can make no moral compromise when it comes to violence.

It's an argument that rages in environmentalist circles (and of course in places where the political context is very different from the UK's). When all life on Earth is threatened, I believe that we urgently need to envision a better future and work toward it together: but Huxley's arguments suggest that, paradoxically, that future is already here. It is immanent in the present moment, in all our capacities to be mutually respectful of each other and the Earth. Deflating SUV tyres or gluing hands to the motorway look, to me, like necessary ways to demand that respect from others who flout our very right to life, but if green activists everywhere began forming armed militias and shooting 'traitors' in the movement, I don't know that I'd want to live in the world we were co-creating.

Fortunately, we're not there yet. And even if we were, we should still plant what seeds we can. Googling tree-planting at the time that I was finishing this essay, I discovered that it was National Tree Week, an annual celebration to start the mark of the UK's tree planting season, including activities by a local green volunteers forum who won funding to plant 272 trees in 2022. Sounds like high time I heeded my mother!

THE GAPS OF HISTORY

Saeed Khan

'People are trapped in history and history is trapped in them'

James Baldwin

The 11 September 2001 attacks were, as has been discussed widely in the past two decades, a truly historical moment. The twin traumas of both the terrorist acts themselves and the unwelcomed spotlight thrust upon the Muslim American community was a rude awakening for its members who had taken for granted their relatively ordinary condition in the United States. Confronted, perhaps for the first time in their lives, with hostility, hatred and harassment for merely being Muslim, many Muslim Americans began to ask why they were recipients of such sentiment. The shock and surprise they registered seemed in part due to a lack of awareness of historical processes that led to Al Qaeda taking the action it did on that fateful day. It also demonstrated the inability to appreciate the process of cause and effect that had wedded Muslims and the West in a strange relationship for several centuries. It was as if these Muslims had been living outside history itself.

The danger of Muslims feeling they exist outside history certainly does not affect Muslims alone. Western history, the dominant historical narrative for the past three to four centuries, would be incomplete without Muslim history being located in conversation with it. The advent of the so-called modern age, the starting point of what we today understand as the rise of the West, begins in large part at the expense of Muslim defeat. While schoolchildren from London to Los Angeles are inculcated with the familiar couplet, 'In fourteen hundred and ninety-two, Columbus sailed the ocean blue,' they would be less well informed about its causal and contingent realities. The Genoese explorer's voyage occurred after the Spanish conquest of the Nasirids in Granada in January, 1492. The victorious dual monarchy of Ferdinand and Isabella then commissioned

Columbus for his expedition, underwritten considerably by plundered Moorish and Jewish wealth.

For many Muslims, the fall of Spain looms largely over their identity consciousness. To this day, Muslim visitors to the *Mezquita* in Cordoba feel a sense of tremendous loss; the anthropologist Akbar Ahmed has coined this phenomenon the 'Andalus Syndrome'. It constitutes a deep lament for what once was and is now gone. Walking through this magnificent structure, at one time the largest mosque outside the Middle East, tourists are struck by the splendour and the scale of this building. The stunning arches from the period of Caliph Abdul Rahman III evoke a sense of near infinitude for the traveller who walks through the building. In the centre of the *Mezquita* is a fully functioning chapel that holds regular prayer service. And yet along with the arches, the niche, *Mehrab*, that indicates the direction of Mecca for the observant, remains one of the highlights of any tour to the structure. On occasion, Muslim tourists will attempt to make a statement, perhaps out of defiance or even a sense of reclaiming lost territory by unfurling a prayer rug and trying to offer prayer in front of the *Mehrab*. Usually, the security detail of the premises will swoop down on the individual within mere minutes, if not sooner, and politely escort the person from the premises, informing all around that the *Mezquita* is no longer a mosque but in fact now the Cathedral of the Roman Catholic Diocese of Córdoba.

At one time the capital of the Umayyad Caliphate of Cordoba, the city fell to Christian forces from the north in the year 1236; it is from that time that the mosque was reconsecrated as a church. It is remarkable how the former glory of this space, complete with its bell tower, formally the minarets, and the lush gardens and fountains of its courtyard still evoke strong emotions and a sense of nostalgia for Muslims of every background. More recently, efforts to 'rectify' the purported loss of a priceless structure has been attempted elsewhere in the Muslim world. In 2020, Turkish President Recep Tayyip Erdogan announced that the Hagia Sophia would henceforth revert to being a mosque. The Hagia Sophia had been constructed during the reign of Justinian I in the sixteenth century, and had served as the central cathedral of the Byzantine Church and Empire, the site of coronation for its emperors. In 1453, Mehmet II and the Ottomans conquered the city and converted the Hagia Sophia into a mosque; it remained as such until 1935 when Mustafa Kemal ('Ataturk'), the first President of the modern Republic of Turkey (now Türkiye) declared it to become a museum and secular space. One of the impetuses cited by President Erdogan in ending the Hagia Sophia's 85-year tenure as a museum was retribution for what the Spaniards had done to the *Mezquita*.

When does history begin? There are, of course, a multitude of answers available. For some, their sense of history is shaped by their theology. For scientists, cosmology is the critical lens by which to determine that moment. In any case, we are the inheritors of history as well as the legacy of that process. We live inside the history of others, whether it is that of dominant forces that define the narrative or even within the history of our families. Some view history as sacred, others as a trauma.

As the adage is often correct, history is written by the victors. This privilege, often asserted as an entitlement, connotes the ultimate form of agency - those who have the power will exercise it by constructing a narrative that is of, by, and for a version of events and achievements that places them in the best light, distorted and departed from reality though it may be. In 1988, Indian scholar Gayatri Spivak penned her seminal essay with the provocative title, *Can the Subaltern Speak?* Spivak contends that a variety of communities have been marginalised from inclusion in the narratives of history. Their erasure distorts history and has a devastating impact upon the identity of members of those various communities. Currently, Muslims are a subaltern facing the manipulation of their history, an effort that can impact faith, identity and their own place in the world today.

Many people first encounter history in school and associate it with a pedantic list of names, places, dates and events. It is a sad experience that often causes an aversion to an important subject. In fact, history is a study of continuity and change. It is a field where people can actually form a connection with the past, and more critically, the people of the past. History offers an insight to how and why our predecessors coped with conditions they faced. It is a healthy exercise that provides insight to the evolution of communities and even ideas. But the process of studying history requires some important presumptions. First and foremost is the recognition that we are not only students of history, but also agents of history ourselves. After all, we are living through our own as well as someone else's history as it develops in the here and now. This means that one's engagement with history cannot merely be seen as a passive process of study; it is a constant, active exercise.

In addition, history requires vigilance when it comes to learning which elements of the past have been an illustration of continuity and those that are examples of change. All too often, there is an inclination to preserve history out of a sense of obligation to some sense of tradition or obligation to a cultural ethos, irrespective of whether it is even compatible or sustainable with a different time or place. This is a common challenge for immigrant communities that bring with them history of the 'old country' as precious as a family heirloom. That history is frozen in time and place, and is sanitised from some of the reality that may have provided a less than idyllic narrative. But what about the children of these immigrants? Is the history of parents or grandparents really *their* history as well? The fissures of generational gaps can be inadvertently expanded when parents and children living under the same roof exist in different histories: one that is outside the front door, the only one the children might know, comprehend and live, versus a history of sentimentality, possibly perpetuated by satellite television and the internet.

We belong to more than one history at the same time. These can be a family history, an ethnic or cultural history, a religious history and a national history. For Muslims, it is this last category that can be one of the more contentious. For Muslims living in Muslim majority countries, or as large minority communities as in India, there is the quagmire of a national history that has been tainted by colonialism within a fairly recent timeframe. In some cases, like the liberation of Algeria and the independence and subsequent partition of the Indian subcontinent, the memory of these episodes is still raw and rife with trauma, on personal, familial and collective levels. What is fascinating is that these histories also affect the histories of the former colonial powers as well, albeit in complex ways. Despite the destructive role of the Crown in the governance and ultimate independence of India, the history of Partition is not taught in the curriculum of the British school system. Shockingly, it is regarded to be almost exclusively as part of Indian history. At the same, the Algerian war of independence from 1954-1962 is very much part of the French historical narrative; it is unavoidable. But it is an unresolved history where

France, like Great Britain, has never come to terms with the violence and brutality it exacted on the local population, which was, by Western standards, tantamount to genocide and a crime against humanity.

Today, Muslims are categorised as a menace to Western countries, in terminology eerily similar to language used about other groups, like Jews and the Roma. Typecast as an unwelcome presence, an encroaching, even invasive force that is incompatible with so-called Western values, Muslims have become the ultimate 'Other.' They are branded a backward, alien entity that seeks to disrupt and destroy the West. But Muslim history in Europe is actually European history. The Moors were in the Iberian Peninsula since the year 711. Their near seven centuries of rule in Spain is almost three times the age of the United States as an independent country. It is safe to say that the Moors were European, although, sadly, Muslims themselves fail to recognise this simple fact when they claim the Moors somehow still to be African or Arab.

Muslim knowledge production is one of the greatest achievements of Islamic civilisation. In the so-called 'Golden Age' of Islam, which ranges anywhere from the ninth to eleventh to the thirteenth century, some of the most consequential scientific, literary and philosophical scholarship emerged from within Muslim societies. It gave the world indispensable concepts in mathematics, including algebra. Crucial scholarship in the fields of chemistry, physics, medicine are matched with architecture, art and literature. The philosophy of Ibn Rushd (Averroes), a resident of Cordoba, had a profound impact on other famous philosophers like fellow Cordoban Maimonides and Thomas Aquinas. In fact, Greek philosophy was preserved, protected and reintroduced to the West, thanks to Muslim scholars. Western scientists, like the physicist Neil DeGrasse Tyson, officiously ask why there are so few Muslim Nobel Prize winners, implying that this is the only acceptable standard for achievement. Of course, what he neglects to mention is how so many Nobel Prizes are won based on knowledge that was initially produced by Muslims and moved forward by Western researchers today.

Tyson at least acknowledges the splendour of Islamic scientific production in its Golden Age. By contrast, Thomas Kuhn, regarded to be one of the foremost experts on the history of science, barely mentions the role of Muslim scientific achievement in bringing the West out of its so-called Dark Ages and into its own era of scientific progress. The scholar who introduced the concept of the Paradigm Shift somehow ignores how Islamic knowledge constituted a paradigm shift itself. It would be difficult to consider this exclusion to be anything but wilful and intentional. It appears to affirm the suspicion that the West deems it fit to reject any historical narrative or contribution outside its own making, perhaps out of a sense of superiority, bigotry, envy or a combination of all three. Of course, this danger can also be found among Muslims who refuse to acknowledge any achievement, especially in the modern era, to have merit, value or utility, simply because it didn't emerge from within the Muslim world. With the realisation that Muslim history is ignored, disparaged or simply erased from Western history, it is all the more incumbent on Muslims to know their own history, especially its contribution to the world and insist the world acknowledges it.

The absence of the Muslim historical voice is not confined to Western countries. The Hindutva movement in India, enabled greatly by the Bharatiya Janata Party under Prime Minister Narendra Modi, is attempting to demonise, diminish and in some cases, completely erase Muslim contribution to Indian civilisation and history. While the egregious actions of demolishing historically significant structures like the Babri Masjid in 1992 is emboldening Hindutva zealots targeting other buildings, including the Taj Mahal, under the pretence that these were allegedly built on religiously Hindu sites, the more nefarious campaign involves writing Muslims out of Indian history. School textbooks in India are being revised and published, highlighting certain prominent figures like the founder of Hindutva, V.D. Savarkar at the expense of well-known leaders of the independence movement such as Mahatma Gandhi, Muhammad Ali Jinnah, Abul Kalam Azad, and Jawaharlal Nehru. Somehow, they overlook inconvenient truths such as the historic coexistence and collaboration of the Hindu and Muslim communities for the vast majority of Indian history, including, for example, the presence of Hindu officials in the Mughal Court. They also offer outlandish, fantastical ideas as historical and scientific fact, such as that ancient Hindus invented aeroplanes and even nuclear weapons. In their effort to create a 'Muslim-free' India, Hindu zealots have resorted to contorting and distorting the historical record of a region that is renowned for its diversity and pluralism. The fact that the

Hindutva agenda has a scope beyond just the Muslim community reflects how pernicious the situation is in India, but it also allows for the opportunity for a coalition to be formed among Muslims and other groups, including non-Hindutva Hindus to resist and push back on the sinister effort to revise and bastardise history.

Muslim students are particularly susceptible to the plight of a limited lens of history. They are often stuck between the normative and the empirical – a history that they wish had happened and could occur again versus the reality of a historical process that has been authentic in both its successes and deficiencies. This becomes readily apparent in the classroom setting where they are confronted by a narrative that might not be as sanitised as they have encountered within the home or community. Without the experience, and benefit, of a critical study of early Muslim history, many students fall into the trap of becoming defensive at the slightest deviation from an idealised account, or even one that falls short of the expected veneration of the early community.

The weight of a sacralised historical narrative can be difficult to bear even when challenged by ambivalent or benign actors; it can be paralytic when emanating from the hostile agenda of Islamophobes. The days, weeks and months after the 9/11 attacks piqued both curiosity in and antagonism toward all things Islam-related. In the United States, it was common for Muslim Americans to be approached, even accosted at work, at school, in the grocery queue and elsewhere and face the demand of explaining on the spot some aspect of Islam. These unsuspecting Muslims, usually only out for an errand, were now facing an inquisition, and expected to be in an instant theologians, historians, philosophers, economists, jurists, anthropologists and political scientists. These ambushes would also play themselves out for those brave but naïve souls who ventured onto media appearances to explain Islam and contextualise what nineteen hijackers had ostensibly perpetrated in the name of their faith. Ambitious and opportunistic media personalities would frame questions in the form of indictments and force the well-intended to respond either with a reflexive denial that the terrorists were even Muslim or reduce the highly complex landscape of geopolitics and Al Qaeda's actions to the tragically insufficient retort, 'Islam is a religion of peace.' The metaphor of the proverbial deer caught in a car's headlights was certainly appropriate on many of these occasions.

Of course, all of this real-time rhetorical juggling was occurring while many Muslims were seeking an alternate history through the exploration of conspiracy theories, arguing that anybody *but* Muslims was behind the terrorism of 11 September 2001. What causes people to seek explanations that are outside the mainstream coverage? Certainly, there is a justifiable level of scepticism, suspicion and cynicism by which we can approach media accounts. Manipulation of images and narratives is done to exploit emotions and opinions. They are also managed to increase viewership, readership and profit for news agencies that are corporate conglomerates in their own right, as well as for smaller scale enterprises or individuals that crave eyeball traffic on their respective platforms.

Social media has intensified this zeal and opportunity for visibility. It is no surprise that those with the necessary time and internet connection can plunge themselves down the rabbit hole of outlandish theories, presented in slick packages of audio/video pageantry. But at the heart of even delving into the effort of seeking counternarratives of an incident or of history more broadly is perhaps a sense of helplessness and lack of control. For those that seem to benefit, or at the very least, are not adversely affected by the evolution of history, there is both an affirmation of themselves and the absence of incentive to change the status quo. The trouble, however, occurs not because there are people who wish there had been a different outcome, but who also wish there had been a different history to arrive at that point, a futile exercise as history obviously cannot be altered. While history might not be changeable, it can be improved. Often, history suffers an incomplete narrative as too many voices are excluded from it. Historically, so to speak, this has involved the sometime shocking absence of women from historical accounts. It is a phenomenon that is fairly universal; no continent, culture or civilisation seems to be immune to this erasure, despite, presumably, women accounting for half the population at any given time or place on earth.

In Muslim history, there is a similarly scant treatment to women's agency. There are, of course, some important exceptions. The Prophet's first wife Khadija and another wife Aisha are notably featured in his biography, with due reference to his other spouses as well. His daughter Fatima also enjoys an elevated status in general, and an even higher position within Shia narratives, as are other female members of the Prophet's household, including his granddaughter (and Fatima's daughter) Zainab. In general, however, it is difficult to mine the Muslim historical archive for more than a handful of women that feature prominently. There is, it seems, a glaring gap between Umm Kulthum, the Prophet's daughter and Fatima's sister, and Umm Kulthum the legendary twentieth century Egyptian singer.

Is there a single, consensus on Muslim history? On many aspects of the narrative, Muslims can agree upon the accuracy of what has occurred over the past fourteen centuries. But there are some serious and significant exceptions to this fact, especially regarding the historical divergence between the two major sects of Islam. While Sunnis will accept as dictum the way history developed, there is, of course, the disagreement among the Shia. The disparity over the issue of political succession to the Prophet in 632 has led to a divergence of history ever since. The Shia will claim that the political history of Islam was forever tainted by, in their estimation, the disenfranchisement of Ali from becoming the leader of the community upon the Prophet's death. The past fourteen hundred years have at best seen an understanding where the two sects agree to disagree with their difference of opinion, but it has also yielded toxic episodes that have and continue to present themselves through violence and hostility. It also creates the contrast of one party that views history that was and is, and another that imagines a history that could have been. It is doubtful that these two histories can ever be reconciled, but how deeply and adversely the difference impacts the community always rests in the hands of Muslims themselves.

There are other implications associated with the essentialisation of a single, indisputable history as it pertains to sectarian interpretation and making early Muslim history categorically 'sacred'. When, for example, some Muslims insist on learning from and emulating the example of the 'Rightly Guided Caliphs', (Khulafat Rashidun), it is important to remember that those individuals and that era may mean different things depending upon the particular group of Muslims involved. Again, for the Shia, the caliphates of Abu Bakr, Umar and Uthman take on a significance quite different to their Sunni co-religionists and may not possess the example they wish to emulate. It may lead to the Shia narrative being eclipsed or erased from the overall historical chronicle, given the demographic difference overwhelmingly favouring the Sunnis numerically. In a sense, it can lead to the possibility of the Shia living outside the general Muslim historical account.

History is sometimes found in the literature of another. Miguel de Cervantes's *Don Quixote* is regarded to be the first modern novel. Published in 1605, this classic book made its debut a little over a century after the end of the conquest over Muslim Spain. It chronicles the endeavours of a country gentleman trying to make sense of a world that has changed during his lifetime, and his efforts to recapture a bygone era and culture. With his trusty sidekick, Sancho Panza, Quixote travels the Spanish countryside of La Mancha. In one particularly noteworthy episode, the two come upon a place that can best be described as a ghost town. While Cervantes does not divulge too much about this setting, it becomes readily apparent that it was a town that had been inhabited by Muslims, only to be deracinated. It is the silence of the locale that speaks volumes about Spain's Islamic past, one that ended violently and completely. In fact, Quixote's idealism, oftentimes to the point of delusion, evokes memories of a civilisation, culture and etiquette (*adb*) that he had fondly embraced, and futilely craves its return. Cervantes deftly depicts the challenges facing people caught in the vortex of social transition and how some had been acclimated and in favour of the prior Muslim way of life over even the Christianised new (modern) Spain. As a result, Muslims play a critical role in one of the greatest pieces of literature through their noticeable absence.

Winston Churchill is attributed with saying: 'those that fail to learn from history are doomed to repeat it.' Given his rather dubious engagement with the Muslim world, there is a certain irony of invoking an adage from the former British Prime Minister. But there is some wisdom to what Churchill forewarned. At the same time, there are many Muslims who regard their relationship to history not as a matter of doom, but rather a duty and directive to repeat. The Prophetic example is not only a paragon for Muslims to study historically, but it is also a theological source of authority for the community. While no one would argue with the imperative to apply the Prophet's vision today, context is critical, particularly when literalistic interpretations lead to calls to bring the seventh century to the twenty-first in its entirety. There are two major issues that should be considered when such appeals are made, especially as they are often in the realm of political or social engagement. First, the

Prophet's pronouncements were made within a specific context of tribal Arabia. They took into account the cultural context of the region and the time. While the underlying principles and overall ethos that the Prophet intended for community are meant to be universal and eternal, the challenge is how to apply those principles in the current model of the nation-state.

Today, we have countries, some of which are democracies and some are dictatorships. None of these entities operates like the tribal societies of Arabia at the time of the Prophet. After all, the nation-state came about from a specific historical process in Europe that was sparked by Martin Luther's Protestant Reformation and culminated in the Thirty Years' War. The Peace of Westphalia, the 1648 treaty that ended the conflict, offered the concept of the nation-state model as a way for Europe to keep the peace. That is a history that did not occur in the Muslim world. And worse, the nation-state came to Muslims by way of imposition, thanks to colonialism and post-colonialism, when European countries carved up territory that was formerly governed by Muslims, like the Ottoman Empire, the Mughal Empire, other parts of Asia as well as Africa. Muslims didn't have any say over the establishment of these states, their borders and in many cases, the structure and form of government that accompanied them. When most of these countries were established in the Muslim world, after World War II, secularism had become so embedded globally, the notion of a Prophetic example as the national guiding principle in these nations was elusive at best.

Muslims do live inside history, their own and whichever broader historical narrative in which they reside, irrespective of time and space. Given the pressures they experience today, as the chronicle of Islam and Muslims is defined, described, defamed, demeaned, distorted and deleted by others, Muslims need to reclaim both the vibrant scope and scale of their own history and reclaim the role of being its agents and architects. That requires Muslims to learn it, critique it, protect it and add to it. We are all stakeholders in this project, as we are now the ones both preserving history and creating it.

CRYING TREES

Leyla Jagiella

The first story.

A tree was cut down in the Iranian city of Kashmar in the year 861. A cypress. A holy cypress, revered by the faithful Zoroastrians of the region because they considered it once having grown from a branch that Zarathustra himself had brought down from Paradise and planted there. One of the many signs of the Divine that Zoroastrians saw and still see in nature, one among many of the sacred mountains, sacred springs and, of course, sacred flames that for centuries were places of pilgrimage for people of the Iranian Highlands. The holy cypress of Kashmar was cut down on the orders of the Abbasid Caliph Al-Mutawakkil who also had ordered that the wood of the sacred tree should then be used for the construction of his new palace in Iraqi Samarra.

Al-Mutawakkil was someone who had no sympathy for the nature-worship of his Zoroastrian subjects. In general, his religious policies were not characterised by tolerance and leniency. He had abolished the pro-Mu'tazilite 'Mihna' inquisition of his ancestors and had freed imprisoned traditionalist scholars such as Ahmad ibn Hanbal; but only to initiate his own anti-Mu'tazilite inquisition. He ordered his Jewish and Christian subjects to publicly wear clothes that would distinguish them from Muslims, a policy that had also been practiced by some other Muslim rulers before but that today ominously reminds us of the 'yellow star' that Jews had to wear under German Nazi rule. Al-Mutawakkil also re-introduced the long-forgotten Umayyad practice of publicly cursing 'Ali ibn Abi Talib and his relatives and descendants from the pulpits of all mosques, a practice meant to curb Shi'a sentiments but also considered very offensive by a number of Sunni scholars of the time. All in all, al-Mutawakkil wanted to make sure that a tight regime of both politics and religion was firmly in his hands and that all religious minorities would know they had to bow to that regime. As the cypress of Kashmar fell to the ground, he probably hoped that the Zoroastrians of his realm would likewise bend and fall prostrate. And they did, ostensibly. But they also may have seen no need to rebel because they knew that someone who ordered such a terrible blasphemy, as the felling of a sacred tree was to them, would not continue to rule for long. And indeed: before the wood of the holy cypress reached Samarra and before it could be used for the construction of the new palace, al-Mutawakkil was murdered in a palace conspiracy.

The second story.

I have a thing about trees. Wherever I go, wherever I live. In fact, wherever I live for a significant amount of time, a tree always accompanies me. One of those indoor dragon trees that almost everybody has. Someone gave it to me when I was a teenager and it grew, from a small shoot, in my room when I was still living with my parents. That must have been more than 25 years ago. I had other plants in my room at that time. But none of them remained with me. But this tree I have taken with me from move to move, flat to flat, apartment to apartment. And it is still with me now. Which amazes me because I have not been treating it particularly well. I have often been away for months on my travels and would never get around to finding someone who could water my plants during those times. So, the tree just waited there for me in a dark room, until I came back. I have also never bothered to repot this tree and give it fresh, new nutritious soil. Each year I swear that I will eventually do so because the tree really deserves better. But it never happened. More than 25 years and that poor tree is still surviving on that bit of soil that it received back then and the water that I give it only occasionally. And still it survives. Sometimes it looks as if it is almost about to die. But then it always renews itself. And it still keeps me company.

The other day I again swore that I would repot it this year. And I told him so (I am sure the tree is male). And I apologised to him and thanked him that he is such a loyal companion, even though I do not treat him so well. I do think, however, that there must be some kind of symbiotic relationship between the tree and me and that it is that relationship that may have made his survival possible. He survives on the CO_2 that I breathe out, after all. Just as I breathe in his oxygen. Over the decades I must have absorbed a number of his particles. Just as he must have absorbed many of my particles. We must have become one body, one flesh, to at least some extent. And I see myself in his amazing survival as well. Just as he always renews himself when he looks as if he is almost about to give up, I have also always renewed myself and gained new strength after every crisis in my life. This tree seems like a simile of myself. Or maybe I am his simile?

This old fragile-but-resilient dragon tree is not the only tree that I have a thing about, however. There are many others. There have always been others. I still fondly think of the huge sacred fig tree that grew in front of the house of my Kathak teacher in Kolkata. A huge thing in whose crown a large number of crows nested and every now and then a koel as well. A shrine had been built under it and the tree had slowly grown around the shrine and had become 'one flesh and one body' with it. The tree must have been there first, of course. It may have already been considered sacred before this area had become urbanised.

When I was living at my Kathak teacher's house I often spent hours just sitting on the balcony and watching the tree, watching the crows, watching the coming and going and the *pujas* at the shrine. And marvelling at the intriguing connection between natural phenomena and beings and the sense of the sacred that they could evoke in human beings. Indeed, I also felt that this huge tree was something holy. And as in the case of my little frail dragon tree, I realised that here as well the holiness of this tree embraced its relationship with us a well. All of us who lived around it, whether only temporarily as I did or permanently, benefitted from it. From its oxygen as much as from its cooling shade. Often my Kathak teacher's mother joined me, sitting on the balcony and watching the tree, the crows and the coming and going at the shrine. And we had many conversations on the world, on humankind and on meaning and religion.

Many years later my Kathak teacher visited me in Germany and we talked about that time and the tree and the conversations that I had had with her mother. And then a shadow flew over the face of my Kathak teacher. And she told me that the tree wasn't there anymore. People in the area had wanted a fancier and more modern looking little temple than the old and dilapidated shrine and so they decided that the shrine shroud be renovated and expanded. But given the strong symbiosis between tree and shrine, the tree wasn't able to survive those measures and it had to be cut down. How ironic! The tree that was the actual sign of the sacred had to go so that the shrine, which actually had no real meaning without the tree, could expand. Unlike in the case of the cypress of Kashmar, nobody had to die for this act that was more an act of absurdity than of sacrilege. At least as far as I know. But punishment still followed. The ground has become unstable and easily subject to the damage of floodings ever since the roots of the tree withered. And the street is now open to the unmerciful scorching heat of the sun, no shade is found there anymore, neither for leisure nor for work.

A third story.

This one you will have heard or read before. It is a story commonly told in Friday sermons because it is a story found in some of the most authoritative collections of traditions from and about our Prophet Muhammad. In this story we are told that after the *hijrah*, the flight of the early Muslim community from Makkah to Madinah, the community still found itself living in very simple and humble surroundings. The courtyard of the house of the Prophet had become their mosque there. And when the Prophet was giving his sermons he was simply leaning or sitting on an old withered date tree. Some narrations say it was a tree, some others say it was a mere trunk, but it was something like that. One day, however, the community suggested that the Prophet should have a proper pulpit to preach his sermons from and so some carpenters had come together and built what was to be known as the first 'minbar' of Islam. On the following Friday, the Prophet rose on this minbar to give his sermon. And in that very moment the whole community heard the tree cry. It cried because it yearned for the Prophet. The Prophet went over to the tree, hugged it (original tree-hugger that he was) and comforted it with his words. And only then did the tree stop crying.

We know this story well. But do we believe it? Can we believe it? As I mentioned, it is found in some of the most authoritative collections of

Prophetic hadith. And both Sunni and Shi'a authorities have confirmed its reliability. For centuries the majority of Muslims would never have doubted that this miraculous event did indeed happen and that it happened exactly as reported. But the modern Muslim has a broken relationship with such stories. The modern Muslim yearns for his religion to be rational and logical and he can not afford to have faith in crying trees and in speaking rocks (whose existence is attested to in other narrations). In fact, not rarely does the modern Muslim look down on adherents of other religions (and on his allegedly uneducated *jahil* co-religionists who are only real Muslims in name) who still entertain such notions.

Islam is not a religion of fairy tales. The Qur'an describes the development of the embryo in the mother's womb and knows about the mummy of Pharaoh Ramesses II, as every devoted Bucailleist knows. A religion built around such scientific coherency should not be telling tales of trees with human emotions. So what do we do with such stories in modern times? Stories that, after all, are very well-established in our traditions but that our modern minds cannot accept anymore? We can go down several roads with this one. We can walk the path that deems all traditions as unreliable and be happy that this story is just more proof for the fact that the hadith are a collection of fables and legends. We may try the road of the rationaliser who would suggest that maybe the event did happen in some way but that the tree just caused some sound for some very natural and physical reason (we know about creaking wood, right?) and that the uneducated people of seventh century Arabia just exaggerated the incident a bit. We can follow the track of the mystic and philosopher and perhaps suggest that the story is not to be taken literally and that it has a different, symbolic value. We may also adopt the good old tradition of the average believer who does not worry too much about things that she does not agree with and just largely ignores the existence of such stories. But only very few of us will still be able to literally believe in the veracity of this story. Most of us just can't believe in crying trees anymore, even if we wanted to.

Three stories about trees, three branches you might say. Branches of a larger question that I would like to ask. A question rooted in the soil of our own existence as fragile human beings in a natural world. A fragile existence of whose fragility we now become more and more aware again.

After a few centuries in which we probably thought that we could truly conquer nature and then just do with it what we want, we now come to understand the hubris with which we have been treating the world that we live in and finally realise that nature may eventually still triumph over us. Whether in the form of virus pandemics or in the form of climate change, we cannot escape it. We are still helplessly dependent on its moves and we need to deal with the fact that we have to work with nature if we want to survive as a species. Work with it, not rule over it. We are, in many ways, like Al-Mutawakkil, who wasted his life thinking that the wood of the holy cypress was only meant for his palace.

Our modern hubris is often understood as an extension of premodern religious hubris. Our treatment of the natural world is often described as an effect of the Biblical verse in which God speaks to Adam, 'Be fruitful and replenish the earth, and subdue it: and have dominion over the fish of the sea, and over the fowl of the air, and over every living thing that moveth upon earth' (Genesis 1:28). The Qur'an does not confirm these divine words but Muslims have nevertheless often understood the place of humankind in the cosmos in similar ways, given that we are *ashraf ul-makhluqaat*, the most noble of creation.

Indeed, the words of the Bible, especially in its King James version, have given much support to the rise of an anthropocentric vision of the world in which humans could do all that they want to the planet they inhabit. But it is worth considering that in both Judaism and Christianity there have always also been other traditions of translating and understanding these words. And Islam in particular has always stressed that the specific place of humankind in the cosmos also entails an *amana*, a trust that God has given us. We may have special blessings in our exercise of rational thinking and free choice, but God expects us to use these blessings for the benefit of all. When the Qur'an says that God has created humankind to be his *khalifa* on earth, many scholars point out that a *khalifa* is supposed to be more a caretaker than a ruler. Our rational thinking and our free choice give us a responsibility that no other created being has. And we do best if we fulfil that responsibility in a way that preserves God's creation.

Before the especially neurotic situation of post-industrial urban existence arose, most common Muslims would have understood this special responsibility as also guiding us towards a way of organic existence in this world. In some rural regions of the Muslim world people still live accordingly, or may at least have done so until recently. We may here take as witness anthropologist Reinhold Loeffler, who studied and described the life of a number of Iranian Muslim villagers in the 1970s and 1980s:

> The Zagros villagers studied by Loeffler uniformly held that being a good Muslim meant being good to others and not inflicting harm on other creatures. Even the mullah held animals to have souls. According to an old hunter the jinn would appear as animals, and one could hurt them by killing them as game animals or snakes, or by bothering them as cats, if one did it without first invoking God. It was lawful to kill game, he said, but it was sinful to do so excessively, beyond what one needed. 'But why do we kill these animals?', he asked. 'They have lives too and their lives are dear to them. Why do we kill this chicken?' Again he affirmed that it was both lawful and sinful: anything that did harm to other beings was sinful. Another villager said that it was impossible to live without sinning, giving as his examples having to throw a stone at an animal to keep it out of a field and hurting it thereby, or having to kill a chicken that had been hit by a stone: 'Then I shall have taken a life', he said. Apparently, it was the unintended nature of the animal's death that bothered him, for he said nothing about killing animals for food and he approved of sacrificing animals and distributing the meat to the poor to avert misfortune. These villagers did not have a coherent set of principles, but their sentiments are clear enough.

Here I actually quote a summary of Loeffler's observations that one will find in *The Nativist Prophets of Early Islamic Iran: Rural Revolt and Local Zoroastrianism* by controversial late scholar Patricia Crone. I do so not just because Crone summarises these observations in a way that I could not have done better myself but also to point to Crone's argument here. Crone in her work suggests that sentiments such as the one described here could not actually be 'originally Islamic' but that they must be a residue of older Zoroastrian ideas, ideas such as the one surrounding the holy cypress of Kashmar. If Iranian Muslims are kind to animals and conscious of their natural surroundings, this can not be an inheritance of Islam, right? Islam obviously being, for Crone, the religion of those who 'subdue earth and have dominion over everything that moveth upon earth', the religion of those who cut down holy trees, not the religion of the one who hugged and comforted a crying tree.

Notwithstanding the fact that Loeffler's Zagros villagers all articulate their sentiments in clearly Islamic terms and in a language peppered by references to Qur'an and Sunnah and the Shi'a Imams. Also, notwithstanding the fact that similar sentiments can be found among villagers all across the Muslim world, even in regions where Zoroastrianism has not played the same historical role as in Iran. I have often been told by Moroccan friends about very similar attitudes common among the rural people of the Islamic Maghreb. Jonathan Parkes Allen on his beautiful 'Thicket and Thorp' blog has in a recent blogpost (dated 20 December 2022), documented similar attitudes in stories surrounding the Algerian Sufi saint Sidi al-Hasan Abirkan who in the sixteenth century had been reported to miraculously converse with lions, dogs and snakes. The whole animal kingdom takes part in the story of such saints, the beings of creation are not just bystanders, they are part of the social fabric of the saint as much as other human beings and supernatural creatures such as angels, devils and jinn are. Saints such as Sidi al-Hasan, or at least the people who wrote down the certainly embellished and exaggerated biographies of such saints, lived in a world not only of crying trees but also of speaking animals and they knew of the numerous relationships and responsibilities that we as human beings have with and towards other beings.

This was a way of living in the world that was not only known in the Maghreb or in Iran. I am here also reminded of the attitude I have personally often encountered among rural Muslims in Punjab or Uttar Pradesh in India. An attitude that centres around the idea that we human beings have a special responsibility to take care of everything that is be-zubaan, without tongue. Neither animals nor plants can cry out with a voice that we human beings can usually understand (unless a miracle happens, just as in the courtyard of the Prophet in Madinah). Thus, we have to make an extra effort to not ignore their voices.

Sarra Tlilli, author of *Animals in the Qur'an*, suggests that Islam is in its essence is not an anthropocentric but a theocentric faith. And that theocentricity implies love and care for all of God's creation. But I think that Islam goes even further than that when it speaks to our relationship with the natural world. When we look closely, we may understand that the boundaries between us are porous, that the boundaries between the *ashraf ul-makhluqaat* and the other beings of the natural world are actually not as firmly drawn as we often think and that we are, in fact, beings that are constantly in transition. That already starts with Islam's central myth of the creation of humankind, the creation of Adam from kneaded earth and water, from clay. No 'earthier' vision of the human being is possible. We literally are soil, in that myth. At least our materiality is.

It is also for this reason that a narration of the Prophet tells us: 'Be mindful of the earth because she is your mother'. And the Qur'an says: 'God has made you grow out of the earth as a growing thing' (71:18). Our relationship with the earth and its soil is therefore to be understood as a truly organic one. And it doesn't stop with the pure soil itself. It extends to everything else that has grown out of that soil as well. For another narration attributed to the Prophet tells us that 'the date tree is the aunt of mankind'. Another narration that has a well-established place in Muslim tradition but which we find difficult to understand literally in our modern day and age. But maybe we should? Maybe it would help us do better on this planet if we would truly realise that we can even consider a tree a close relative? And are we not constantly urged to do good to our relatives in our religion?

We have grown out of earth and we grow alongside all the other beings that have grown out of it. But in the course of that process we ourselves also become part of all beings and all beings become a part of ourselves. Our transitional state continues. This is something that Muslim thinkers have realised very early on and have elaborated on. We find this expressed in the proto-evolutionary theories of a number of medieval Muslim scholars, from al-Jahiz to the Ikhwan al-Safa to Ibn Khaldun, who many centuries before Charles Darwin suggested that the different species of creation may actually go through a process of development and change until they truly reach their eventual stage of being.

This idea was also taken up by the mystical tradition where it was transformed into the vision of a constant ascent of all beings through different stages of creation, best expressed in the famous words of Maulana Rumi: 'As a mineral I died and rose again as a plant, a plant I died and rose again as an animal, I died an animal and was born as a man. Why should I fear what comes next? When was I ever less by dying?' The same idea also prompted the sixteenth century Iranian philosophy Mulla Sadra to develop his theory of substantial motion, according to which there is a constant transformation going on within the inner structure of things: every being and every little particle of creation is constantly moving towards self-perfection. Except those who may actually chose to not progress, as some humans may who in the afterlife may even acquire non-human forms.

These traditions of thinking nevertheless express a hierarchical view of existence. They suggest that we all have been minerals, plants or animals at some point and therefore are all intimately related to all of these beings. But they nevertheless do think of human existence as the 'crown of creation' and the eventual goal of all these transformations. While I wonder, whether we should not more clearly also incorporate a more horizontal view of our human existence in the midst of all creation into our Muslim thinking as well. If the date tree is our aunt, then she is also our wise elder, she is the one we should look up to instead of expecting that everything shall always look up to us.

We are therefore not simply just the successful end-point of a transition. We remain in a state of transition even as human beings. The boundaries and limits of our existence as humans are not absolute because we constantly merge into other beings and they merge into us. Be it through the air that we breathe in and breathe out, be it through the other beings that we consume, cooked or uncooked. Be it through our own bodies that become nutrition for others both during our lifetimes and after death.

I would like us as Muslims to think of our relationship with earth and nature much like the ideas of the spiritual writer Sophie Strand. In *Your Body is an Ancestor*, she writes:

> ancestry isn't a lineage. It is a nonlinear tangle of animacy with multiple points of entry. For me, ancestry extends beyond the human. It is rhizomatic, rooting into different species and deep time... Every one of your cells holds an ancient and anarchic love story. Around 2.7 billion years ago free-living prokaryotes melted into one another to form the mitochondria and organelles of the cells that build our bodies today.' And who reminds us: 'If you live in a valley, chances are the ancient glacial moraine, the fossils crushed underfoot, the spores from grandmotherly honey fungi, have all entered into and rebuilt the very molecular make up of your bones, your lungs, and even your eyes.

That is, I would think, a kind of ancestry that was understood by the Zoroastrians of Kashmar but not understood by the Abbasid al-Mutawwakil.

It was also understood by the people who once started to worship in the shade of a sacred fig tree in Kolkata but not by the Bengali upper middle-classes who yearned for a fancy and proper shrine many decades later. I would believe it was also understood by a Prophet who hugged crying trees and who reminded us that the date tree is our aunt. Curiously, it is a kind of ancestry that establishes itself anew every morning, every day, in every moment. With every new breath we take. Thus, our ancestries, our physical existence, our embodied presence in this natural world remains constantly in transition and at the same time in connection. And if we are willing to truly listen to the flow of that transition – like the Prophet who was willing to listen to the cries of a tree – then we may also be able to stay in perpetual renewal, just as my frail little dragon tree does. And maybe we may also understand that we cannot preserve ourselves if we do not preserve the soil that we have grown out of.

MY CONVERSION

amina wadud

Islam is my choice: I pronounced the *shahadah* on Thanksgiving Day, 1972, in the city of Washington, DC. Often when I say I am Muslim by choice, both Muslims and non-Muslims ask why. This curiosity leads me to tell the same basic story because I hardly think my individual entry into the doors of Islam lights up any bulbs of excitement. That may be because no light bulbs went off for me at the time.

I was a seeker, raised in a loving Christian environment. I was close to my dad. We called him The Rev. As a Methodist minister my father led a fascinating life with his own light of faith. I witnessed him leading both his private and public life within that light. Imagine how devastating it would have been to hear him profess faith in public, but then do horrendous things in private.

I adored my father. I had my first experience of transcendence sitting in his lap. As a child I was deathly afraid of thunderstorms. I felt like there was a message being hurled at me for my shortcomings. Oddly, it was not the lightning—which could actually do some harm if it struck something—but the roaring noise of thunder that I found most upsetting. One evening, my father took me onto his lap and told me the biblical story of Noah's Ark and the flood. He told me God's promise never again to destroy the world by water. The symbol of that promise—he leaned in to whisper—is the rainbow. For a brief moment, I was suspended beyond the material world. Time stood still as joy and serenity flooded through me as if to confirm the divine promise.

As a teenager I began to look into more diverse expressions of faith. I also spent high school living with Jewish, Catholic, and Unitarian Universalist families. I pursued more of this religious diversity in my early years at university by studying Eastern faith traditions. By my second year, I had moved to a meditation ashram and began practising Buddhism. I still carry light from both of these earlier experiences of faith. From Buddhism I carry a profound experience of tranquillity and transcendence through daily meditation practices. Once a year I take myself off the beaten path to spend ten days in silent retreat with ten hours of meditation a day. From the Christianity of my father, I carry sincerity and love. Despite the benevolent patriarchy of my father, he bequeathed to me an enduring sense of Divine Love. I chose my Arabic name Wadud from the Loving God.

Actually, I made *shahadah* without intention. Because of my interest in the diversity of faith I had started to read about Islam. I knew there had to be more to it than just what I found in books. I noticed a small mosque in a row house around the corner from my parents' house one Thanksgiving Day visit. I had intentionally chosen to cover my legs, arms and hair in recognition of the trauma my African ancestors experienced when stripped naked on the auction block and sold into slavery. This modesty was a reflection of other African-American women who chose to project bodily integrity by leaving off popular revealing fashions.

On the evening of Thanksgiving Day, I went to the mosque and was met only by men. They thought my choice of modest dress meant I had come to make the confirmation. So they said, if you believe Allah is One and Muhammad is His Prophet, you should pronounce *shahadah*. So, I did. Despite my lack of intentions, I took the statement to heart and went to read more books. The men gave me a small daily prayer book and I learned to recite these in Arabic.

With my *shahadah* I entered a global awareness with a sense of history that I had never considered in my mere 20 years. I made my way through those first few months by reading as many books as I could from my University library. Four months after that Thanksgiving Day event, on a mild early spring afternoon, I was introduced to the Qur'an. If it were up to me, I would make a huge deal about the Qur'an for anyone interested in Islam even without conversion. I started regularly visiting my family in Washington DC so I could attend *jumu'ah* (Friday prayer) at this small mosque. No one there emphasised reading the Holy Book. In another way, this could be seen as a blessing. It gave me time to acclimate to being Muslim first. Once I was introduced to the Qur'an my life changed forever.

One afternoon after visiting the mosque I bumped into a childhood friend. I chatted mostly about what I was reading and learning. Her youngest sister said to me, I know something about that. To be sure, their house was a block away from the mosque. The men went out in the neighbourhood to make *dawah*. That word means call or invite. It can be an invitation to Islam or to reinvigorate one's Islam. One of them had given her a Qur'an. She gave it to me. Fifty years after that gift, I can tell you it was the single most important moment of my life. I took the gift and began to read. Then, I fell in love—even while reading a translation that I can no longer abide today.

Imagine, fifty years have passed and I am still in love with the Qur'an. The more I am in love with the Qur'an, the more the incentive I felt all those years ago makes sense. I wanted to understand it unencumbered by any limitations. Thus, I started Arabic study at a mosque near my university while waiting for the full academic course to resume in September 1973. The Qur'an was the goal. To get there over the next ten years, I immersed myself in the language. This included living twice in Arabic-speaking countries, Libya and Egypt. The year in Egypt, almost a decade later, was for an immersion course that would culminate my Arabic studies and put me at a level of proficiency equivalent to a native university student. While there, I studied with a Qur'anic studies professor from Ain Shams University whose resistance catapulted me into my life's work. Namely, it makes a difference who is reading to how they are interpreting. Reading as an African-American woman who was not born into Islam meant I had questions that had not been given consideration for a millennium and a half. I then applied myself to those questions and arrived at insights that would help shape the mandate of reading for gender and eventually reading intersectionally.

To this day, I am still surprised by the Qur'an. I am still learning. I am still challenged by it. I could never have imagined how a single gift would become the central focus of my life, creating a public and professional trajectory that was inspired by love. What a blessing. As I look back now, I see how all the important moves in my life were revolved around this gift. Still today, if things are off kilter, I return to read only the Qur'an.

In the ten years between taking *shahadah* and attaining proficiency in Arabic, the politics of conversion would come into my life in full force around self-naming. Some Muslims by choice are adamant to identify as 'reverts' to Islam. I don't know the politics of rejecting the term 'convert' but I can see the appeal. There is an often-cited statement from the Prophet: 'Everyone was born Muslim... and then their parents make them Jews, Christians, etc.' The actual Arabic says, *kullun 'ala al-fitrah*, which translates literally into everyone was born in/with *al-fitrah*. The word 'Muslim' does not occur in that statement.

According to the Qur'an, al-fitrah is a primordial predisposition toward faith. The commentators contend that it is also a primordial predisposition to surrender, which is another word for Islam. Unfortunately, this is then concluded to mean, 'Everyone was born Muslim or in Islam'. I have a problem with collapsing the primordial state with historical and anthropological Muslims. I think it misses the point of expressing an idea about the natural make-up of the human person. We were created with the potential to believe in something greater than ourselves. What that something is, to me, is not one and the same as Islam as a historical or cultural phenomenon. Having the capacity to believe in the transcendent— which is denied our animal cousins—is a special quality in the very creation of the human being. Not all humans choose to develop this faith capacity. Al-fitrah is not coercion.

I stay away from 'revert' as it feels like over-compensating. Most reverts choose it to say, I am the original Muslim. Those born into Muslim families are secondary Muslims. Reverts try to reclaim their original nature because born Muslims often make them secondary.

After more than thirty years as a Muslim by choice, I learned I had Muslim ancestors on my maternal side. The first member of my family from Africa identified as Moors, or Muslim. I shared this genealogy with a born Muslim friend who said, 'Now you are really one of us'. After three decades of conscious practice I need a lineage to be a real Muslim? So, I get it with reverts. Islam is more than just a person's bloodline. It is more than a way of naming the self and affirming Islam as a choice.

I mean, think about it. A man named Muhammad started receiving revelation at age forty. He died at age sixty-three, as Prophet. That would make twenty-three years as Muslim. I chose Islam at age twenty and yet even after more than thirty years I would all of a sudden become 'one of us' because I learned of my ancestry. I don't get that math. Completing my most recent book, as a faithful Muslim for fifty years, I am beyond both the blood of it and the conversion to it. Any person who chooses

Islam and remains faithful for more years than the Prophet's twenty-three, yeah, that's gotta qualify for being unconditionally Muslim: no defence, no math and no wordplay required.

Okay, I know, I should probably unpack what I mean by 'remain faithful'. These days online trolls attack my faith as I often make statements contrary to their conservative Islam. Some feel that Islam is under siege from the imperial West, the colonisers or Islamophobes. As such Islam needs gatekeepers to protect it. Most of these gatekeepers hurl their vitriol against other Muslims who have ideas, practices and experiences that differ from a more conservative norm. I don't have a siege mentality. On the contrary, I have confidence that Islam will continue to thrive even through torrential times. It has lived through nearly a millennium and a half with major issues of preservation coming and going to the periphery. Meanwhile, and more importantly, it has adapted to include a greater diversity of perspectives. Sure, we must address anti-Muslim sentiment or Islamophobia. But we do this by aligning with the order of the universe that confirms Islam as a way of life. I remain faithful to that way of life. It is that orderly universe that makes me Muslim. Meanwhile, it increases the sense of love and serenity I received when practising Buddhism and Christianity. Today I identify as an eclectic Muslim.

I will repeat several times that I fell in love with the Qur'an. By some special grace this love has never faltered. I have had a more tumultuous relationship with the Prophet of Islam, upon him be peace. So let me introduce him through some of the waxing and waning of my love for him. The second part of the *shahadah* is, 'I bear witness that Muhammad is the Messenger of Allah'. This second mandatory part begs a few questions: what does prophethood mean and who is this particular Prophet? First you will notice, I will often follow his name by keeping to the etiquette of offering peace and blessings: *sallaLahu alayhi wa-sallam*. In writing I put (s) at least once after his name. This reflection of honour and esteem is itself a ritual act.

An ordinary man in seventh century Arabia, Muhammad, the son of Abd-Allah and Aminah (from whom I took my name), was peaceful, sensitive and deeply spiritual, and became a guide to communities of Muslims across time and place. He was called al-Amin, faithful or reliable, because he was honest and open. He had a sense of humour. A few of my favourite stories will show my love. At the age of twenty-five he was hired to manage the trade of a wealthy widow, Khadijah. Later, she would propose marriage to him and he would accept. They had a long and loving monogamous relationship for about twenty-five years until her death. She was his senior by fifteen years. They had four daughters. Although he would contract multiple marriages (only after Khadijah died), he would never have additional surviving children.

His habit of going into spiritual retreat was afforded to him in part because of his wife's wealth but mostly because it was his nature not to emphasise the material world except in harmony with the Unseen. During one such retreat he had a phenomenal experience. Something or someone pressed him to '*iqra*: recite or read, iqra'. At first, he resisted. 'I do not know how to read'. When instead he asked, 'What should I read?' the Qur'an began to be revealed. He was forty years old. The experience of revelation continued until his death some twenty-three years later. By then he had migrated to a city called Yathrib where he established the first Muslim polity or *ummah*: a collective dedicated to establishing life in accordance to the message of the revelation and as exemplified in his behaviour. Muslims still use the term ummah today although we are a much more complicated collective.

As I started my journey in Islam, I did automatically connect to this desert Arab from my location as an undergraduate student and a Black woman in the city of Philadelphia. Later, I would read Nabia Abbott's book *The Beloved of the Prophet* about his wife Aishah. Then I got my first glimpse of him as a person who was also a prophet. Something about the loving way in which Aishah described him gave me a sense about him as a real person, kind, gentle and funny. For example, despite the cultural taboo around menstruation, she describes him resting his head on her lap during her cycle.

One challenge in following his legacy has been to determine when he is a person of his time and place and when he is an exemplar for all humanity— no matter the time, place or gender. As a Cis-Het man, his gender identity was in part typical and within the normative seventh century patriarchy and heterosexuality and at the same time exceptional. As a self-identified non-binary Black woman in the twenty-first century, I could not come to love the Qur'an except through its being revealed to this person.

There are more complex answers to the question of the legacy he bequeathed us. Throughout history those answers have never taken a single route. There are twists and turns as related by communities of scholars and believers across their own identities and politics. It is enough to say that Muslims fundamentally accept that the Prophet's behaviour embodied the Qur'an. Thus, his behaviour, the *sunnah*, became a secondary source for understanding how to live as a Muslim and was deeply encoded into Islamic law. His statements while living as a Muslim were captured and preserved. These are called *hadith*. In my case, I am sometimes erroneously accused of being anti-hadith or Qur'an-only, just because I choose to focus my study of the Qur'an from a multitude of academic disciplines in the study of Islam. This just shows how little such people know about the various disciplines. There is a dynamic relationship between sunnah, hadith and Qur'an which cannot be claimed as one single thing.

As my plans for Hajj, the pilgrimage to Makkah and Medina, came together I sought advice from my Shaykh or spiritual teacher in Sufism. He suggested I follow the light of the Prophet(s) or al-Nur al-Muhammadi. This is a favourite Sufi preoccupation. They say the first thing Allah created was the Light of Muhammad. It's a metaphor. I get that. I also get when the Qur'an says, 'We have *not* sent him *except* as a mercy to all the worlds'. Whichever path one follows of the prophetic legacy is impacted by a number of factors debated across time. Thus, when my perspective follows the ebb and flow, it is part of developing my understanding of Islam as both a way of life for the Prophet and also a way of life for me: it grows as I grow.

Recently, while researching sexual diversity and Islamic classical sources, I learned something that also enchained my love of the Prophet (s). His time on earth was characterised by an immersion amongst women and the feminine. I have never seen this emphasised to the extent that I experienced it during this recent study. For example, he was a child without a father, since Abd-Allah died while he was still in the womb. Instead, he had two mothers: Aminah, his birth mother and Halimah, his wet nurse. When he returns from the desert with Halimah, Aminah's life too is cut short. He comes under the guardianship of two senior Quraysh men: his grandfather, and then upon his death, his uncle. Both of these men left off war and pillage to enter into a more feminine part of their lives. This was demonstrated by the way they would nurture this boy-child with love and tenderness.

He goes to work for a wealthy widow, Khadijah, who is senior to him. She makes the proposal of marriage. He accepts and remains faithful to only her, despite the wide practice of polygamy. With her he becomes father to only daughters. Thus his life was surrounded by loving feminine energy all the way through his prophethood. This love would be infused in the manner in which he stood for this new role. Ibn al-Arabi says the Prophet loved prayer, perfume and women. Most people read his love of women as romantic or even erotic love only. From my perspective this is clearly more universal love. For example, when the Qur'an emphasises the need to take up military struggle, I sometimes think perhaps how this would have been contrary to his peaceful nature. Others recount the story about him helping to resolve a dispute between the leaders of the Makkan tribes over who should replace the Ka'bah stone after the building had been destroyed. He laid his own garment on the ground, placed the stone on it and directed each tribal leader to hold one piece. Together they replaced the stone. When he conquered Makkah he granted pardon to all. This also expresses feminine nature. As a statesman, I think certain stories about him appeal to those who like doing things the way kings do. But I am not so sure that was how he saw himself.

In reality, much of his normative behaviour is typical of seventh century customs. Yet he was a Messenger of Allah. I do not marvel at seventh-century Arabian civilisation, to be honest. Despite the lowly origins of the Prophet in this peninsula, he was exceptional to his time and place. Part of how we understand the objectives of Islam combines not only what he did that was typical but more importantly what he did that was exceptional. I love that he was a person of moral excellence, spiritual devotion and unusual sensitivity. His expressions of excellence and devotion exceeded the standards of his time and place, making him a representation for all of us to move into our own excellence and devotion in our own time and place.

The universe is organised around the principle of God's abiding beauty and unity. In Islam this is called *tawhid*, the Arabic word for monotheism. This unity of Allah is living and dynamic. Since the word tawhid comes from the second form of the verb its meaning is emphatic. It is more than just saying God is One. That is true. God the Creator is also unique from the creation, and yet intimately connected to what It has created— especially the human creature. Thus, I tend to use the word unity for tawhid to express the unifying capacity of the One Divine Ultimate Reality, Allah.

Have you ever seen computer-generated images of a fractal? A fractal is a pattern based on a repetitive mathematical formula that adheres to its unity and form at the most minute levels and when projected out to its largest manifest levels. One such fractal, the Mandelbrot set, has been called the 'thumbprint of God'. No matter the scale, it remains harmonious and beautiful. It may be difficult to 'see' eternity and unity; however, the images generated with the mathematic of a fractal give us a clear visual idea of beauty and harmony in the universe.

Discovering these visual depictions of a metaphysical idea gave me both relief and challenge. On the one hand, giving form to the abstract idea for the Unseen might take away the mystery in belief. The Unseen is made manifest within everything in the universe: I was humbled and in awe. On the other hand, I am primordially predisposed to acknowledge the underlying unity in all creation as a manifestation of the unity of the Creator: from the many we return to the One. Fractal images bring the magic of the whole to confirmation by the sense of sight. It clarified my ambiguous belief through the beauty of its visual imagery. Thus, I came also to greater clarity of purpose: my life is an alignment with this sublime unity. It predisposes me to respond in action, thought, and emotion. Tawhid is the ultimate order of the entire universe: visible and invisible.

Although I identify as Muslim by choice, at this juncture in my life, there can be no other choice except to embrace this unity at every level. It is just the way I see all the worlds. However—and this needs to be stated explicitly—this is not a condemnation of other worldviews or other responses to the Sacred and Ultimate, nor of those who choose to reject faith. On the contrary, once my vision of this unity became clear, greater love and mercy towards others followed.

When the Qur'an says, 'There can be no compulsion in religion', it follows by saying 'Truth is (manifestly evident or) clear against falsehood' (2:256). You cannot force a person to see Truth. It can only be seen by complete volition. If truth must be forced, it is corruption and that is antithetical to faith. I have grown in love for any perspective of faith that allows one to act in devotion to the coherence of the Divine Unity of all the universe.

I draw the line when someone pretends their faith is justification for closing off others from engaging in their own independent exploration of sacred goodness and divine grace. As the medieval thinker Ibn Qayyim said, 'the root' of Islam is 'love for God, intimacy with Him, and yearning to encounter Him (sic)'. This perspective leaves no room for petty prejudices.

As my life unfolded and my global experiences expanded, my sense of tawhid as an active principle was enhanced. My faith in Islam was freed from the need to prove myself to others and left to embrace the enchantment of being connected to others through an intimate relationship with the One. That is what tawhid means.

Extracted from amina wadud, *Once Upon a Lifetime,* Kantara Press, Manchester, 2022.

SHIAPHOBIA

Sarah Shah

The international Muslim community is diverse, comprising many sects and outlooks. The increasing diversity sometimes leads to isolation; thus, there is a strong desire for unity in the *ummah*. Such a desire is rooted in faith; multiple Qur'anic verses are used to justify this notion (3:103; 6:159, 30:31-32). However, some have (mis)understood this concept of unity to mean sameness, and show no tolerance for the rich diversity in the ways Islam manifests in different contexts. Some believe only one form of Islam is 'correct', and all other forms are in error, dismissing them as cultural or ritualistic. This extends also to sectarian social politics, as many Sunni Muslims continue to exclude Shia Muslims from the folds of Islam. And even when Shia Muslims are accepted, it is done so as long as Sunni normativity is not interrupted.

It is impossible to hail unity driven by sameness given the globalisation of Islam. If we are to respond to the Qur'anic call for a united *ummah*, we need to build not only tolerance for, but also acceptance of, our differences. This also means becoming aware of how certain privileges make it easier for some Muslims, while disadvantages and exclusions can make it harder for other Muslims, to comfortably fit within the *ummah*.

The attitude of some Sunni Muslims towards the Shia can be described as Shiaphobia, which mirrors Islamophobia as the systematic and everyday exclusion of, or hostility towards, Shia Muslim minorities. In the same way that Muslims are made to feel othered by Islamophobia, Shias are made to feel othered by Shiaphobia. This happens sometimes intentionally, and sometimes innocently, through the centring of Sunni experiences, practices, beliefs, and worldviews as the norm.

Shiaphobia can be witnessed in Muslim-majority settings, in countries like Pakistan, Afghanistan and Saudi Arabia, where the Shia are systematically oppressed through political, economic, and social injustices that lead to disadvantaged life circumstances and even death. While some of these incidents receive public attention, like the widely criticised Saudi torture and execution of the late Ayatollah Sheikh Nimr Baqir al-Nimr, many murdered Shias die anonymously, with Sunni Muslims unaware of such violence happening around them. This is especially egregious when deaths result from targeted killing, like mosque bombings or assassinations. The silence of this violence in effect normalises it, and Sunnis take for granted that violence against Muslim minorities is just the expected reality, albeit an unpleasant reality best left ignored. Shias in immigrant settings, including the US, Canada, and Europe, experience the echoes of this violence – sometimes more directly when victims are family or when the violence takes place in one's hometown. As Shereen Yousuf has identified, the silencing and erasing of these violent realities create harmful experiences for Shias in immigrant settings. But experiences of Shiaphobia also go beyond the wilful ignorance of the Sunni majority of global anti-Shia violence.

As a sociologist studying immigrant Muslim experiences of discrimination, I spend a great deal of time in the field, listening to life stories. I often ask about experiences of marginalisation, exclusion, or hostility from others. Most Muslims share how these experiences happen outside of Muslim communities, and that they find solace and comfort within Muslim communities and especially mosques. However, this is not an experience shared by all Muslims. Shia Muslims often share stories about unpleasant experiences within mosques and Muslim communities. Even some chapters of the Muslim Student Association (MSA), a supposed haven for the diverse Muslim students on university campuses, refuse to include Shia and Ismaili students, insisting that they are not Muslims.

I was born and raised in New York, and like other Shia Muslims in immigrant settings, I was somewhat protected from the more physical forms of anti-Shia violence. Most of my experiences of Shiaphobia emerge from the constant othering by the Sunni majority in North America. Nonetheless, vivid memories from my visits to Muslim majority countries serve as stark reminders of the vulnerability of being a sectarian minority.

I have always called Turtle Island/North America home, but have visited Muslim countries across the years—namely, Pakistan, Saudi Arabia, Lebanon, Iran, and Egypt. With the exception of Iran, these visits include ambivalent experiences of Muslim unity and, simultaneously, Shia exclusion. Three experiences especially stand out: in my mother's hometown in Pakistan, and in Mecca and Medina during Hajj.

Though I identify as Pakistani, there is a deep woundedness of nonbelonging in this identity. Even as a child, I was aware my family left Pakistan due to sectarian violence, but my family shielded me from many of these details. Several of my mother's cousins have been killed by the Sipah-e-Sahaba, a vigilante terrorist group that targets influential and educated Shia community leaders. As an adult, I came to learn about a childhood experience kept hidden from me. When talking with my brother about Pakistan, I asked him directly, 'Why do you hate Pakistan so much?' He raised his brow and stared at me, then he slowly asked, 'You really don't remember?' I shook my head, and he began to tell me about my first, and only, trip to Pakistan.

I was eight, he was twelve, we had travelled with our family for our uncle's wedding. We were staying in our grandparents' village in Sialkot, Islamabad. This village was composed of Shia residents, and, as implied by the name Syedanwali, most were descendants of the Holy Prophet. At some point, my brother and our eight-year-old cousin left the safety of the family home to run an errand in the village. Sometime later, we heard loud commotions from the street, and the children in the home were rushed into an inner room. The adults – women and the elderly – were tense but tried to maintain calm. Hours later, my brother and cousin returned, and the adults expressed sheer joy and relief. I thought it was strange but thought nothing else of it, until years later my brother explained what had happened.

In their typical attack style, two Sipah-e-Sahaba came to the village. One sat driving a motorbike, the other sat behind him wielding a machine gun. As the driver rode through the streets of the village, the gunman opened fire on anyone he saw. These acts are not uncommon in Shia neighborhoods, especially at that time, and the authorities do little to respond to anti-Shia violence—as well as violence against Ahmadis, Ismailis, or any Muslim minority community. While the children were kept unaware, the adults of my family fretted about the likelihood that my brother and cousin had been targeted in the mass shooting, but were unable to leave home given the danger. As luck would have it, my brother and cousin had gotten lost in conversation, both figuratively and literally. They walked out of the village, and out of harm's way, without realising it. When they grew weary of walking, they realised they must have gone off track, and retraced their steps to come home—witnessing the aftermath of devastating bloodshed as they entered the village. Though I learned about these details over twenty years after the fact, this knowledge still shook me to the core, and I begged God to protect my brother. I reflected on the story of Karbala, my heart trembling at the thought of Zainab bint Ali praying for her brothers' protection.

My experience in my mother's hometown was violent, but as a child I was protected from the reality. This contrasts with the experiences I had during Hajj, where I was immediately aware of my otherness as a Shia Muslim. The Hajj is where Muslims celebrate their unity among siblings of shared faith, regardless of socioeconomic class, language, and race/ethnicity. A unity so profound it transformed Malcolm X's view on race relations. In this unity, I was reminded of my otherness, first in Medina and then again in Mecca.

In Medina, on the last Thursday before the pilgrims left for Mecca, I was sitting with my caravan inside the Prophet's Mosque. We were rudely removed by the guards, so we found a quiet corner outside to sit and continue reading our Thursday night supplications. We observed the armed guards blocking off entire sections of the courtyard but felt fairly certain they wouldn't come to us, in our quiet and remote corner. Then two armed guards spotted us, and came directly towards us. We began packing up our things to leave before they even uttered a word, but apparently our pace was too slow for their liking. One derisively snickered, '*yalla Shia*', instead of '*yalla hajji*'—hajji or hajja being a term of respect, and 'Shia' being used as an insult in this case.

Indignant beyond words, I turned around to face him, set my jaw, and looked him straight in the eye daring him to say it again. He stood his ground and waved the machine gun slung over his shoulder to indicate I should turn around and keep walking. Locking my angry gaze, I took a step towards him, and he flinched. This was not the reaction he anticipated, and he threw his machine gun behind him, lifted his hands as if in surrender, and apologetically said, '*yalla hajja, yalla*'. I glared at him for another moment, then slowly turned back to walk with my group as we were kicked out of the Prophet's Mosque. I caught my mother's expression and expected she would be cross with me, having risked a rather dangerous situation. But instead, her eyes glimmered with tears, a mixture of pain and pride.

I do not know if the rest of the group saw the confrontation, but on the way to Mecca, several members of the caravan shared horror stories of pilgrims mysteriously disappearing, being found dead in garbage dumpsters, or rumoured to have been forced into modern slavery. The disappeared included Shia Muslims and western women, among others. Such disappearances are made possible because of the anonymity of hujjaj. When you enter Saudi Arabia for Hajj, you hand your passport over to the authorities, and retrieve it after Hajj upon your exit. During the time between arrival and departure, you have no identity. While this suits the spirit of Hajj, it also creates the potential for individuals to disappear, or be disappeared, without a trace. Thus, the naive bravery I embodied in confronting the guard in Medina melted away, and my courage was quickly replaced by caution and even cowardice.

Despite the transformation, I took a risk in Mecca. While entering *Masjid al Haram*, I noticed piles of *turbah* sitting with the guards at the gates. A *turbah* is a clay disc, usually made of dirt from Karbala, which Shia Muslims place under their foreheads during *sajda*. This is following the *sunnah* of the holy Prophet, who had made a *turbah* out of the dirt where his uncle, Hamza, was martyred and buried. Looking at the piles of *turbah* next to the guards, for a moment I thought they were providing the *turbah* for Shia pilgrims. But my mother told me they were confiscating them, and to make sure I hid my own *turbah* well lest I be caught with one.

After my caravan had been to *Masjid al Haram* a few times, I was comfortable with the layout of the space and wandered off to explore. The muezzin called us to prayer. I was separated from my group, but I found a quiet corner to pray. No one was around, so I decided to take a risk and put my *turbah* in front of me. This was not necessary, since the floor was made of marble and no carpet covered the stone in the corner I found. But I had not yet had the experience of using my *turbah* and wanted to take advantage of the solitude. As I raised my hands for *takbir*, I saw someone stand to my right, and then another man come to my left. A moment later, I registered their khaki uniforms, and I realised I was standing between armed guards. My heart froze, and having broken my concentration, I raised my hands for *takbir* again—this time, with full conviction that this could very well be my final prayer. I concentrated on the prayer as best as I could manage, my heart racing loud enough to prove a distraction. We prayed in congregation uneventfully, and then it ended. I stayed seated, expecting them to haul me off, or at the very least confiscate my *turbah* and chastise me for praying with my hands unfolded. But they walked away without saying a word to me. Frozen in shock and confusion, I stayed seated for a while longer. I stared at my *turbah*, tears welling in my eyes and obscuring my sight as the shock slowly wore off. I did not use the *turbah* again at *Masjid al Haram*.

While this third experience of Shiaphobia contrasts with the first two—of mass murder and of forced removal at gunpoint—it is an experience I would consider to be Shiaphobia nonetheless. Because of how Sunni practices are taken as normative, Shia practices, including use of the *turbah*, are often met with violence. While the two guards said nothing to me, they nonetheless wielded guns. The fear of being exposed to violence was enough for me to avoid Shia-typed practices.

In the US and Canada, I have had countless experiences of Shiaphobia within Muslim spaces. In these immigrant settings, Shiaphobia manifests as the centring of Sunni normativity, erasing non-Sunni experiences of Muslimness and Islam. It can also manifest as the problematising or othering of non-Sunni identities, experiences, practices, beliefs, and worldviews. The kind of Shiaphobia that manifests in more exclusivist spaces differs from the kinds that manifest in more inclusivist spaces.

In Sunni-majority Muslim spaces that tend towards exclusivity, there is a lack of acceptance of non-Sunni Muslims. I have been outright told that Shias are not Muslim, that Shias are going to hell, that Shias are *kaffir* — this, immediately after sharing that I am Shia. Sometimes I would receive looks rather than words. When I started university, I was thrilled to finally pray Zuhr and Asr on time, as the MSA had a prayer room on campus. On my very first day, I gleefully entered the prayer room, and recited my prayers with a heart full of gratitude. This experience was short lived. When I finished my prayers, I felt the eyes of the Muslim woman sitting next to me and turned to smile at her. She gave me a sour look, looked at my *turbah*, rolled her eyes, and left the space. She had finished her prayers well before me, but waited till I had finished mine perhaps to ensure I witnessed her dramatic portrayal of disapproval. Having been rejected as 'that Muslim kid' throughout my post-9/11 middle and high school years, I felt the bitter sting of being rejected as a religious minority yet again. After similar experiences of being made to feel unwelcome, I stopped using the prayer room. For the sake of self-preservation of my mental health, I now avoid these kinds of exclusivist Sunni Muslim spaces. However, Shiaphobia manifests even in inclusivist Muslim spaces.

Immigrant Muslim spaces that tend towards inclusivist social politics are seen as progressive and claim non- or anti-sectarian politics. Yet, there remains a lack of appreciation or understanding about how Sunni-normativity pervades the spaces, creating Shiaphobia. By normalising Sunni experiences, practices, and beliefs as *the* Muslim approach, non-Sunni Muslims are in effect othered. This is most evident in two specific and interconnected practices: by adding descriptors for non-Sunni approaches, but not for Sunni approaches, and by rejecting any sectarian identity, instead identifying as 'just Muslim'. Both practices in effect equate Sunniness as Muslimness, reifying Sunni normativity.

Descriptors are added when a characteristic stands outside of the norm. For example, because of gender segregation in occupations, doctors are socially constructed as men and nurses are socially constructed as women. Though these assumptions are becoming undone over time as genders are represented across the health care field, it is still common to hear someone say, 'female doctor' instead of just 'doctor' (who is assumed to be male). Likewise, it is common to hear someone say, 'male nurse' instead of just 'nurse'. In the inclusive Muslim spaces I frequent, I often hear (Sunni) Muslims say 'Shia adhan', 'Shia salaat', 'Shia hadith', but rarely do I hear Muslims add 'Sunni' as a descriptor to any of these practices.

I was once part of a mosque that identified as non-sectarian, but was Sunni in practice. Whenever a Shia would offer adhan or lead Jumma prayer, the Imam would hastily remind everyone that the person was Shia and would do things 'differently', and to 'not panic'. This happened enough times that I grew curious and asked the Imam, 'has anyone said or done anything?' To which the Imam responded: 'No, but just in case.' Though he was a Shia ally, his actions continued to other Shias. This was addressed by another volunteer, who began calling the normative adhan 'Sunni adhan', and normative prayer 'Sunni salaat'. By providing descriptors for the Sunni practices to mark them as 'Sunni' rather than taking for granted as normative for all Muslims, the othering of Shia and additional Muslim minority practices can be addressed.

Likewise, calling oneself 'just Muslim' when one holds fast to Sunni Islam reifies Sunni normativity. Those who identify as 'just Muslim' may do so out of sincere desire to represent a united *ummah*. However, equating Sunni tradition to (all of) Islamic tradition erroneously erases other Muslims while denying sectarian differences, in effect further dividing the *ummah*. The equivalence of someone refusing to accept the reality of sectarian difference—and thus, inequality—in terms of race would be akin to a white person refusing to see colour, denying being aware of race.

Similar to how race-based privilege makes it difficult for white folks to understand racism and the experiences of racial minorities, or how gender-based privilege makes it difficult for men to perceive sexism and the realities that confront women, sectarian-based privilege also makes it difficult for Sunnis to recognise Shiaphobia and other forms of discrimination and exclusion against Muslim minorities. Thus, it is imperative for those in positions of social power to listen to the experiences of the marginalised and mobilise their privilege and ally with those who experience marginalisation.

To create a united *ummah* that includes all Muslims, we need to critically address the ways that Sunni normativity is often taken for granted and left unchallenged. Practices that reify Sunni normativity keep minority Muslims outside the folds of Muslimness and Islam. In an already divided world, such practices reinforce separation between Muslim communities, exacerbating the tense discord within the *ummah*. Scholars of race warn us that words can quickly escalate to actions; we observed, and still mourn, the brutal 2021-2022 killings of four Shia Muslim men in Albuquerque, New Mexico, by a Sunni Muslim. In order to prevent such atrocities from reoccurring, or escalating and becoming a norm as it is in several Muslim majority contexts, it is important we address Shiaphobia and the exclusion of Muslim minorities however it manifests.

At a recent Qur'an halaqa in a progressive community, a 'just Muslim' man countered the suggestion that we should take the Qur'an as a standard to question hadith and said, 'that's what the Shia do, we don't do that'.

The issue with this statement is twofold: first, it makes a generalisation about another group, and second, it rejects a practice on the basis of sectarian otherness. When people, especially those in positions of social majority, make broad generalisations about others, especially those who are minorities, it is often based on stereotype rather than fact. Even when the generalisation is based on fact, it rarely represents the diversity of minorities, and creates a false us–them dichotomy by creating a monolithic category for the 'other'. I have often heard 'that's what Shia do', and it has almost always been in a negative critique: 'Shia join their prayers, we don't do that'. 'Shia do *muta*' (temporary marriage), we don't do that'. 'Shia cry for months, we don't do that'. I have also heard outrageous accusations about what Shia do that are based on offensive stereotypes and rumours. Whenever I hear such generalisations, made by anyone about any sect they do not belong to, I ask for a collective agreement of respect—namely, I ask that we refrain from speaking on behalf of other sects, that we speak only about and from our own approach to Islam. If I feel safe, I may also share how tired I am as a Shia to have others make (often false) claims about Shias.

Additionally, by stating, 'that's what Shia do, we don't do that', this 'just Muslim' man rejected non-Sunni practices and reified Sunni Islam as the only approach to Islam. Sunni Muslims who identify as 'just Muslim' may do so with sincere desire to unite the *ummah*. While there is nothing inherently wrong about identifying as 'just Muslim', it becomes problematic when one's approach to Islam is based solely on Sunni Islam. If a 'just Muslim' does not recognise the Sunni normativity in their own practices, they are in effect equating Sunni tradition to (all of) Islamic tradition, and naively erasing minority Muslims, in turn further dividing the *ummah*. In other words, their intentions and actions are completely at odds.

Unless one actively incorporates non-Sunni approaches, including the diverse practices of Shias and other minority Muslims, one is in effect actually Sunni and not 'just Muslim'. To truly be 'just Muslim', one may choose to actively incorporate the diverse practices of Muslim minorities and challenge one's own Sunni normativity. Such inclusivity in one's own practice would do justice to the 'just Muslim' descriptor, and also unite the *ummah* in ways that are critical, holistic, and healing. Engaging with the responsibility to incorporate more diverse Muslim practices may also be a way to learn about the beauty in the diversity of Muslims and Islam, as enjoined by the Qur'an (49:13; 3:103), while also exploring the complex realities of Shiaphobia, from Muslim-majority countries to immigrant contexts. In this way, we can effectively transition from Sunni normativity to an inclusive Muslim *ummah*.

FOLLY

Raha Rafii

I. Landscape

The first time I flew across the Atlantic to England on a work visa was to catch a train from London Paddington Station to Exeter St. David's. As I settled in for the two-and-a-half-hour trip, gazing at the moving frames outside my train window, I lost myself in the landscape—*if there is a paradise on earth, it would be this*—a landscape so beautiful it angered me.

Hills rolled by in shades of gold and green, their horizons crowned by round-topped trees.

Black-faced sheep searched for brambles on their gentle slopes, which soon gave way to pearly smoke and bales of hay, signs of life pointing to a lonely barn or thatched-roof cottage. Within a sea of green my eyes would rest upon a glassy creek, a red-iron bridge for crossing, and bushes, neatly-hedged, marking an ancient right of way. Train tracks dutifully marked the borders: long grasses wild and spilling on one side, neatly trimmed on the other. Nature, funneled into place, rolled in its thousand life-giving shades of olive, emerald, and lime. Blades, leaves, and buds reached out and reached up, guided by the touch of those who work the land. The kind of calm seen in most people's dreams, and missing in the rest, the kind of calm that kindled anger in my breast.

The kind of calm that is borne from the privilege of existing outside of the last century's mandate of decades-long subjugation by war or chokehold by economic sanctions, IMF, or World Bank. It is true that bombing during World War II burned up much of the wooden buildings in the city centres, leaving very little of the old cities behind. But England was not touched again by war after that, and was left unmolested to rebuild. Even the war did not manage to interrupt its imperial holdings, just as warring never interrupted the first (but not last) English slaving expedition from Plymouth, nor stopped the first Lieutenant Governor of Tasmania from sailing off to subjugate the island in what would eventually lead to genocide.

The kind of calm wrapped up in a particular kind of Britishness post-Brexit, where 'PROUDLY GROWN IN BRITAIN' was mercilessly tagged onto items as benign as chicken breasts. It is no wonder that Devon County is one of the most sought-after housing markets in the UK, with its temperate clime and frequent blue skies (a Godsend in England!), its pride in rustic living and farm-to-table traditions, its long-lined coasts of stone and sand and clay.

Bucolic, idyllic, lush. So beautiful it soothed but would then, inevitably, give rise to anger. What the north of Iran, marshes of Iraq, western Syria, valleys of Kashmir and Afghanistan looked like, what they could have been. *If there is a paradise on earth, it would be this, and this, and this.* What literally every other country, every people, deserved. My frustration only deepened as the train hurtled past another thatched-roof cottage on yet another rolling hill.

II. Sonnet

David Lester Richardson spent much of his career in the Indian subcontinent, first as a soldier in the Bengal army and then later as an agent of the East India Company. He eventually settled in a position teaching English literature and, by his own presumption, civilising the natives at Hindoo College. Despite his astounding privilege as a white English coloniser in the employ of one of the most violent capitalist corporations of the nineteenth century, Richardson had a wandering eye. He would not be satisfied with his artificially elevated social rank as an Englishman in India, nor with his role as an imperialist gatekeeper of 'civilisation'. Frankly, he couldn't care less about how many natives he could turn over to the superiority of English literature. What David Lester Richardson really wanted was to be validated by his fellow white man back in England.

The first time I ever came to know of David Lester Richardson was by chance. I had moved from Exeter to London during the first lockdown and stayed with Mark and Linnie, a charming, older Salvation Army couple, whenever I had to come back for university business in Exeter. By the time the second lockdown dialled down, I hadn't seen them in six months. Although my post-doctoral fellowship had made little impression on them, Mark warmly remembered my attempts at writing poetry. He gifted me a tiny book of poems he had recently picked up at an estate sale, noting that I would appreciate it more than he ever could. It was barely larger than my palm, with a dark cover embossed in swirls. I opened it to the title page, 'Sonnets and Other Poems, by David L. Richardson', with a portrait of the author on the opposite page. I let it open at random, and to my surprise, it landed on Sonnet XXVIII, 'To Devon':

> *THY pleasant Valleys, Groves, and verdant Hills,*
> *Clothed in their summer beauty, all must own*
> *Unrivalled in the land.—But not alone*
> *Thy fair domain, romantic Devon, fills*
> *The gazer with delight…*

A pastoral poem carefully worked into the strictures of a Petrarchan sonnet, and to be honest not half-bad, albeit undistinguished. Written almost entirely in enjambment, the poem resists proper excerption, demanding to be reproduced, reprinted, replicated in full—a coloniser's dream.

Struck by this unexpected connection to Devon, I returned to the title page, noticing for the first time the publishing date—1827, fourth edition—and another drawing under the title itself. It is initially perplexing: two shirtless figures in turbans flanked by coconut trees, with some vaguely Taj Mahal-ish onion domes across a river behind them—until I flipped to a few pages later where the title was repeated with the rather euphemistic subheading, 'partially written in India'.

Despite having been comfortably well-off in India, where he was installed as an authority on English literature, David Lester Richardson had wanted more than anything to be published in a poetry journal to the acclaim of his fellow countrymen. Specifically, David Lester Richardson wanted to enjoy this acclaim as an Englishman in England.

Although his collection of poems was not exactly a stand-out, David Lester Richardson was certainly deserving of the mild praise from the journals that were blurbed at the end of his collection. 'A volume of miscellaneous poems, many of which possess much beauty', wrote *The Star* in typical English restraint.

Along with the requisite love and memorial poems, for every idyllic reference to England—with the distinct exception of London, where 'morning wakes, and through the misty air in sickly radiance struggles' —Richardson included somber reflections on various parts of India. Always in juxtaposition to the verdant, life-giving hills of southwest England, they were places that were marked by their misery and desertion—with endnotes (!) to let the English reader know precisely how awful they were. Despite waxing poetic about the morning and evening light in the various sonnets written 'in India', Richardson had less gracious opinions of the places and peoples upon which it fell. Richardson kindly summarised his thoughts in Sonnet XXVI, 'On Leaving India':

NOW for luxuriant hopes, and Fancy's flowers,
That would not flourish o'er thy sterile soil,
Grave of the Wanderer, where disease and toil
Have swept their countless slaves !...

What is a sonnet? A sonnet is a 14-line poem in iambic pentameter with a tight rhyme scheme. A sonnet features two contrasting beliefs, events, or emotions. A sonnet idealises someone you love. Richardson's sonnets would only depict India as a sterile, lifeless place that a white man, with his privilege of movement, had to leave behind. The irony of Richardson's own role in the rapacious colonisation which decided the inferiority of these places was certainly lost on him.

III. Garden

There has always been something precisely engineered about the English landscape. When I first read Zadie Smith's essay 'Love in the Gardens', an almost throwaway line forever changed the way I would be primed to see English greenery:

The English lord looks out on his creation and sees just that—'creation'—
unspoiled by workers' cottages or beasts of burden.'

The first time I moved from Exeter to London I was struck by two
things. First, how parched I felt by the relative lack of foliage in London
after having lived in Exeter, and second, how wild London parks—St.
James, Hyde, Victoria, Tower Hamlets Cemetery, Greenwich Ecological
Park—appeared to be, with their long grasses and riotous meadow flowers
and forageable plants. It wasn't until my friend Jalal mentioned the recent
re-wilding projects that the city parks' casually wide range of biodiversity
began to make sense.

The southwest of England—at least, the landscape outside the window
of a South Western Railway train—had that effortlessly natural effect, with
its preternatural calm. But, for many English lords and stewards of the
landscape, it had been almost too natural, too devoid of proper history and
civilisation. So, they sought to rectify this issue with that peculiar British
architectural feature: the folly.

A folly is as odd as it sounds. It is a distinct, lone structure in a place it
has no ties to. It could appear as a misplaced pagoda, rustic shelter, or even
as a mock ruin, such as a crumbling tower, to ornament the landscape.
Follies such as Lawrence Castle imparted an imagined history onto the
land, while ruins were meant to funnel one's thoughts through romantic,
melancholy meditation on the fleeting nature of life, particularly through
poetry. This was not lost on David Lester Richardson, who wrote a sonnet
on the actual ruins of nearby Netley Abbey. Unlike the current incarnations
of the city parks of London, which had nothing to prove in a city marbled
with memorials to empire, these landscapes preserved an aspiration to
civilisational veneer, to a well-deserved, sleepy peace long after whatever
supposedly important marks on English history had been made. The
original thatched-roof cottages by now have become so much rarer and
expensive to maintain that they have in turn become symbolic of rustic
village life: relics by a process of gentrification, then symbols of
gentrification itself.

You could almost be forgiven for being lulled into this mute, picturesque
testimony to rural innocence, as if the southwest had not been built on the
backs of exploited and enslaved labour, as if it had not settled its haunches

on empire and extraction. As if the very compulsions to move migrants, refugees, and asylum seekers across the English countryside weren't the same compulsions to build railways to move oil and grain and bodies out of entire countries. As if people of colour were there by the mere goodwill of the inhabitants and the rest of the country, to dot the landscape as surviving ruins. As if England had no hand in destabilising the rest of the world, or even now with its part in the world order, as migrants and refugees and asylum seekers are turned back on boats crossing the Channel and left to drown in the gray, rolling waters, the never-ending rolling waters, this waterscape of death, day after day after day, in that inhuman calculus of bringing their numbers down to zero. You could almost be excused for falling for such a folly; after all, misdirection is its very purpose.

IV. Metropole

The first time I ever heard the word 'metropole' I was 35 years old.

I had come to London to spend the summer after not having seen England for a decade since my early graduate studies. I did not decide to spend that Ramadan there because I particularly missed it, but because at that point in my life it was the only place I could still find friends living in one city. During the day, while my friends were preoccupied with going to their jobs and making rent, I would wander around various neighbourhoods. Eventually I ended up in Kensington, one of the richest and fanciest areas, walking past the Royal Albert Hall, where my eyes alighted upon the Albert Memorial for the first time.

The Albert Memorial is a shrine to Queen Victoria's Prince Consort Albert, a royal of no real consequence other than dying an early death. It is an elaborate, Gothic canopy-like building projected high onto columns onto platforms onto steps. With a shiny gold sculpture of Prince Albert sat squarely in the middle, it creates a framed blank space in the air as if to colonise the sky. At each of the four corners of the platform are allegorical sculptures of the 'Continents', their respective bases proclaiming which land mass they represented: 'Asia', 'Africa', 'America', 'Europe'. Apparently, Australia was too inconvenient for a four-cornered monument.

Unsurprisingly, the 'Continents' are grossly self-indulgent and crass, with 'Europe' merely a collection of stylised Greek muses representing the epitome of civilisation. The sculptures, erected as part of the memorial in the mid-nineteenth century, are classic monuments to imperialism: the vast colonial holdings that Queen Victoria ruled over, and the imperative of the civilising mission. The 'America' sculpture—really, Anglo North America—has the next highest number of stylised muse figures. What is depicted as an almost complete civilisational mission is really one of genocidal displacement, with white figures—including one of a pioneer—outnumbering a lazy attempt at an indigenous figure in a made-up headdress. Notably, Black figures were nowhere to be found.

The 'Asia' sculpture has a stylised female figure, an allegorical reference to South Asia, topless yet attempting to cover her hair, atop a collapsed elephant. To her left are what can only be described as stereotypes of an East Asian man and an Arab in keffiyeh, while on her right stands a statue of a Persian ambassador in full 'native' attire. Behind her sits a Bedouin-like figure, with a saddle and a water skein.

The figure of the long-robed Mohammedan appears in the 'Africa' sculpture as well, which is dominated by a terrifyingly unnatural-looking pharaonic figure. It is notable that this sculpture contains the only naked figure of all four 'continents': that of a Black African man, tucked away in the back while being 'taught' by yet another stylised muse. Even through Orientalist tropes the sculptors reinforced the internal racial hierarchies of the non-white man—always a man, of course—in which the Arab and East Asian prevailed over the Black African, a figure so maligned and marginal that he lay beyond the realms of Orientalism itself.

What is Orientalism? Orientalism is studying Arabic and Persian poetry under neoclassical arches while Persian and Arabic speakers drown in the Mediterranean. It is the political danger of the Muslim, always bearded or in hijab, always a threat to whiteness yet almost always light-skinned. It is not incidental that the news never dwelled on the Eritrean and Congolese men, women, and children who were also on those capsized boats.

My friend Michael happened to text me as I walked back toward the Royal Albert Hall, trying to figure out where the entrance was. 'Why are there so many random memorials to Prince Albert here?' I wrote to him. 'They don't seem to serve any purpose than to remind you of empire and stolen money.' I looked at those three little bouncing dots as he immediately responded.

'Welcome to the metropole.'

V. Occupation

The first time I flew on a plane by myself I was eight years old.

A few weeks before, my mother and I had boarded a plane from Juan Santamaría to John F. Kennedy airport. Three decades later, Trump would stir up paranoia about the 'criminals' and 'unknown Middle Easterners' in the migrant caravans heading from Central America to the US in an impressive combination of anti-Latinx, anti-indigenous, and Islamophobic racism. Other than the fact that my mother and I flew to the US rather than walked, we were those unknown Middle Eastern infiltrators that were so feared; my father would come over less than a year later. As my mother went to work full time in Manhattan, speaking no English and watching her wages get stolen, she didn't know how she'd be able to take care of her only child. So she put me on my first unaccompanied flight to Vancouver to stay with my uncle—a veteran of the Iran-Iraq war who himself had only immigrated a few years before—as she managed her life as a lone, newly-arrived migrant. With my father still behind working 12-hour days on a mountain plantation, for several weeks all three members of this tiny family—mother, father, daughter—were separated across three different countries in the Americas.

I write this as I'm back in the United States after not having been able to see my family for 18 months in a Rubik's cube of pandemic and visa restrictions. Although I had lived on my own in other countries, finding employment abroad was by far the hardest transition I had to make. Before, I had merely been a student, a safe, recognisably temporary type. Now, a doctoral degree and institutional research title could not make up for what kind of work this was: limited-term migrant contract labour. Meanwhile, back on the other side of the Atlantic, inadequate health insurance and indefinite unemployment awaited.

It is not lost on me that I can trace my life back to the outbreak of the war that turned my father into a migrant, looking for work on any continent that would take him, shuttling his wife and child from visa to visa, country to country. Unlike my father, I did not have a family to bring with me, and unlike me, my father did not speak the languages of the countries he moved us to. Yet my fancy Tier 2 Skilled Worker visa did not make my transition any easier, as if the United States and the United Kingdom had just had a thawing of uneasy relations instead of existing as mere shades of each other, as colonising forces that displaced people like my parents in the first place. Yet despite these dysfunctional interactions, these metropoles remained wildly successful as border regimes, rolling visas into place like guillotines to slice through communities, families, and lives, hoarding their precious resources to uproot and displace again and again and again.

What is a visa? A visa is a prize. A visa is a ticking time-bomb. A visa is a way to separate those on one side of a border from another, to let a few in while keeping most out.

I had come to work in England in 2019 with much hesitation; my inability to find an academic position in my own country had not left me with much choice. I had thought a PhD, with my degrees in politics and history, would help me put fact and fact together, figure out timelines, understand the greater forces that set my family in motion in the first place. It wasn't until the end of my PhD that I began to see higher education for what it really was: a border regime, with its own mandates of language assimilation and self-colonisation, surrounded by walls to keep out the majority of the communities it judged from afar. Instead of answers, I found Orientalism at every turn— repackaged, renamed, and rehabilitated, but still recognisable—sculpted into garish, four-cornered texts, with Europe as its centre. These disciplines, these studies, were nothing but a folly, a white man's vanity project, alone and crumbling on a green hill overlooking a murderous shore.

It was on a preliminary visit to Exeter that the lushness of the landscape convinced me I would have respite there, in the peaceful refuge of nature. A pandemic and three lockdowns forced me to realise how tenuous my grip was in that place, how superficial the façade, as I placed more space between me and the university that employed me, fighting for the community and mental subsistence I needed that went beyond mere permission to move. Instead, that wide expanse of land only exacerbated the precariousness, the isolation of even the most privileged migrants like me. Yet all this remained invisible to white people chafing against restrictions on their God-given rights to holiday abroad or hunkering down in a family cottage in their home country. We remained foreigners, trapped and isolated and alone in the middle of nowhere, dry drowning in full sight.

What would David Lester Richardson think as I rolled my own words over the manicured terrain he idolised in verse, as I picked out the migrants in the far distance and their labours? How many David Lester Richardsons wax lyrical about the fertile beauty of their own tolerance and humanity as they haphazardly fleck the English countryside with refugees? The ones that made it, small enough in number to be unthreatening but enough to dot a landscape and stand as monuments to gratitude, as follies to the magnanimity of the metropole? How many David Lester Richardsons force us all to clap for a choreographed idyll that belied the basic human fact that no one should have to ask permission to sit, stand, migrate, breathe, exist; as if the real aspiration isn't to sit in ease and dignity among relatives, neighbours, and friends, eating off the land that gave ancestors its name, gazing out into the turquoise lakes and emerald valleys and copper mountains unravaged by war and sanctions and greed: *if there is a paradise on earth, it is this, it is this, it is this.*

How naive I was to think that I could take refuge in the pristine beauty of the landscape, as I crossed the Atlantic to go from one empire to another. Arriving with my degrees, my English, my Tier 2 visa, hitched to a fence post that pinned others to the bottom of the channel, the bottom of an entire ocean; at least my visceral anger at those rolling hills served me well in that respect, before my mind could fully comprehend what lay before me. How naive I was; truly, what folly!

*personal names have been changed.

TŪQĀN AND AUTOBIOGRAPHY AS HISTORY

Sameena Kausar

Climbing a steep mountain is a challenging task. Not everyone can endure the rigours of climbing a mountain. Mountains represent adventure, escape, and conquest. Mountains also symbolise the edge of possibilities. Life is an uphill climb on mountains, says the Palestinian writer and poet Fadwā Tūqān (1917–2003), who titled her autobiography *Mountainous Journey: A Difficult Journey*. Her autobiography, which challenges conventional academic accounts and established genres, blends autobiographical with academic and fictional writing, providing an alternative to traditional historical narratives and methodology.

Tūqān, best known for her resistance poetry against the Israeli occupation of Palestine, connects the dots between resistance, victory, patriarchy, and feminism. In her gripping memoir, her narrative is immersed in many layers in which she depicts the self, womanhood, and many other themes. Also known of as 'the mother of Palestinian poetry', Fadwā Tūqān was perhaps the most famous female Palestinian poet. Her title, the 'Poet of Palestine', suggested that her fame goes further.

In an interview Tūqān was asked, despite being a Muslim woman, what made her write a poem on the birthday of Jesus Christ? Tūqān spontaneously responded that we Muslims believe in Jesus and his messenger-hood, and the second reason for writing this poem was that Jesus was the first Palestinian martyr.

The political turmoil of 1948 and 1967 shook Tūqān. At that moment she turned to both active politics and poetry to reflect her political struggle. The Palestinian poet Mahmoud Darwish considered the events of 1967, which started the Palestinian occupation, as an 'earthquake'. This was the decisive event that made Tūqān stray from her exclusive poetic interests to become engaged in politics.

In his poem 'Fadwā', eulogising her, Darwish captures her dilemma of not being fully content with the deteriorating conditions of the Palestinian people. Darwish asks: 'what does the poet do at the time of catastrophe? Suddenly the poet is forced to emerge from her own interiority and reach the external reality. Poetry then becomes the witness.' He goes further to add, 'She visited us in Haifa… a hostage seeking hostages, and read us her first poem about the new ordeal: "I will not cry".' But on that day, Darwish said, 'she was crying like a dove. Love songs ceased to be the answer to hate and inhumanity.'

Can autobiography serve as a source of history? Some contemporary historians exaggerate the unreliability of autobiographies as a historical source. However, autobiographies, written at a specific time and geographical area, deal with essentially the same conditions that a professional historian engages. I do not wish to make an equivalence between the science of history and the art of autobiography despite their interdependence on many occasions. What I wish to bring to the attention of the reader is that the account Fadwā Tūqān wrote of her life is highly reliable. She reliably documents the struggle of the Palestinian people — the war — as well as the social and political events of the conflict in meticulous detail. She was a historical witness.

This is what we can call an intersection of history with a form of self-representation. Though historians have traditionally doubted personal narratives as critical documents, in recent decades, experimentation and theorising on forms of life writing from the field of history have grown considerably. Historians started to discuss how autobiographical narratives may contribute to understanding both the past and the processes of accessing it.

Autobiography is a strange genre. It can be placed in the realm of both literature and history, but cannot entirely be placed in one or the other. Historians have always been using autobiographies and life experiences as *a* source of their writing, but they have seldom given this genre the status of *the* primary source of their writing. The way life writing enriches our understanding of the past cannot be done by any other single source or material. Aside from the formal use of autobiography by historians, it takes a much more historical root in being a primary method for the preservation of one's or a people's history.

The Arabs of pre-Islamic times practised a type of oral biography in the form of short narratives called *akhbar* (sing., *khabar*). When reciting his genealogy, a tribe member would add identifying remarks and accounts of memorable incidents associated with certain figures in the lineage. Similarly, a poem would be transmitted along with reports about the poet and the occasion for the composition of the verses. These paired elements, the informational *khabar* and the transmitted text (whether a list of names or a poem), affirmed each other's authority and authenticity, and the joined elements of anecdote and poetry, or anecdote and genealogy, commonly remained together in oral tradition as a single discursive unit. For this reason, perhaps, the *khabar* remained unitary, limited in focus, and never expanded to become the summation of a life. With the advent of Arabic writing and the proliferation of literacy, it was primarily by the accumulation and combination of *akhbar* that biographies (along with various sorts of extended history accounts) were first constructed. The pattern of linking poetry and prose into a single discourse imprinted itself very firmly on early Arabic written literature and greatly influenced the formation of written historical and literary genres during the early Islamic period (the seventh to the ninth centuries).

Al-Imad al-Katib al-Isfahani wrote an account of himself in an independent work which he titled *The Syrian Thunderbolt;* the jurist Umara al-Yamani wrote an account of himself in an independent work; Yaqut al-Hamawi wrote an account of himself in his *Mu'jam kuttāb, Biographical Dictionary of Writers*; Lisan al-Din ibn al-Khatīb wrote an account of himself that occupies a half-volume of his book *The History of Granada*, the whole work being eight volumes long; Ibn Hajar wrote an account of himself in his book *The History of the Judges of Egypt*.

The fifteenth century Egyptian polymath Al-Suyūṭī's emphasis on passing on the knowledge of his 'circumstances', 'conditions', or 'states' (*ahwal* or *atwar*), words commonly used by medieval Muslim scholars to describe the contents of autobiographies, reflects a widespread conceptualisation of life as a sequence of changing conditions or states rather than as a static, unchanging whole or a simple linear progression through time. Life consists of stages dictated not merely by one's progression from childhood through youth to adulthood and old age but also by one's changing fortunes, which were often contrasted to those few areas of life in which genuine accrual over time was thought possible: the acquisition of knowledge and spiritual understanding, the creation of scholarly and literary works, and the fostering of offspring and students.

These motivations for presenting one's life – as an act of thanking God and for others to emulate – stand in marked contrast to the confessional mode of some medieval and premodern European autobiographies that emphasise the public recognition (confessions) of one's faults, sins, and shortcomings as a warning to others. One tradition seems to be framed to make the statement, 'these are the ways in which I have enjoyed a moral and productive life – imitate me in them,' while the other seems to imply, 'these are the ways in which I have been deficient or in error – beware of similar pitfalls!' Each frame produced its own moral tensions and anxieties of representation, as well as literary strategies for resolving those issues. Although this comparison is a very broad one, and this general orientation certainly did not fully dictate the content of autobiographies in either context, it serves as a useful background against which to read contemporaneous autobiographies from European and Islamic societies in earlier periods.

In more recent times, allowing autobiography to stand as a worthy primary source amongst historians has gained significant currency. The British historian, Carolyn Steedman, specialised in the social and cultural history of modern Britain, exploring labour, gender, class, language, and childhood. Steedman's *Landscape for a Good Woman* is a lucid diagnosis of and proposal for social history using a hybrid strategy that straddles the conventions of the autobiography of childhood and a historian's autobiography. This helps us understand autobiographical literature as not only a personal account contained in the realms of a personal trajectory but as a source of historical events and the past contained within.

Tūqān's autobiography is no exception. The details and the information contained in the autobiography of Tūqān show literature and history can be interconnected and that the facts of history presented in an alluring and impressive form of narration can offer a treat to the reader. Texts that blend personal experiences and history deserve scholarly attention because they allow us to examine our access to both individual lives and the past. The noted British historian E. H. Carr in his famous book *What is History?* had long ago taught 'that the facts of history never come to us "pure" since they do not and cannot exist in a pure form: they are always refracted through the mind of the recorder'.

'The striking fact about the historiography of women is the general neglect of the subject by historians', remarked Gerda Lerner in a 1969 article titled 'New approaches to the study of women in American History'. Lerner's explanation of 'general neglect' was that women were outside the 'power structure' and, therefore, could be easily neglected. Assessing the credibility of Lerner's statement requires a deep inquiry into the subject. Writers like Tūqān received less attention from historians, even though while writing her autobiographical notes, she took more than a documentary interest in her autobiography, which makes it a formidable historical record of her time's events and the political and social issues around them. Whether historians consider these records as source material or not, they do form and narrate history. Tūqān was not in the 'power structure', and neither did she try to be included in it or be inside it. But her voice was strong enough to be heard by the common reader, and the cries of her pain echoed and resonate till today. Her narrative records her personal experiences as a woman, writer, poet and also as a person who was witness to the political and social tremors created by the events that shook Palestine and left the entire world dumb and stricken.

Although Tūqān was writing about her personal experiences and the social and political life in her home city of Nablus, she raised an important issue over the course of her narration: the connection between women's personal and national freedom. Tūqān's question covers the entire history of the Palestinian women's movement and women's struggles, searching for a balance between the two freedoms. When writing poetry was supposed to be something only men could do, Tūqān wrote poetry and dared to challenge a patriarchal and male-dominated society. When Tūqān started documenting her life in the form of an autobiography, there were very few women who could have dared to do so. Tūqān's honesty and courage left a lasting mark on modern Arabic literature. She did not try to romanticise her life with fake words or by hiding the truth. She put her life in the hands of the reader as it was. Perhaps the beauty of this document made Tūqān the ambassador of truth and a model for future generations of writers.

The first steps towards an unknown and unexplored destination are always challenging and mysterious. You are afraid and hesitant to explore unknown terrains. But the magical spell of those first steps never evades your memory. This is exactly the case with human expression. When your emotions and sentiments are suppressed, your soul feels suffocated, and if, in such a situation, a window of new opportunities opens up to you, even if the window is just a hole in the wall, your joy knows no bounds. It is a feeling of flying into the horizon like a bird, careless and free. This is the experience young Tūqān went through when her brother Ibrahim started teaching her poetry.

Poetry is a revelation of truth, and all poetry is founded on this truth, wrote Percy Bysshe Shelley, the well-known romantic poet, in *A Defence of Poetry*. Edgar Allan Poe, the famous nineteenth century American writer and literary critic, also stated the same about poetry in his essay *The Poetic Principle*. For Poe, this truth is not told directly but through a 'harmony' or 'metaphor' previously unrealised by the reader. While creating this 'truth' through the poetic device, the poets undergo numerous emotional and psychological experiences. These experiences flow through the past and present. A poet is born through various encounters with their tradition and experiences accumulated through reading and comprehending the philosophy of traditional and classical poets. It is rare to find a poet who has never connected to the beauty and authenticity of the past. Fadwā Tūqān saw her tradition as the source of her being. Being a modernist in her approach to poetry, she used free verse frequently; she believed that to find oneself, it is essential to stay attached to one's roots. One of her first favourite poets was Ibn al-Rumi. His elegy for his son left a lasting impression on her conscience:

Though it is vain your weeping giving some ease; be lavish then, my eyes,

for one is lost as dear as you to me.

My son whom my hands to the earth consigned, noble the offering, miserable the giver.

She wrote her first verse about his love and longing for Ibrahim in the same meter and rhyme as Ibn al-Rumi's elegiac poem titled 'Longing for Ibrahim':

The distance has increased the longing in my heart,

Does Ibrahim also feel the same for me?

Tūqān's autobiography carries aesthetic complexities and literary intricacies. Patriarchal traditions and masculine structures surrounded her childhood. These traditions did not allow a woman to write poetry, dress as she pleased, and enjoy life on her terms. It created a psychological dilemma for her. The creative person in her was puzzled. She wanted to fly high and touch the far-away horizons, but these social obstructions were the mountains that did not allow her to soar as she wished. This blockage made her start her poetic journey. This led her on a journey within herself. The first poem she wrote was in the style of the elegy of Ibn al-Rumi for his deceased son. Melancholy and sorrow prevail in these first lines by her. Her brother, Ibrahim Tūqān, a well-known Arabic poet, was her mentor and guided her in this journey.

Literary expressions bestow a feeling of liberation on the writer. Writing and expressing oneself is like a mysterious healing touch on the human soul. Tūqān realised this fact and utilised the power of writing and expression to soothe her soul and found solace in it. She recalls this moment as that which freed her from the shackles of society for the first time in her life. Sometimes writers unconsciously become the historians of their time. Tūqān, while penning down her thoughts as memoir or diary writing, did not know that she was recording a historical overview of her time and that her autobiography would serve a historical purpose for the coming generations.

The text of the autobiography delineates the poet's personal struggle against subjugation and oppression in her conservative Muslim environment, her tradition-bound literary journey, and her success at finding her voice. Moreover, the individual self's biography is amalgamated into the public history of the home, 'school', city, and country.

Tūqān's study of classical writers like al-Jahiz, al-Mubarrad, Abul Faraj, and the modern classics of al-Aqqad, Taha Hussain, Aḥmad Amin, Muṣṭafa

Sadiq al-Rifa'i, and May Ziadeh provided vigour to her thinking and enriched her. She had the saying by the famous Chinese philosopher Confucius pasted on the wall of her room: 'young birds can also fly if they have the will. Nothing is impossible in the world.'

Tradition had a special place in her brother Ibrahim's conscience. He saw tradition as sacred. The writings of modernist poets did not appeal to him and he disapproved of them. He warned Fadwā too of memorising the works of modern poets except for Ahmad Shawqi, Ismail Sabri and Khalil Mutran. These writers were modern but their approach to literature was traditional, according to Ibrahim Tūqān.

In the Islamic tradition, poetry and autobiography have often served as sources for history. The famous saying about Arabic poetry as the archive (*diwan*) or 'the register of the Arabs' is an indication that Arabs have acknowledged the status and value of poetry as a source of historical heritage. 'Poetry as the register or Arabs' was initially attributed to Abdullah ibn Abbas, the cousin of the Prophet Muhammad. From the earliest stages in the Arabic literary tradition, poetry has reflected the most profound sense of Arab self-identity, communal history, and aspirations.

Tūqān believed that women need to explore their collective consciousness and share experiences to surpass and transcend the stereotypes and isolation of their lives. Patriarchal society considered it taboo for a woman to write love and romantic poetry. This is what Abdul Lateef Ashur admitted in his preface to *Nuzhat ul Julasa'a fi Ashaar al Nisa*, a collection of poetry by forty women compiled by Jalaluddin Suyuti (1445-1504). He describes the odd reaction of critics to the publication of the poetic collection of Ayesha al-Taimuriyyah (1840-1902), which contained 554 couplets on love or romantic poetry out of 1,936 couplets. A debate started in literary circles about whether women could compose love poetry. If yes, then who would they write it about, who would be the addressee? Taimuriyyah had indeed broken down this taboo with her strong voice. Her romantic poetry charmed hearts like a nightingale singing from behind a veil. These societal obstacles forced Tūqān to hide her authentic self behind a pen name, 'Dananeer'. The name was borrowed from the famous slave poet of the Barmakid period (during the eighth and nineth centuries) about whom Isfahani writes in *al-Aghani*: 'she was noble and chaste'.

The unrestricted soul of Tūqān disapproved of hurdles and hitches in the expression. She felt as if some barriers were blocking her way in the process of writing poetry in the traditional mode, following meter and rhyme. The conventional style of verse required a non-natural imitation of rhyme for her. It felt hollow – she wanted a free explosion of emotions and a smooth expression without putting effort into matching the complexities of rhyme and meter. Free verse poetry has no rhyme scheme and no fixed metrical pattern. Often echoing the pulses and tempos of natural speech, a free verse poem makes artistic use of sound, imagery, and a wide range of literary devices. It allows greater freedom for rhetorical effects than the confinement of meter or rhyme. She was introduced to Mahjar literature, diaspora literature in Arabic, by Mohammad Mandur, the great critic, and she found the works of these poets in the diaspora precisely what she was looking for. This was the time when Tūqān came to know about the School of Apollo in modern Arabic literature and was inspired by its manifesto and writers.

Inaction and stagnation are against the nature of this universe. Everything in this world is undergoing a change and transformation. This change is a universal principle. The same goes for poetic expression. Why do we deny the application of this law to verse? Our demand for sticking to the old tenets of verse writing without making a minor change and breaking a single rule is like asking for something against nature. Something against the law of existence and development. In Tūqān's view, this change in the form and structure of poetry was a natural phenomenon. Her understanding of life and its philosophy was simple. She believed that this movement and revolution in the form of poetry called 'modern' would also change over time, and some new experiences would emerge from the same natural change phenomenon and replace it.

Literature, to Tūqān, is a tool to understand humanity. She saw novels as a source full of thoughts, philosophy, poetry, and psychoanalysis. Novels deal with life. They talk about every living thing. Their dealing with 'man' is so detailed that every heartbeat of this creature is transferred onto the paper. His shortcomings and his characteristics, sorrow and happiness all get covered. In novels, Tūqān was more inclined towards the philosophical. The encounters between good and evil or the problems of death, diseases, and the like attracted her. In her quest for answers to the questions relating to man, his destiny, and life, Tūqān would refer to the Old Testament sometimes. She felt that due to its narrative style, many human stories come alive on the pages of the sacred book and help understand life and its complexities.

On her journeys by air, she always recalled 'the Epistle of Forgiveness' by famous poet Abul Ala al-Marri (973–1057), where the poet describes his trip to the heavens and meeting with famous Arabic pagan poets there. She also mentioned an excerpt from Marri's book *al Fusool wal Ghaayat*, dealing with the same scenario. Her poetic and artistic mind would travel from the imaginative world created by writers to the real world she lived in. Marri was a controversial rationalist of his time. He believed reason to be the chief source of truth and divine revelation. Mentioning the excerpt from *Fusool wal Ghayaat*, Tūqān connected the fictional narrative to the present and made it a point that Abul Ala could imagine flying in the air like birds a thousand years ago. Sometimes, poets can see what a normal eye fails to observe, which is why the translation of the word 'poet' in Arabic as *shaair* literally means one who feels or knows what others do not know or feel. The root of the Arabic word *shaair* means consciousness. Tūqān's approach to literary history and obtaining insights from it are impressive. Her modern views did not deter her connection to the past. Her rootedness in her tradition gave her the confidence to face the present.

The second volume of Tūqān's autobiography, titled *The More Difficult Journey*, is talked about significantly less in academic circles. This volume is a record of Palestinian history after the Israeli occupation. It deals with the minute details of the war between the two sides, the elements that may hide from the eyes of a historian but can be seen by the eyes of a poet and a woman fighting for the rights of human beings through her voice.

When the author of a biographical compendium came to a point where it was logical or desirable to write his own entry, he did so in either the first- or third-person voice, and the result was termed a *tarjamat al-nafs,* self-*tarjama,* or the author was said to have written a *tarjama* of himself. Tūqān not only immortalised her own *tarjama* in that compendium known as the human story, but give words to the *tarjama* of the Palestinian people and their struggle that otherwise would have been lost to memory and knowing.

MUM'S THE WORD

Robert Hainault

Pick an evening from my late teenage years when I was living at home with my mother and the chances are that you'll find us arguing about race. My mother's father was a Pakistani immigrant who came to Hartlepool some time in the late forties or early fifties, and for most of my upbringing I had been warned not to let anyone know because if they find out they will think about me differently. Perhaps they won't speak to me any differently, or treat me any differently, at least not to my face, but things will be different.

Up until this point, mum's been the word, but I've started to grow uncomfortable about it: uncomfortable about what that says about the people around me, and even more uncomfortable about how emotional my mum gets when I try to challenge her about it.

As a teenager, I simply didn't understand what it was like for her growing up mixed race in the North East, and the threats and violence she faced on a regular basis. To me, these are stories from a different time: I had been an out-and-proud gay man for several years, and had grown accustomed to the unkindness of strangers in my native Scunthorpe whenever I'd gone out with a full face of make-up, Cuban heels, and a silk scarf, but I never backed down from a lively exchange of ideas with hecklers on the High Street of a Saturday afternoon, and so far no-one had ever tried to hit me. In fact, more often than not, after spending some time talking to me, most people came to the conclusion that despite looking very strange to them, I was actually not so bad. To me, my mum's attitude was outdated. Having never encountered physical violence, my frame of reference for the kinds of experiences my mother faced was woefully inadequate for the kind of mature conversation we should have been having. So instead I resorted to being pompous and any attempt at conversation would end in tears and the slamming of doors.

The irony is that my mother barely knew her father. My grandmother was a widow with one child from her first marriage, my mother's half-sister, when a friend introduced her to my grandfather. They were married by an imam in the fifties, and had two children together: my mum and my uncle Phil. Then my grandfather went back to Pakistan for a time, and returned with his previously-unmentioned Pakistani wife and children, much to the horror of my grandmother. They separated immediately and my grandmother found she was back where she started, only now the single mother of not just one but three hungry children. While my mother did see her father occasionally, he wasn't a big part of her life, and she was far-removed from his cultural heritage: she didn't learn to speak Urdu, she wasn't raised Muslim, and the most connection she seemed to have with her father's culture was a recipe for curry and the skill of folding up pieces of chapatis to use as a scoop. But despite being raised a Christian by a white woman from Birmingham and having fair skin and green eyes, she had a foreign surname, an Asian father, and jet black hair, so to everyone around her that meant she was 'half-caste'. Standing in our kitchen I would observe that if the smallest denomination of a caste is a half, then surely no-one would even register the dilution of my Englishness by a quarter. This was the kind of smart comment my mother knew was wrong but couldn't answer, which made me feel terribly clever and made her terribly upset. Looking back on these evenings I don't feel very clever at all, and wonder how I could ever have been so stupid and so cruel.

Nevertheless, I felt proud to be something other than just another boring old Saxon, and I still do, no matter how much of an imposter I might feel when talking to British Asians with legitimate cultural credentials. My olive-coloured skin, thick wavy head of hair and plenteous coarse body hair are from my grandfather, and I think they're gorgeous. As far as I was concerned at the time, it was just a fact, and hiding it was giving in to the prejudices of people whose opinion should be worth nothing to us; regardless of anything that had happened in the past. Continuing to hide it in the new millennium was just cowardice. Yet over the next decade I was to learn that the reality of being even remotely associated with Islam in Britain, even amongst my own socially liberal generation, was far from simple, and would be asking myself how, despite being once so determined to defend my Islamic heritage, I would end up entrenched in anti-Islam politics. Over the next few years I would shift from being an active member of the Doncaster Socialist Workers' Party and a committed Marxist marching against the war in Iraq, to being asked to contribute material to the British wing of the French far-Right movement Generation National Identitaire. And I was not alone in undergoing a significant Rightward shift in my politics. This is how that happened.

From Left to Right

Fast forward to Monday 16 January 2012. I am greeting people in the foyer of the Geography building of QMUL in my role as Secretary of the newly-founded QMUL Atheist, Secularist and Humanist Society. We have organised a talk about Sharia Law by a human rights lawyer recommended to us by the National Secular Society (NSS). The speaker is called Anne Marie Waters, and to us, well-versed as we are in the arguments of Richard Dawkins and Christopher Hitchens, the protesters from the Islamic Society (IS) who are gathered outside are just further evidence of the opposition between post-Enlightenment western liberal democracy and conservative Islam. Of course, we think, the IS feels threatened by the talk: they segregate their meetings into men and women, and they invite speakers to their events who espouse extremely regressive sexist and homophobic views: why would they not want to disrupt a talk about the rights of women like our society's president and homosexuals like me? We plan to proceed as scheduled, and if anything, are enjoying making a bit of a stir.

But the event was not to proceed as scheduled. Shortly before the talk began, a man came up to me and the treasurer, filmed us on his phone, and told the treasurer he knew where he lived. Either by lucky guess or by genuine research, he at least got the area right, and promised to 'hunt [us] and [our] families down' if we said anything that disrespected the prophet. Baffled, I wished him a good evening and he left, and a moment later the society president and Anne Marie came out of the auditorium saying that someone had just made a threat against their lives, and that someone had come in and left a large bag on the stairs. At the behest of security, the talk was cancelled, the building evacuated, and the police called. The bag turned out to be just a bag. We gave statements and then decamped to the pub, joking that at least our assailant was unlikely to follow us there. For the next week I stayed with the president of the society answering the flood of press enquiries that followed, and preparing a meeting with the Students' Union to demand better protections for our society and its members, and to ensure that speakers for the Islamic Society who held regressive views be more carefully vetted, as our research into the views of their speakers over the past few months had revealed a number of them had anti-gay and anti-women views that we felt was leading to the radicalisation of IS members culminating in the threats we received.

The event was covered by the *Independent* in its crime section and Joan Smith in commentary, and by Nick Cohen writing in the *Spectator* online, as well as by several smaller publications including the National Secular Society, and the *East London Advertiser*.

At the time we released the following statement, which was printed by the NSS in its coverage: 'Only two complaints had been made to the Union prior to the event, and the majority of the Muslim students at the event were incredibly supportive of it going ahead. These threats were an aggressive assault on freedom of speech and the fact that they led to the cancellation of our talk was severely disappointing for all of the religious and non-religious students in the room who wanted to engage in debate.'

These two complaints, which came from the Islamic Society, were regarding Anne Marie Waters' history of making anti-Islam statements, chiefly through the organisation One Law for All, a pressure group headed by Iranian ex-Muslim activist Maryam Namazie, and for whom Waters was a spokesperson at the time. We felt that lobbying for the restriction of religious courts, both Islamic and Jewish, was not only ethically but legally justified, and argued successfully against the complaints in a meeting with the Union, allowing our talk to be scheduled on campus. We sincerely believed that the complaints were part of a general trend to oppose freedom of speech in universities where it threatened the perceived right of religious conservatives to behave in ways damaging to the civil rights of women and LGBTQ+ people.

Perhaps they were. Waters, however, turned out to be a fascist. Three years later in 2014 she stood for Ukip in the Lambeth Council election. She stood for Ukip again in the 2015 general election, contesting the seat for Lewisham. In 2016 even Ukip wouldn't have her, and she was deselected from the 2016 London Assembly election after her involvement in Tommy Robinson's far-Right anti-Islam group Pegida UK, which she co-founded, was reported on. After failing to win the Ukip leadership election, she would go on to found the far-Right political party For Britain. Writing in *The Times* in 2017, Sean O'Driscoll wrote: 'For Britain hopes to inherit the far-right support previously enjoyed by the BNP before its descent into obscurity, largely brought on by allegations of corruption and infighting. Ms Waters has previously said that allowing Muslim immigration would encourage "sexual dysfunction" and "child rape", comments which were widely denounced by more moderate members of Ukip.'

You might wonder how we could have been so naïve as to have invited this obvious lunatic to come to address our society, and to have been so blind to her political leanings. As is often demanded of those who knew serial killers: surely there must have been signs? Indeed, in hindsight we can suppose her political views did not emerge suddenly after the event, though it's possible they may have been catalysed by it, and it is impossible not to associate her specific interest in human rights violations under Sharia law with her later public stance in open opposition to Islam and her association with other figures on the far-Right. But while it is certainly true that her views did not come out of nowhere, she had previously allied herself not with the Right but the Left. Prior to joining Ukip, Waters had made four attempts to stand for election, all with the Labour Party.

One Law for All itself, the organisation with which Waters was affiliated when we invited her to speak for us, was headed by Maryam Namazie, an Iranian ex-Muslim and Socialist-Feminist whose opposition to the Islamic oppression of women and free speech ostensibly comes from a sincere sense of loss at the suppression of radical progressive political thought in Iran following the Islamic revolution. She is not the only Left-wing figure to have ended up with Right-wing bedfellows through her involvement in secular humanism. Christopher Hitchens claimed until the end of his life to be a Marxist.

There were three of us who co-founded the QMUL Atheism Society, and we all identified as Left-wing. I had been a member of Doncaster Socialist Workers' Party prior to going to University. While the political views of undergraduates might, to some extent, deserve their reputation as going only skin deep, there was no sense in which any of us felt any affinity for the political Right: we were in favour of equality for women including the right to reproductive freedom and the de-stigmatisation of sex work, the right for people to be gay, queer, or transgender, and deeply sceptical of any institution that claimed absolute answers to ethical questions we felt were best determined by the personal choice of individuals. We believed in a strong welfare state, and forward-thinking policies on immigration and asylum. In other words, we were somewhere between libertarian socialists and Left-liberals.

Yet by 2012, I had become involved with the libertarian Adam Smith Institute after attending their summer school at Sidney Sussex College, Cambridge, and had campaigned for Boris Johnson in the London 2012 mayoral election. By 2013 my new friends included fans of Ayn Rand and Enoch Powell, and by 2016 I had lost old friends over my vehement criticism of Hillary Clinton in the American Presidential race. I had hosted a radio show modelled on the American conservative talk show *Firing Line with William F. Buckley, Jr.,* and had been approached to contribute political writings for Generation National Identity, a British political movement modelled on the French far-Right *Generation National Identitaire* which was particularly anti-Islamic in focus. From a position of committed Marxism I had moved through libertarianism with an emphasis on socially liberal values within free market capitalism, through conservatism, to a hard-Right nationalism that, while it never tipped into fascism, brushed very close against it on some issues. This Rightward spiral ended in November 2016 when a friend of mine excitedly shook me awake at the pro-Trump election results party where I had fallen asleep on a beanbag to tell me that Donald Trump had been elected the forty-fifth President of the United States. I can still remember the feeling I had watching the others in the room celebrating and knowing that this wasn't supposed to have happened, and worse, that I had absolutely no right to regret it. It was then that I realised: this is never what I'd wanted to believe in.

Over the next few years I began to reflect on how I'd ended up advocating political views that five years earlier I would have found repellent, how I'd gone from arguing with my mother that she should be proud of her Asian heritage in the face of suspicion and distrust, to absorbing a politics that was inherently defined by the suspicion and distrust of Muslims. I started to wonder too what had happened to Anne Marie Waters to take her from standing for the Labour Party in 2010 to managing Tommy Robinson's Pegida UK some six years later, and how Christopher Hitchens had gone from being synonymous with the British and American Left to defending an aggressive interventionist foreign policy against the Islamic world on the part of the United States and Britain. I began to ask: how was it that the values of secular humanism, with its strong liberal traditions of anti-authoritarianism and individualism transformed itself so neatly into a new anti-Islamic political ideology?

While a full exploration of this political trajectory is clearly beyond the scope of this essay, there is a particular phenomenon at work that has presented itself as of particular importance to my understanding of my own political transition, and that is especially illustrative of the latent tensions and contradictions in the political self-image of British and American liberal democracy which persist today and which played out through the evolution of the New Atheist movement between 2004 and 2015.

New Atheism in Britain and America

In understanding what New Atheism is, it is helpful to consider its place within the history of popular ideas and its emergence as a cultural phenomenon. The beginning of the movement is generally attributed to the publication of Sam Harris's *The End of Faith* in 2004 in the U.S. which, when released in paperback in October 2005, remained on the *New York Times* bestseller list for 33 weeks and won the PEN/Martha Albrand Award for First Nonfiction. In 2006, the British evolutionary biologist Richard Dawkins published *The God Delusion*, and for many of my colleagues in British secular humanist circles this signalled the beginning of the movement proper in the UK, and a formative book in the crystallisation of a contemporary anti-theist school of thought.

It is relevant to distinguish between the different flavours of these two books and their relevance to contemporary political discourse in America and Britain respectively. Harris's book is a direct response to the threat of religious, and particularly Islamic, extremism in the wake of the 2001 September 11 attacks, beginning with a literary description of the moment of a terrorist attack from the perspective of a suicide bomber. Its fourth chapter is titled 'The problem with Islam' and isolates the faith of Muslims as especially dangerous and likely to inspire terrorism.

Dawkins, however, is more cautious about making generalisations about any inherent predisposition towards violence within the Islamic faith particularly. While he cites the *fatwa* against Salman Rushdie in *The God Delusion* and the violence that was stoked in response to the 2005 *Jyllands Posten* Mohammed cartoons controversy, he is quick to point out that while early Islam was spread through conquest, so was Christianity through the crusades, and that it is religious faith itself, not any particular religion, that so enables violence, citing the famous quote from Steven Weisman 'Religion is an insult to human dignity. With or without it, you'd have good people doing good things and evil people doing evil things. But for good people to do evil things, it takes religion.' However, while Dawkins' approach is, at least superficially, concerned with a more scholarly assessment of Islam within his critique of the fundamental nature of faith itself, there is subtler foreshadowing of the kind of dubious bedfellows that New Atheism invites.

In his chapter 'What is Wrong with Religion?', Dawkins draws on both Ibn Warraq's *Why I Am Not a Muslim*, calling him 'a deeply knowledgeable scholar of Islam', and a 2005 *Spectator* article by Patrick Sookhdeo, 'The Myth of Moderate Islam', to argue that the contradictions present within religious texts make applying an ethical standard to a faith impossible, and, in the case of Islam, that 'Islamic scholars, in order to cope with the many contradictions that they found in the Qur'an, developed the principle of abrogation, whereby later texts trump earlier ones. Unfortunately, the peaceable passages in the Qur'an are mostly early, dating from Muhammad's time in Mecca. The more belligerent verses tend to date from later, after his flight to Medina.'

Ibn Warraq, a pseudonymous anti-Islam writer, has been criticised by the likes of Fred Donner, for his limited knowledge of Arabic, over-reliance on Christian polemic, and for creating misunderstandings about the Islamic faith, with the American Islamic scholar Asma Afsaruddin saying that his book *The Origins of the Koran* 'needlessly poisons the atmosphere and stymies efforts to engage in honest scholarly discussion'. Writing in the Journal of the Royal Asiatic Society, François de Blois calls the book 'a decidedly shoddy piece of missionary propaganda'. Clearly anything more than a peripheral glance at Warraq's reputation suggests that the description of him as 'a deeply knowledgeable scholar of Islam' is misleading. Nevertheless, Warraq's *Why I Am Not a Muslim* was described by Christopher Hitchens in 2003 as his 'favourite book on Islam' and Warraq received similar praise from Douglas Murray, founder of the Centre for Social Cohesion, in a 2007 article for *The Spectator*, referring to him as a 'great Islamic scholar'.

While I do not think Dawkins had an especially anti-Islam agenda when writing *The God Delusion*, he demonstrates he is inadequately equipped to tell the difference between rigorous, well-intentioned Islamic scholarship, and anti-Islamic polemic that will ultimately be used to prop up the neoconservative political positions of Hitchens and Murray, despite criticism of Warraq's work having been made by serious academics several years before *The God Delusion*. It is in these cracks that the potential for New Atheism in the UK to tend towards the neoconservative agenda of the War on Terror resides, not, as in *The End of Faith*, an explicit belief that Islam is, in its very essence, a violent faith, but in an ignorance about the field of contemporary Islamic discourse and Qur'anic scholarship within the academic mainstream.

Ignorance amongst non-Muslims about matters pertaining to Islamic scholarship is, in many ways to be expected, for it comes from not only an ignorance of the subject itself, but a lack of awareness of the extent to which one is ignorant at all. The Dunning-Kruger effect dictates that a little knowledge of something can cause a gross overestimation of one's competence, and in this case a little bad Islamic scholarship can easily be confused with a more thorough understanding of the field, particularly by those who have good reason to afford weight to their own intellectual abilities. Consider any of the so-called 'Four Horsemen' of the New Atheist movement and we find all are distinguished in their own fields: Harris is a respected neuroscientist, Dawkins a professor of evolutionary biology at Oxford, Hitchens was a well-regarded journalist, particularly on the Left, and the lesser-talked-about Daniel Dennett a notable professor of philosophy within the field of philosophy of mind.

Even though New Atheism has been considered 'dead' since 2015, its impact on British Muslims remains something that many of my non-Muslim friends remain oblivious to. In speaking to a number of friends and colleagues about this essay, the response I most often got from non-Muslims was one of bafflement at why I would be writing about something like New

Atheism in 2022. Muslim friends and colleagues, however, reacted with interest and seemed to understand instinctively why this is still a relevant issue. What this suggests is that the experience of Muslims during the popularity of the New Atheist movement was something that didn't even register for most non-Muslims, who remain unaware of the way in which many Muslims in Britain had felt especially under attack from a rise in Islamphobic rhetoric fuelled both by the political conditions of the War on Terror and the discursive environment of hostility towards religion, and especially Islam, engendered by the confrontational anti-theist attitude popularised by the New Atheists. What is clear, then, is that, for most non-Muslims, the world of Islamic ideas and Muslim experiences exists in a state of alterity so removed from their field of vision that even the quality of discourse about it remains impossible for many to accurately assess. It is under these conditions of alienation that the New Atheism, ostensibly to many of us involved in it, a continuation of the tradition of British secular humanism, began to dovetail with the political agenda of the far-Right.

'Social cohesion' and multicultural alienation

In 2007, Douglas Murray founded the Centre for Social Cohesion (CSC), a supposedly impartial think tank, that, at the time, defined the need for its work as follows:

> Civitas has established the Centre for Social Cohesion following widespread and longstanding concern about the diminishing sense of community in Britain. Why is social cohesion an issue at all? Several developments have each in their own way put questions about our sense of national allegiance on the map. The threat from Islamist terrorists is the most prominent, but a sudden increase in large-scale immigration has also raised questions about the number of newcomers who can be absorbed without dramatically affecting house prices and job prospects. Simultaneously, growing doubts about multiculturalism – in the sense of very different, even antagonistic, cultures being pursued by groups sharing the same territory – began to be voiced by thinkers who had previously been enthusiastic about it. And many on the left have sought to revive patriotism in the hope of creating bonds of solidarity that will maintain support for the welfare state in an individualistic age.

While Murray himself made no claims to political neutrality in his own writings – in 2005 he authored *Neoconservatism:Why We Need It* – the think tank clearly felt a need to counter associations between itself and the political Right by presenting patriotism as a cross-party issue, and multiculturalism as a project increasingly under fire from its original proponents. Its current website defines the Centre as 'non-partisan' and 'impartial'. Yet while there are those on the Left who are critical of large-scale immigration and concerned about the compatibility between so-called 'antagonistic cultures', (presumably western liberal democracy and conservative Muslims), there is a general tendency of the Left to defend multiculturalism and of the Right to oppose it.

Writing for *Radical Philosophy,* political theorist Bhikhu Parekh defines a multicultural society as 'one which includes two or more cultural communities', and identifies two responses to this plurality: 'It might respond to its cultural plurality in one of two ways, each of which is in turn capable of taking several forms. It might welcome and cherish the plurality, make it central to its self-understanding, and respect the claims of its cultural communities in its laws and policies; or it might seek to assimilate the diverse cultures into its mainstream culture either wholly or substantially. In the first case it is multiculturalist, and in the second monoculturalist, in its orientation and ethos.' He goes on to say that 'the failure to distinguish between a multicultural and a multiculturalist society has often led to an agonized debate about how to describe a society'.

If we are to favour Parekh's nuanced and considered analysis of what multiculturalism means over the assertion by the CSC that it refers to the sharing of 'territory' by 'antagonistic cultures', then we see that not only does the CSC oppose the idea of a multicultural society, but by the mode of criticism, implicitly argues in favour of a monocultural one. The implication is that some cultures cannot peacefully co-exist and that some minorities must assimilate to the traditional culture of the country. The focus of the CSC on issues specifically related to radical Islam gives a clear idea as to which minority they believe needs to do more to assimilate.

This in itself may seem uncontroversial. Many people in Muslim communities are concerned about radicalisation, but they are also concerned with what appears to be a disproportionate focus on it at the expense of sincere engagement with their communities by non-Muslims in Britain, something which British non-Muslims are understandably less concerned about. This is often complicated further by the ambiguity within political discourse between Britain as a multicultural and as a multiculturalist society, for it is when the failures of multiculturalism are miscategorised as failures of multiculturality (that is to say the simultaneous presence of people from different cultural backgrounds), that concerns about social cohesion become naturalised within a hard-Right rhetoric in which there is political opposition not to the plurality of culture but of race.

It is not a coincidence that Murray, Dawkins and Hitchens all converge on the same writer as the source of their Islamic scholarship. When the popular discourse surrounding an issue is undertaken at a level of superficiality in which these kinds of conflations can readily occur, even the most well-intentioned actors are prone to making naïve errors about the authoritativeness of the ideas in which they are dealing. This in itself would contain little danger within the field of serious academic scholarship where protections are in place to ensure work is reliable, but the role of the public intellectual is, by definition, to mediate between the intellectual realm of scholarship and a public audience that is necessarily comprised of laymen. As such, while Richard Dawkins was eminently qualified as an evolutionary biologist to convey scientific ideas in his role as Professor of the Public Understanding of Science at Oxford University, that is no measure of his credentials as a writer about metaphysics, theology, or religion. Harris and Hitchens particularly, despite self-evident intellectual prowess, expressed no interest in any field of learning within Islamic studies, be that Islamic theology, Qur'anic exegesis, the Arabic language, or Islamic culture and society, beyond the implications of radical Islam as perceived by the west, and as such it is little surprise that both tend towards generalisation and caricature, identifying international jihad as an existential crisis for liberal western democracies despite religiously-motivated terrorism being far from a new phenomenon, and Islam being but one of many religions that has been used as a justification for political violence.

The Empiricism Paradox

Throughout *The End of Faith* and Christopher Hitchens's *God is Not Great*, and touched on by Dawkins in his quotation of Weisman and Pascal, there is the assumption that acts of terror in the name of Islam are *solely* driven by faith as a result of that faith's nature.

Harris claims that the fictional suicide bomber at the outset of his book might have any kind of background but we can be sure of his religion, and is critical of any attempt to include political, economic, or personal factors in the analysis of the actions of Islamic terrorists. In interviews and debates Christopher Hitchens was reliably scathing about anyone who dared to suggest that a rise in Islamic fundamentalism in the Unites States and Britain could be in any way linked to aggressive interventionism of the two states in the Middle East, calling any association between terrorism and American involvement overseas 'masochism'. Dawkins uses Sookhdeo's explanation of abrogation to explain that 'Islam is war'.

There is, here, an agreement between the three authors about an essential quality of violence within Islam. Yet the consensus amongst serious scholars in the field of terrorism research is that Islamic terrorism is a result of political instability caused by disastrous British and American foreign policy, and even a cursory literature review reveals links between the actions of the west and the political turmoil in the near east. Furthermore, the west is not the primary target of Islamic terror groups: most of the victims of Islamic terrorism have been Muslims and those living in Muslim-majority countries according to the National Counterterrorism Centre's 2011 report. As Mona Siddiqui argued in *The Guardian* in 2014: 'The appeal of the Middle East wars to some young British Muslim men can't be reduced to an "Islam and the west" debate', instead suggesting that it is the pursuit of power and the oppression of women that is expressed through the surface narrative of Islamic conquest.

There is, then, a complex confluence of ironies within New Atheist thought insofar as it translates from its surface appearance of an ontological enquiry about the existence of God into a political position predicated on an existential threat posed to western liberal democracy not only by Islamic fundamentalism, but by Islam itself and the presence of a practising Muslim population. Just as Siddiqui argues that Islam provides a surface structure for a deeper motivation amongst Islamic terrorists, New Atheism uses the surface structure of ontological enquiry for what is, in reality, a politically-motivated discourse. Through this ideological apparatus, the New Atheist is able to create a discursive space in which their own argumentation is very difficult to refute.

First, it is necessary to attribute to Islam a privileged position of being especially warlike based on the belief that conquest is the only form of evangelism consistent with Islamic theology, a view derived from the work of writers considered by many Islamic scholars to misrepresent mainstream Islamic thought. While a Muslim who believes this assertion is a fundamentalist and extremist, an atheist who believes it is simply recognising the fact of the matter. In this way the role of the 'moderate Muslim' who values peaceful components of Islamic teaching is erased from the discourse while their vocal condemnation of acts of terror is simultaneously demanded. When that is, as a consequence, absent from the sphere of New Atheist discourse it is cited as evidence of at best complacency amongst moderate Muslims, and at worst tacit approval that proves moderate Islam is a misnomer. When condemnation is forthcoming from prominent public Muslims, their Islamic perspective is dismissed as having no standard by which to condemn in the first place.

As a result, the Muslim community finds itself predestined to be considered suspect. Operating not unlike the doctrine of original sin within Christianity, the very presence of faith in someone's life renders them ethically void *in essence*, and as such they are pre-emptively denied sufficient ethical agency to challenge problems within their own community. As such, the field of discourse about Islamic fundamentalism is reliant on self-appointed non-Muslim advocates of 'social cohesion' and 'western liberal values'. This ensures that anti-Islamic rhetoric remains the white man's burden despite the majority of meaningful engagement about the issue of extremism within Islam being undertaken by Muslim scholars.

Second, within this discourse so structured as to exclude any critique of Islam from within genuine Islamic scholarship, New Atheism is uniquely well-positioned to explain away the problem created by this void by virtue of its epistemic approach. By emphasising an exclusively empiricist epistemology which can be summarised by Hitchens' razor that 'what can be asserted without evidence can also be dismissed without evidence', all truth statements are forced into the epistemology of the scientific method, regardless of whether the statement pertains to physical reality. Debates framed as explorations of the existence of God are not, in fact, ontological in nature but epistemological, with New Atheists demanding metaphysical claims be expressed in empiricist terms in order to demonstrate any kind of validity. This, in a quasi-Wittgensteinian fashion, presupposes that metaphysics can be reduced to falsifiable claims about the measurable properties of the material world. As metaphysics does not operate within the epistemological apparatus of empiricism, this is bound to present metaphysics as inherently absurd. We might note, of course, that ethics does not fall within the scope of empirical epistemology, and yet this apparent absurdity within metaphysics is also assumed to favour the empiricist in making ethical claims, despite empiricism's self-evident uselessness in addressing any of these claims itself.

Regardless, since the late 1960s, such an austere approach to metaphysics has fallen out of favour, succeeded by attempts to synthesise the logical empiricism of the analytic school with the emphasis on phenomenology found in the traditions of continental philosophy of the likes of Alain Badiou. Meanwhile, logical empiricism finds its legacy thriving in the field of philosophy of science.

Not only, then, are the public intellectuals of the New Atheist movement either intentionally unwilling or psychologically incapable of engaging with prevailing trends within Islamic scholarship, they are also resistant to engagement with any tradition of secular metaphysics that might create space for the consideration of phenomena beyond those which can be accounted for by an empiricist epistemology. This places them in a uniquely contradictory position of being both intellectually unequipped for the ontological discussions they invite while at the same time creating rhetorical spaces in which the validity of scientific epistemology is tested against metaphysics. Necessarily this false equivalency favours the scientist: the metaphysician has no opposition to empiricism as an epistemic approach, but is interested in questions which, as the term 'metaphysics' suggests, lie beyond the scope of empirical enquiry. The empiricist, on the other hand, is not interested in questions that lie beyond the scope of empirical enquiry, and as such has no real interest in the question of God's existence. The framing of the debate in these terms is a bait-and-switch in which the limitations of the empirical approach in realising specific kinds of knowledge is assumed to delineate the bounds of knowledge itself. In this way, the unspoken premise of this kind of argumentation is that there is an axiomatic meta-epistemology in which empiricism is not only the *summum bonum* of the scientific approach, but the final word in all forms of philosophical enquiry, an assertion which itself does not pass the test of Hitchens' razor.

It is in this space in which the logical axioms of the discourse are self-contradicting that various kinds of hypocrisies emerge. While simultaneously scaremongering about the dangers of Islamic radicalisation on British university campuses such as Queen Mary, the radicalisation of secular humanists is enabled by the foundational undermining of logical processes within rationalism itself. This creates both the conditions for a kind of rhetorical discourse in which New Atheist ideology is, like religious faith, presented as all-encompassing, as well as an imbalance of representation within sociological and political discourse amongst New Atheists, reducing the visibility of contributions made by Muslim scholars, and lending disproportionate weight to the ideas of non-Muslim critics of Islam. In asserting its own modes of discourse as the only ones necessary to consider the issues of cohesion between Muslims and non-Muslims, the question of what 'cohesion' means is gatekept by predominantly conservative commentators, exploiting ambiguities of understanding about the nature of multiculturalism to conflate the failure of a monocultural project, which was never a political goal in mainstream British policy, with a failure of multiculturalism. Finally, the commodification of ideas by the class of 'public intellectuals' allows for ideas not subject to proper academic scrutiny to be more widely disseminated than rigorous scholarship, reducing complex discourse to a kind of intellectual populism that predictably achieves the greatest reach when it gives the appearance of greater respectability to prejudices and anxieties.

It is therefore no surprise, at least in retrospect, that New Atheism acted as a vehicle from the liberal principles of secular humanism to the conservative agenda of the British and American states during the War on Terror. What follows, according to a 2013 study by Kielinger and Paterson, is that between 2008 and 2012 Muslims were the target of almost half of all recorded faith-based hate incidents in London (which excludes a significant spike in anti-Muslim hate incidents following the 2007 London bombings).

While it is impossible to accurately ascertain the specific contribution of the New Atheist movement to a rise in anti-Islamic prejudice, we can see a clear link between the kinds of anxieties about Islam identified by Right-wing populists and by New Atheists, and that where these anxieties are heightened we see both a rise in anti-Muslim hate incidents and the success of anti-Islamic Right-wing populist movements.

By denying a broader political and socio-economic context for the analysis of Islamic extremism in favour of a reductionist argument in which faith ideology can fully explain the violent actions of radical Muslims, as well as by establishing a rhetorical framework in which logical empiricism is not only presented as a total epistemology but also as symbolic of the pinnacle of western thought in opposition to the superstition of religious faith, particularly Islam, New Atheism in the UK constituted a reinvention of common anti-Islamic Orientalist tropes within an apparently respectable discourse of 'public intellectualism' linked to the progressive tradition of British secular humanism. As such, it appeared to be a liberal movement with clear roots in the secular Left while undergoing a transition from liberal to conservative ideals. Similarly, it maintained the appearance of being an intellectual movement while, in fact, operating as populism. By framing the opposition between the history of ideas in the West and the East as mutually exclusive, and the rise of Islamic terrorism as a result of this tension, as well as an existential crisis for the liberal democratic way of life, New Atheism succeeded in convincing many of its adherents that the ideal of multiculturality that so characterised the ideals of western liberal democracy, relies for its success on an end to multiculturalism. In other words, under the banner of multiculturalism it argued for monoculturalism as the only solution for dealing with the problem of Islamic radicalism.

It is not surprising, therefore, that so many secular humanists who were initially liberal when they came to New Atheism, found themselves radicalised against the values they initially considered central to their political identity. For some, like Anne Marie Waters, hard-right ideology has become an inextricable part of what it means to them to be a secular humanist. For others, it has been a long road of unpicking the stages by which we became alienated from our core political beliefs in order to find our way back to a political worldview that feels representative of the kinds of people we are. I remain grateful to my boyfriend Alfonzo for challenging me over the years, and for his mad belief that, despite being his political polar opposite when we met, that somehow I would end up finding my way back to the Left. And while I am embarrassed to have been drawn in to such hardline Right-wing politics, it has given me a new perspective on my own Islamic heritage, and a new enthusiasm for discovering more about this part of my identity. I am currently in the process of reaching out to my extended British-Pakistani family and hopeful that I'll be able to meet and get to know them in the near future, something which my mother now supports.

ON THE RIGS

Yassmin Abdel-Magied

Released as part of the 40th edition of The Griffith Review *in April 2013, this was my first formally published piece of work. I wrote it at urging of the incredible Julianne Shultz, editor of the Review at the time, whom I served with on the Queensland Design Council. She saw in my 21-year-old self a storyteller, the potential of a writer, possibilities of a future inconceivable to me at the time. The essay came together in the mornings after 12+ hour nights shifts, lying cross-legged on the rough pale blue sheets of my single bed in an ice-cold donga, somewhere in outback Australia. 'Show, don't tell', Julianne said to me at the time, and through draft after draft, I worked to try show the world what it was to be a young, Sudanese engineer on rigs around Australia. Who knew it would be the beginning of an entirely new career? A personal transition that began its trajectory with a glimpse into an industry in the throes of change.*

'You're working on the rigs?' one of the drillers from my camp asked, his voice heavy with surprise. 'We assumed you were just with the camp. Respect hey, that's awesome, we love having chicks actually on the rigs.'

Another chimed in. 'Yeah, that's great. What do you do?'

'I'm a service hand, a "measurement while drilling" specialist. You really think we're really welcome here?' I asked.

'Yeah! We need more of it.'

Later that day, I had another conversation that challenged this view. Clearly women in the oil and gas industry are not universally welcomed. My rig manager was quite clear about his views, 'I said nope, no, absolutely not. There was no way I was going to let a female be on my crew. Everyone agreed. Sean (the manager on the other shift) even said to me that if she was hired, he would quit.'

The rig manager shrugged as he explained the reaction to a 'lady' applying to be a leasehand on the rig – the lowest level job, responsible for cleaning and errands.

'I just didn't want to deal with the extra hassle that it would bring,' he said.

I am the only woman on the twenty-five-person rig in Central Western Queensland.

Later that evening as I begin my regular twelve-hour night shift, I touch my iPod screen and select my current favourite anthem. In a flash Seal's velvet voice reverberates through the white earbuds. 'This is a man's, man's world…'

Accepting that your 21-year-old Muslim daughter is going to work on remote oil and gas rigs is not easy. I am fortunate to have parents who understand (although perhaps not always share) my interest in adventure and not being ordinary. Their view is simple: as long as the rules of Islam are followed and there is a coherent and beneficial reason for me doing the things I choose, they will support me.

My parents say they weren't sure what to expect when they immigrated to Australia almost twenty years ago, fleeing the oppressive political regime of Omar al-Bashir in Sudan. They may not have had a concrete idea of where it would lead, but I certainly inherited from them a willingness to seize opportunity and embark on adventures. That may explain how they found themselves with a daughter who boxes, designs racing cars, and while visiting family in Sudan last year, got wrapped up in an attempt to overthrow the same oppressive government that forced them to leave.

They came to Australia looking for a new beginning, now they are parents of a female, Muslim rig hand.

As part of my faith, I wear the hijab, and have been doing so since I was ten, as a personal choice. It is truly something that has become a part of my identity, and I like to be flamboyant and creative with colours and styles. My head covering on the rig is a little less obvious and obtrusive, the turban and bandana combination combine with the hardhat and are a little cooler. In true Australian fashion, however, religion is one topic that is fastidiously avoided on the rig, and people don't always realise the significance of my head covering. It makes for some interesting conversations.

'So when's that tea cosy come off?'

I turned around to my colleague and chuckled to myself.

'Nah, it doesn't come off, I was born with it, eh!'

His jaw dropped slightly and he looked at me in confusion. 'Wha-a-?'

I laughed out loud. 'Nah mate! It's a religious thing. We call it a hijab, I guess this is the abbreviated hard-hat friendly version...'

'Oh yeah righto...'

He nodded, uncertain, then shrugged and went back to his meal.

When I told my family at home, my father couldn't get enough of it.

'Let's call you Tea Cosy now!'

The oil and gas industry in and around Australia has existed for decades. The onshore coal seam gas industry has, however, only begun to boom in the mid-2000s, and become a subject of vocal controversy. Companies like Santos, Arrow Energy, Queensland Gas Company and Origin are battling it out throughout the Bowen and Surat Basins, drilling as fast as they can to have enough gas to fulfil the contracts they have signed. The numbers advertised by the companies are incredible, going from just ten wells in the early 1990s to more than 600 in 2010–2011 and peaking at 1,634 wells drilled in 2013–14. They predict this will increase to a whopping 40,000 wells by the middle of this century.

This means that there are many job opportunities in the gas industry for new mechanical engineers, like me. Many opt for graduate positions in one of the large client companies that produce the liquefied natural gas from the coal seam gas that has been extracted. There they work on the design, procurement or project management aspects of drilling and production.

Others want to get their hands dirty, to see what is happening in the field, and they take another route. This suited my sense of adventure and I opted for field experience. As a field engineer, I live, eat and work on remote oil and gas drilling rigs throughout the country and the world.

It is unusual and full of challenging learning experiences. It is also an extremely humbling opportunity to be part of a world that is unknown to many. What has been most surprising about the experience, however, is not the physical aspect or the male-dominated environment – studying engineering will accustom any woman to this, only five women graduated in my year (2011) in a class of 200 – but the constant reminder of gender.

What I considered an innocuous detail looms as the most important for many others.

Drilling rigs drill holes — wells — in the ground in order to reach a 'payzone'; usually either oil or gas. Onshore and offshore drilling rigs look similar, despite the obvious difference in location. Australia has both onshore and offshore operations, but the onshore rigs are typically smaller. I work mostly on these onshore outfits, often in remote locations anywhere from thirty minutes' drive to a few hours flight away from the nearest town. They operate twenty-four hours a day, seven days a week, every day of the year. I spent Islamic Eid celebrations, Christmas and New Year at work. This is common, the drilling and pumping never stops.

In a typical operation, a rig will be set up on a cleared piece of land — a pad — and the operating crew will live in a camp up to (and sometimes over) twenty minutes drive away. The rig is basically made up of a rig floor (where the main rig operations occur, usually at least four metres above the wellbore ground level), the derrick (the tall mast that holds the pipe as well as the drive system, and ranges from ten to thirty metres high), the dog-house (a small room on the rig floor for the driller) and varied tank system on the ground nearby, housing the fluid (usually mud) which is pumped down the drill string (as it is called when the drill pipe is joined together). The 'catwalk' attached to the rig raises the pipe to the rig floor while drilling. There are also various water tanks, other equipment (generators, pumps) and shacks for the personnel. All up, this can all be housed on a piece of land that is less than a hundred metres square.

The quality of the camp depends on the company; generally there are between five and twenty 'dongas' (converted shipping containers) with three to five rooms each. Each room houses two people, on opposite shifts; one person sleeps the other works, and depending on the camp, there are either camp-wide communal bathrooms, shared bathrooms or individual ensuites.

It is not luxurious, but crew are compensated for the lifestyle. Most rig workers, like mining workers, work a rotational fly-in, fly-out shift — two weeks on, two weeks off. The contractors who provide supplementary services to the rig tend to have on-call arrangements with no formal rotation: you work when you are needed. I have been fortunate and have not had to work extremely long 'hitches' yet. To my parent's relief, my longest attachment was twenty days in central Queensland. The longest hitch I've heard about is eighty-four days straight, with not a single day off. Such is the life of a service hand.

The environment is unapologetically male. It is also isolated and basic: all everyone does is sleep-eat-work. I found it relatively easy to acclimatise given my studies and interests, but I underestimated the impact that being the only woman for most of my time, in a group of between twenty and sixty men, would have on me. I found it more challenging than I expected to navigate work/life nuances on the rigs.

There are few workplaces where a woman is made more aware of her gender: where you must learn to find the balance as a woman in such an overwhelmingly male world. Many, most, of the men who work in oil and gas still consider the industry to be a 'man's domain', and even those who welcome women have particular expectations of how a woman should act to be fully accepted.

'This is a man's world,' I was told once by an older male colleague, 'so as a woman you have to learn the rules and fit in. You can't change the men.'

Most surprisingly for a Muslim woman focused on academic and formal equality, 'learning to fit in' has included navigating the sexual double standard that is ever present in the field. I became weary of being seen as a woman who would come in to 'change the ways of the men'. Such a reputation would make life very difficult for me. So when I was on a rig I would make a point of joking with the crew and let their comments roll. It was a way of showing that 'I could take it.' I had four years of mechanical engineering under my belt after all, where females made up less than 5 per cent of the class, so I thought it was something I was used to. I soon discovered that I was not.

Things were turned on their head, and I had to rethink the best way of coping, one afternoon when a rig worker made an announcement over the two-way radio.

'Yassmin, I'll give you $100 to wrestle in the mud with Bazza!' the voice cackled over the speaker.

I scoffed to myself, who did he think he was?

'You wish – I wouldn't even dream about it for less than half a million,' I shot back, secretly proud at myself for fobbing him off in what I thought was quite an effective manner.

'Half a million! Do you know what I could get with half a million?' the voice came back, incredulous.

Not me rolling around in the mud on a rig for you, I thought.

Later that night, an older colleague took me aside.

'You gotta put a stop to that kind of talk you know,' he said. I looked at him, puzzled.

'It diminishes you. People will start thinking you're a slut.'

I was shocked – how did they interpret my comment like that? The double standard of sexual promiscuity for men and women took me by surprise. How could I, as a young, practicing Muslim woman on a rig, standing up for myself, possibly be considered as promiscuous?

The same banter that makes 'men, men' on the rig, is not open to women. Too much backchat and your value is 'diminished', too little, and you're perceived as uptight and hard to work with. A fine line and not one that I never expected to walk, but not the only one in the bush.

Drilling rigs are places where large groups of men are isolated for at least two weeks at a time and left to their own devices. Many of these men are not well educated – I know several illiterate drillers – and so it becomes an environment where base instincts take hold. Humiliating hazing, that should be illegal, like tying people up and urinating on them, is, according to stories I have heard from other rigs, surprisingly commonplace. In this environment women are seen as fair game. Adolescent-like practical jokes are common and almost everyone talks about viewing of pornography openly. On my second job in the field, a colleague offered me free access to his one-and-a-half-terabyte pornography collection. 'Take what you want!' he said. 'I've got stuff from almost any country, and there is exotic stuff in that folder,' he indicated. 'I collect it!'

I politely, but firmly declined.

I had thought pornography was something people grew out of in high school. Not so, I was assured by a motorman on my first job.

'If the dongas aren't perfectly level, you might feel the room rocking when you're trying to get to sleep. That usually means someone in one of the rooms is having a...' I interrupted at that point; not wanting to hear the details. The image stayed in my mind, though, and I involuntarily cringe every time my donga moves now, even though usually it's someone walking up the stairs.

It is not all rough, and the industry has changed significantly since the turn of the century. Despite the traditional male dominance, there are strong factors forcing welcome change. Two catalysts for change are the increasingly strict Occupational Health and Safety regulations and the presence of women on rigs. While there are relatively few women in the physically demanding rig environment, there are increasing numbers of women working as geologists, engineers, and in wireline and drilling and measurement services.

The transition has not been easy and as my experiences show, reactions vary from acceptance and encouragement, to fear of the change the presence of women might bring. 'It makes it feel more like the real world,' several rig hands have told me. 'When there is a woman around, people argue less, talk about different things and it doesn't feel like such a strange place to come to. This perspective was slightly surprising and equally encouraging. The more common opinion however, is shaped by fear. Although some men enjoy having women as part of their workforce, they still believe it is their domain and women are 'more trouble than they are worth'. I have heard this many times. In part this stems from the fear of sexual harassment claims, which are not uncommon in the industry in both the field and office environment. Numbers are difficult to come by, but anecdotally, it seems that two thirds of the rigs in Queensland have had some sort of sexual harassment complaint from a woman in the recent past.

I have found it takes an average of three shifts (tours – three consecutive twelve-hour days or nights), before the crew begin to interact, even after making an extensive effort to get to know the individuals. By the third tour, crews may start having conversations in my presence. It usually takes a week or two on the same job before I can walk into a room and the conversation doesn't completely stop. It is rarely an aggressively threatening environment, although it can be extremely intimidating. It is more that the crew don't know how to behave with a woman in their midst. Do they act normally? Should they be on their best behaviour? They wait for cues.

'We gotta suss the chicks out,' an assistant driller commented. 'You don't know if she's going to just report you on a joke you didn't even realise you made. I don't want to lose my job, so I just stay quiet.'

This view is not uncommon; a lot of people have said the same thing in different ways. On one hand, it is heartening to see the system working, to see that women's rights in the field are taken seriously. On the other, it instantly causes an 'us and them' rift. The men band together; their view is that 'the women are the same and out to get them' or that they are 'too sensitive' and won't be privy to the men's banter. Unfortunately, on most sites there are not enough women to form their own gangs.

The men are right to be uncertain about how their banter will be received. It is usually extremely racist, sexist and offensive. It can't be just excused as 'rig talk'.

Charlie is a 68-year-old directional driller. He grinned at me when he decided he could talk to me and said with a smirk, 'Oh yes, I have some blacks in my family tree!' I was naively impressed (and surprised) that we may have some shared heritage, as Charlie looked like an average 'Aussie battler'.

'Oh yes, yes I do. I think they're still hanging there out the front of the house!'

His wizened face creased into a smile as he began to chortle. I began to laugh as well, mostly in shock. 'Charlie, you're a terrible man!' I replied, shaking my head.

'I know! It's great isn't it!'

I find I am constantly asking myself the question: Does one adopt and accept the mannerisms of the rig to 'fit in', and become 'one of the boys', not causing waves by accepting the status quo? Or should I, and other women, stick to our guns and demand change, that the men working in these isolated and testing environments change their culture and mannerisms in order to incorporate women?

It is not easy to answer. My mother sat me down before I left for my first 'hitch' and gave me some advice. 'Don't forget Yassmina, that you are not a boy, and you will never be "one of the boys". At the end of the day, you are and will always be a woman, and a Muslim woman at that, so you must act like one and guard yourself.'

At the time, the advice jarred. I had always been 'one of the boys'. It was difficult to understand why this had to change now.

The more I work in the field though, the more I realise that things are different. Being 'one of the boys' may have been appropriate at university. In the field no matter what I do, my gender will never be forgotten. This was one of the reasons the rig manager refused to have women on his crews. 'The guy that was pushing for this woman to be hired, he had hired his twin sister way back in the day on the rigs so had a soft spot for women on crews. He ended up having to fire her though, because she hooked up with another crew-member. What does that tell you?'

We are faced not only with entrenched attitudes within the industry of what women are capable of, but also individual prejudices. In an industry where it seems every second man is going through or recovering from a divorce (partly due to the lifestyle), the cocktail of emotion and misunderstanding can be toxic. If I had a dollar for the number of times a co-worker has said, part mirth and part seriousness – 'All you damn women are the same' – I could probably retire.

Even as I write this, I feel I should apologise and add a disclaimer. Not all the oil and gas fields are like this.

Or is this just me, explaining away behaviour that is common on rigs so I don't 'rock the boat' or disturb the peace and become an unwanted entity? I haven't been able to answer these questions yet. Working on the rigs has, however, allowed and forced me to reinterpret my understanding of what it means to be a strong woman.

I was always one for doing things differently, partly because I could, and partly because I just did what I wanted. Being the first girl at a Christian ecumenical school, and the largest in Queensland, to wear the hijab when I started there in 2002, was pretty exciting. Being the first woman in my company's department in Australia was even better. I broke the bench press record for girls at school, topped the two male-dominated classes of graphics and technology studies (woodwork) and I prided myself on being able to 'hold my own among the men', physically and in banter. Although I was proud to be a woman, I had always been even more proud of my 'masculine' qualities. Perhaps this is what frustrated my mother the most.

In the rigging world though, there is no mistaking the fact that I am a woman. I am not as strong as all the guys, though I can hold my own. I am not as foul mouthed, but I can come back with a quip to keep them quiet (or laughing, depending on the situation).

'Gosh, you've got it pretty good don't you? You get your clothes washed, your bed made, your food cooked for you and on top of that, your choice of twenty-five men! With no competition!' John, the campie, chortled as he opened the crib room door.

'What more could a woman want, eh?'

His lined, weather-beaten face flashed a grin, showing off his multiple silver fillings as he left the shack. I shook my head slowly and laughed. What more indeed...

This job has made me realise that it is actually okay to be a woman, and being 'strong' doesn't necessarily mean being 'masculine'. It's ironic that it has taken a world renowned for its toughness, to make me appreciate my femininity.

There is no doubt that it is a man's world, but it is changing. Australia is lagging behind other countries – in Norway and Europe women are much more routinely employed on rigs. How women change the field or change ourselves to fit in remains an unanswered question, but it will be exciting.

On another rig, I need to find the amenities. 'Are the loos working?' I ask the lease hand in charge of keeping the rig clean.

'Nah, they're probably filthy. I haven't been in there in ages, I just piss in the paddock!'

I laughed as I walked towards the amenities shack.

'Hover!' he yells faintly.

Hover I did. As I pushed down the pedal of the Portaloo and the stench wafts up, I shake my head and wonder: why did I choose this job?

But I do remember. I chose this job because I love a challenge, I love working in the field and I thrive on being forced out of my comfort zone and into environments where I have to prove myself. If I manage to smash a few stereotypes along the way, so much the better.

THE BOOKROOM

Robin Yassin-Kassab

I.

My friend Will has built me a bookroom. It sits at the transition point of our property and the farmer's. From the large window I see the two-year-old hedge on the boundary, and sheep fields and drumlins, and beyond them the rising Galloway Hills.

It's built of larch, with a metal roof. The ceiling and walls are plastered with clay, and the shelves are cut from sitka spruce. I've dreamt of this room for years. With Will's help, I've dreamt it into existence. It's my own *bayt al-hikmah*, this one a working temple to the printed rather than the calligraphed or digitised word – something which readers of languages in Arabic script missed out on for a long and impoverished three and a half centuries. True there is one calligraphed *mashallah* hanging from a beam, but no internet connection – this radically cuts down distraction and creates a mental silence.

The first task is unpacking the books from the boxes they've lived in for the last four years.

This evokes warm feelings. It's like recognising the faces of old friends. But it also involves a mourning for absences. Those missing include Albert Hourani's *Arabic Thought in the Liberal Age*, Timothy Snyder's *The Road to Unfreedom*, *Black Jacobins* by C.L.R. James, *The Man who Mistook his Wife or a Hat* by Oliver Sacks, *The Eden Express* by Mark Vonnegut (Kurt's son), *The Tibetan Book of the Dead*. And quite a few others. O I have been too liberal a lender. I hope they're happy, wherever they are. There are also all those I shed when I left a country, when I left a life behind – something I've done at least six times. And there was a major purge four years ago, before the survivors were packed into their boxes. Still, there are so many books. Too many books even for this generous shelf space. So I set about another, more minor purge now.

I get rid of some I read to potentially review – 'for work', as it were – and which I didn't much like. And some, even after the earlier purge, of which I discover I own more than one copy. And some I've outgrown.

Here is *Quotations from Chairman Mao Tse-Tung*. I can't remember where or when I acquired this. It's a book so cocky and unjustly sure of itself I want to hurl it into the bin. Published by Foreign Languages Press, Peking, in 1967 – as part of a state-driven propaganda project, therefore. 'Once Mao Tse-Tung's thought is grasped by the broad masses,' says the foreword, 'it becomes an inexhaustible source of strength and a spiritual atom bomb of infinite power.'

I don't hurl it into the bin, nor into the fire. However bad a book might be, burning books is worse. Book burning is a symbolic violence and a historical echo too terrible to allow. Not even if the book has been painted with poison. Not even if you're dying of cold.

Though the flames do tempt. Here is *Voice of Hezbollah: The Statements of Seyyed Hassan Nasrallah*. An interesting historical document, no doubt, but these days – after the bloody victory of counter-revolution in Syria – the sight of it gives me a trauma response. Even the name of the publisher gives me a trauma response. So I pass that one on to an interested friend. I feel comfortable doing so because she understands the severity of Nasrallah's crimes. And for now I keep the Mao book, more for the absurd enthusiasm of the foreword than for the platitudes of the genocidal Great Leader. Also because it's pocket sized, and it won't take up much space.

I will judge politically those books authored by political actors, those which demand to be taken seriously for their politics first and foremost. Otherwise it makes no difference to me if an author is a conservative or a radical if their writing is beautiful or perceptive or of some other inherent worth.

Take Saul Bellow. In the opening passages of *Mr. Sammler's Planet*, an animalistic Black man exposes his penis to the cerebral, highly civilised Holocaust survivor Mr. Sammler, an act resonant of everything that's supposedly going wrong in the American nineteen sixties. It's ugly stuff. At first sight the racism might actually be a stylistic as well as a political and moral defect, in that it disrupts the reader's immersion in Bellow's densely-woven world. On further consideration, it might not be a defect at all, because the later reappearance of the Black man complicates Mr. Sammler's response, as does the reader's greater knowledge of Mr. Sammler, what he did in the war, as well as what was done to him. More difficult for the Muslim reader is the rapport struck up between Sammler and an Indian scientist based in part on their common fear of Muslim enemies apparently threatening the Indian and Israeli states. And more difficult for a woman reading the novel would be the misogyny, which is not really in any way complicated. I note these flaws, or rather, these distances between Bellow's sense of the world and mine, but I still love the book. I'll definitely be pleased to have it on my shelves, alongside the rest of Bellow's novels, the collected stories, the collected non-fiction, and a biography. The non-fiction, by the way, shows Bellow as much as Sammler to have been a fierce supporter of Israel, and somewhat disdainful of Israel's victims. This has never put me off. Indeed my most fiercely anti-Zionist phase coincided with my most intense fascination with Bellow's writing. Bellow is a great writer. Whether I share his politics or his cultural positioning is neither here nor there.

But then take Martin Amis — perhaps Bellow's greatest advocate — who made a series of distressingly offensive Islamophobic remarks in the aftermath of 9/11 — some of which he's distanced himself from since. I remember this when I look at his book (it's the comic novel *Money*), and it distresses me, it stains the book somewhat. Unlike Bellow's book, which remains unstained. Perhaps this is because Amis is younger than Bellow (Bellow died in 2005, aged 89), and is British like me, and is less of a stylistic genius than Bellow. Closer to me, therefore more easily sullied. But still *Money* isn't stained enough in my eyes to be cancelled. It goes on the shelves, and the five or six other novels I've read by Amis would sit there too, if I hadn't lost them.

On the other hand, there are a couple of Palestinian writers who I can't read anymore for revulsion at positions they took on the last decade's revolutions in the Arab world. I give these away to the same interested friend.

What's the difference? Where is the transition between a perceived flaw which adds nuance to sheer delight and one which provokes outright disgust? In part, the answer is time (for I am still living through the counter-revolutions). In part, it's the proximity of the wound.

After giving some away, I end up with two piles of unwanted books. One contains political polemics which once impressed but now appal me, and which I can't in good conscience pass on to others, ones which my friend also has no use for. Plus those which are falling to bits. I can't burn them so I use them to build a ring in the grass in front of the bookroom. I will plant a tree at the centre of the ring. The books, with rocks on top, will protect this sapling from the wind.

The second pile I donate to our village library.

I'm about to do so when I decide to give one – *Bad Moon Rising* by Gilles Kepel – another chance. I read a few pages and decide it's not all that bad. I read to the end and decide it's really quite perspicacious. Now I can't understand why I wanted to throw it out. I'd based that decision on a judgment made some years ago, on what basis I can't remember. It must have offended me in some way. It must have traduced some viscerally held notion.

Here's a transition: from me then to me now. If I met that earlier self, we'd soon start fighting.

This is one of the most interesting things that a personal book collection can do. It reflects you back to yourself in a complicated way. It's a mirror in which you see many faces. It renders your current face insubstantial.

II.

The books in their provisional groups are piled high on the floor. It's as if they emanate a beautiful perfume. They give me a pleasant feeling of respect for myself – or for the earlier iterations of myself – that I have engaged so deeply with so many subjects, ideas, and cultures. There are lots of books on Syria, several shelves worth, in several languages, books literary, political, historical, archaeological. Lots on Palestine and Israel (though most, I admit, are from the Palestinian point of view). A pile of books on Iraq. And on Islam, Buddhism, prehistory. On cosmology, consciousness, art. On the natural world. On Scotland. There are more novels than anything else, especially American, but also Latin American and Russian.

There are piles of certain particularly prolific writers whose work I have consumed in full, including the aforementioned Bellow, and Calvino, Vargas Llosa, Bolaño, García Márquez, Tolstoy, Mahfouz. (My current fascination is with George Saunders.)

There are books from the Caribbean, a real crossroads of cultures. There are books concerned with or exemplifying the Black American experience. And the Jewish experience. And the immigrant experience. In fact there are books concerned with just about everyone's experiences. For this is perhaps the first point of books. A book is the transitionary point between my experience and somebody else's. The text is an interface between consciousnesses, the reader's and the writer's, just as sex is the transition or interface between bodies. The readerly-writerly experience is as profoundly intimate as any. And texts produce children too – in this case there's no reliable contraceptive – in the form of new ideas and ways of seeing which may long outlive human children. These intangible lives which live within and beyond us, for good and for ill.

The next task is to organise these volumes on the shelves. Which leads to the question: How? That is, how to divide them from each other, according to which principle?

I ask our neighbours' daughter for advice. Aarni is an eleven-year-old bookworm, a devourer of audio books in particular. Harry Potter is her repeat favourite, but her tastes are expanding. On Wednesday mornings she skips school and visits me in the bookroom, where we talk about the world, and mainly, read stories (last time we read 'Some of Us Had Been Threatening Our Friend Colby' by Donald Barthelme). In recognition of her bookishness, the school has tasked her with organising its library. Or rather, its libraries – the school has a room for fiction and a room for non-fiction. Within those two rooms, Aarni sorts the books according to their level of difficulty.

It's great the school still has a library. In a surge of misplaced enthusiasm for the digital future, so many schools and other institutions (including, in my experience, British Council teaching centres abroad) got rid of libraries when they installed computers. According to Nicholas Carr's book *The Shallows*, plenty of evidence shows that students engage less, remember less, think less critically, and enjoy the learning process less, when a topic is presented in 'multimedia' form on screen rather than simply as a text on a page. And anecdotal evidence abounds that the internet is a monstrously poor substitute for books. From the Trump phenomenon to people's reported increasing inability to concentrate, it's clear that the shift from print to screen is bad for the mind and worse for society. But too late, the damage is done and seems irreversible.

Except in my bookroom. Which still needs to be organised.

Aarni's best friend Bea, she tells me, sorts her books by colour.

Well, I'm not sorting according to colour, nor according to difficulty. Not least because the concept of difficulty is itself difficult. What I find difficult depends on my mood, my approach to a text, and even the time of day. Where, for example, if I sorted by difficulty, would *Finnegans Wake* sit? Because if it's considered as writing on the page, the Wake is by far the most difficult book I own. But if it's consumed in audio form, that is read out loud, it becomes one of the easiest, because then it's a music to be listened to, and sometimes to laugh at, not a text to understand.

III.

Here is how I've done it: by chronology, geography, and language of composition.

On the upper wall to my right – if I sit at the desk facing the large window – are three shelves of American novels sorted by author, alphabetically. These merge into Black American non-fiction, and then the Caribbean books. On the lower wall is English Literature arranged by period from Anglo-Saxon to modernism. After that comes contemporary English language fiction, from England, Scotland, Ireland, Canada, and Australia, alphabetically ordered. Then fiction translated from other European languages, alphabetical again, and not distinguished by country or period (so Dante sits next to Negar Djavadi, despite the centuries between them). On the right half of the long back wall there is a shelf three quarters full of Russians, leaving space for my very small Ukrainian collection to grow (I've just finished *The Orphanage* by Serhiy Zhadan, a war novel which I highly recommend). Below that is a shelf and a half of Latin Americans, and a half shelf of Africans, and then three shelves of non-fiction divided into such vague and overlapping categories as politics, history, psychology, social commentary, philosophy. There's a section of art books and a section for music. Then there are countries in clumps separated by no particular logic. Scotland then Sri Lanka then India then China. The left half of the back wall contains religion books divided as far as possible by religious tradition, and then Pakistan, and various Middle Eastern countries. The left wall houses the Syria books, and a space to hang pictures, and a wood-burning stove.

The books are well enough arranged for me to know where to find them, though the distinctions are often arbitrary. James Joyce for instance sits in periodic English literature, but Samuel Beckett doesn't. I've decided that the transition between canonical and contemporary literature occurs somewhere between these two, though the men knew each other and worked together.

Sometimes I make a distinction between poetry and prose, but often I don't. The poetry and prose of John Donne sit side by side, whereas T.S. Eliot's poetry, unlike his prose, lives in a dedicated poetry section.

This is a distinction in any case which, while useful, doesn't always work. Because there are prose poems. And there is poetic prose. There is also *saj'*, in which most of the Quran is composed, a form producing rhyme and rhythm but no metre, which is therefore neither prose nor poetry.

Poetry and literary criticism fill their own suitable nooks. The sorting principle here is more the shape and spaciousness of the shelving than anything else. The bookroom, as Will has built it, is a nook-rich environment. There's a nook for children's books, and another for science fiction.

As already mentioned, African writing has its own section. By African I mean sub-Saharan African, which makes yet another questionable distinction (Sudan sits elsewhere, next to Egypt). And the questions continue. White Africans (J. M. Coetzee, Nadine Gordimer) are mixed up with the African Africans, though arguably they belong to a different tradition. Abdulrazak Gurnah is there too – he might belong to a different tradition again: the Arab, or rather, the Swahili – the culture of the coasts – although he writes (like all of them on my shelf) in English, and not in Swahili. Of course the Nigerians and the Kenyans belong to different traditions, even if Africanness and the British imperial past in some way bring them together. They all express multiple influences – too multiple, if we look closely enough, to be categorised at all.

In the country sections, literature and non-fiction are mixed together. Under the general label 'Iran', for instance, books as different as Forough Farrokhzad (poetry), Vali Nasr (political analysis) and Marjane Satrapi (graphic novel) huddle side by side.

The novelist Nadeem Aslam sits in 'Pakistan', where several of his stories are set. But *Maps for Lost Lovers* – probably his best book – is very definitely set in northern England. In *dasht-e-tanhai* to be precise, a wilderness of desolation somewhere very like Huddersfield.

Perhaps I should move just that one into the contemporary British books?

The more I think about it the further I am from an answer.

And then there is Laos.

IV.

There are only three books and a notebook in the Laos section. But my experience of Laos, however limited, was enough to open a categorical can of worms. My wife and I spent five weeks in the country in 2017, a visit which upended my ideas, wrecking my former distinctions and divisions.

I used to think that I knew where west and east were. These ideas were wrapped up with the concepts of Christian Europe. Also of the *dar al-islam*. West became east at the Christian Muslim border.

Of course, there is no actual locatable border. Culturally, the two zones interpenetrate. Geographically, there is a collection of grey areas, or multicoloured zones, or colourblind territories. To account for some of these the Balkans have been cast as 'the near east', and north Africa with the Arabian peninsula and its two fertile crescents are called 'the middle east'. The Cold War put Russia in the 'east' only to demonstrate its opposition to the 'west' – a category at that point assigned not to a cultural referent but to a geo-strategic camp.

West and east. Yes, the terms are a mess. Nevertheless I used them. I pretty much understood what they meant.

But in Laos relations between men and women, between adults and children, and between humans and animals, were so different to what I'd experienced elsewhere that I had to reformulate.

Certainly there was the Communist Party, and the remnants of American bombs, so surely the 'west' had reached there too, certainly Laos was globalised. But the major cultural influences were Buddhist,

Hindu, and Confucian, as well as the practices of the 'tribal' peoples of the anarchic uplands. So Laos didn't feel at all like anywhere west of Amritsar.

My point is this. Standing in Laos, it felt to me that *dar al-islam* and Christendom belonged together. In opposition, I suppose, to Laos, now representing the east. I felt that the west must begin in Pakistan, or possibly Bangladesh. Europe after all is a peninsula jutting out from western Asia, and its early history was a later extension of western Asia's domestication of herd animals and grains. Researchers have traced the journeys of western Asian genetics as early farmers colonised the northern Mediterranean and then the Atlantic coast as far north as western Scotland.

Muslims and Christians follow different sects of the same Abrahamic religion. They share, with a few exceptions, the same myths, the same prophets, and more or less the same commands and concerns. And just as they share scriptural origins, so they partake of the same Greek heritage. Renaissance Europe learned Greek literature and philosophy from Arabic sources. Its rationalism was powered by Ibn Rushd. During the convivencia in al-Andalus, Muslims, Christians and Jews formed one diversely divided culture. Similarly the much later Ottoman empire straddled Europe, Asia and Africa and made a melting pot of its cultures. A visit to Greece remains a speedy method of undermining the west-east dichotomy. However fiercely the two nationalisms compete, much of the country looks, sounds, tastes and smells like much of Turkey.

It's this similarity which breeds conflict, in particular over how the shared Greek heritage and Abrahamic myths, prophets, commands and concerns should be interpreted and applied. Hence the crusades, and the eternal return of the crusades, as when in 1920 the French general Henri Gouraud entered Damascus, and before doing anything else, walked up to Salahuddin al-Ayyubi's tomb and heftily kicked it, (allegedly) declaring 'Awake, Saladin! We have returned!' Such essentialist idiocy is practised by both sides. Al-Qaida lists 'Crusaders' amongst its enemies (alongside 'Jews' and 'apostates'), as if a thousand years of history hadn't happened.

The western and eastern halves of this larger west are both fascinated by and resentful of each other, each defining itself in opposition to the other. Each tends to see itself as the other's eternal victim. Indeed a victory for one has often translated immediately into a defeat for the other: in 1492, for instance, when the western westerners drove the eastern westerners out of Granada, and simultaneously launched the colonisation of the Americas. They invested the silver they plundered there in global shipping, and their new trade routes superseded the old land roads, which resulted in the decline of the Muslim heartland.

I'm by no means the first to notice the insubstantiality of west-east labels. I recently read in Tim Mackintosh-Smith's *Arabs* (a wonderful book but one which doesn't grace my shelves, because I read someone else's copy) that in the early days of Islam 'Arabs shared, unconsciously, the old Greek and Roman view of Persians as effete and dissolute; like their predecessors, they saw themselves as epic heroes versus epicene Orientals. Even this early on, they were the West of the East, as Levi-Strauss has described Islam.'

Really the Arabs were neither western nor eastern but a middle people inhabiting a transitionary zone, between tribes and peoples, between *badu* and *hadr*, between Persia and Rome, and their history has been played out in transit, between desert isolation and global migration, on the caravan routes and the sea roads.

After the arrival of Islam, the entire multi-ethnic Muslim community became a middle people. Not a side, not a polarity or compass point, not a category, but an ocean in which all categories could swim.

V.

Categories and the transitions between them are concepts, not objects. They aren't satisfactory. They aren't even real. Still, we need them. Categories serve as the basis of thought.

I sit in the bookroom and gaze on the books, just on the spines of the books. It's like gazing at myself, at my various selves. The books in their groups represent transitions between the sections of my life. Not just my life. My family's lives too.

Here is a book which belonged to my maternal grandfather. Funnily enough, it's called *Tales of a Grandfather*, by Sir Walter Scott. My grandfather's name — Arnold Wilson — is neatly printed inside, with a date, Christmas 1910. I presume the name and date were written by one of my great-grandparents, as in 1910 my grandfather was only two years old.

Here are some books of my mother's, which were also mine: Tolkien's *Tom Bombadil* and *The Hobbit*, *The Nonsense Verse of Edward Lear*, Charles Kingsley's *The Water Babies*.

Here are mine: *Alice in Wonderland*, *The Adventures of Mr. Bumblemoose*, *Hamish Meets Bumpy Mackenzie*. I remember these meaning so much to me. Some of them, beyond that memory of meaning, don't mean so much now. *Hamish Meets Bumpy Mackenzie* when re-examined seems insufferably uptight and snobbish. (On their first meeting, Hamish informs Bumpy that he's a golden hamster, and Bumpy [who is a squirrel] wonders 'what in the world *was* a Golden Hamster? Oh, well, probably a foreigner – so many of them around these days, really, one didn't know where one was.') That little England tone bothers me now but didn't when I was tiny. This is a sign of the death of that tiny me. Dead long ago, and many more me's dead since. The nostalgia provoked even now by the illustrations, the large print, the smell of the paper, is like that provoked by a grave slab.

I had a similar experience when I read my children the Narnia stories by C.S. Lewis. The first time around I'd enjoyed these books straightforwardly, as exciting, imaginative stories. This time I was conscious of them as Christian propaganda, as clunkily contrived polemics. *The Horse and His Boy* was the worst of the lot, its orientalism veering to racism.

The Eagle of the Ninth is still good. So is *Moonfleet*. But most of my childhood books have vanished. I had quite a few. They were what I usually received as presents. My grandfather – Arnold Wilson – spent his working life, from fourteen to sixty-five, in Young's bookshop, central Liverpool. He started as the errand boy and ended as the manager. When I was very young the highlight of a trip into town was a visit to Grampa in the shop, and a wander through the shelves, touching the spines, inhaling the print. When he wasn't busy with a customer, Grampa crouched with me in the aisles, selecting a book as a present, turning it over in his gentle hands, nodding at it respectfully, rocking his pale, weighty, overlarge head.

When he retired he moved to the Scottish countryside, just a few miles from where I am now. He lived so deep in the countryside that every two weeks a mobile library used to visit. I don't know if such things still exist. This one was something like a double-decker bus only with book-filled shelves instead of passenger-filled seats. It struck me at the time as remarkably strange – a moving institution, a vehicle containing worlds – as magically contradictory as Doctor Who's Tardis. As previously in the Liverpool bookshop, Grampa and I pulled down volumes, turned through the pages, conferred in quiet voices.

My paternal grandfather – Haj Ahmad – was illiterate. Though he held a great deal of one book in his head. His children were the first of the line to read with their eyes. At night they would take their schoolbooks to a more favoured, electrified neighbourhood, where they were able to read by streetlight.

I have a book here written by my father, standing in a special nook for books by people I've known personally, and which don't fit anywhere else. It's called *muzakirat tabib*, or *The Memoirs of a Doctor*.

Most of the canonical English literature books became mine when I was a student. They contain underlinings, jotted notes and doodles done by that student who shares my name. I can remember glimpses of the person but I can't remember doodling, because the person who doodled was not I.

I might have done it differently. I could have arranged the books by the chunks of my life. So rather than putting together books about Turkey, I could group the books I read while living in Turkey, when I owned that particular mind. Books in chronological order, from *Hamish Meets Bumpy Mackenzie* onward. From the head space of the reading child, through the other minds that have inherited the head space since. So many minds I can't count them. Minds replacing each other like water rushing over rapids.

These books have made me, the succession of me's, though I have forgotten most of their contents. Each one marked a change in my soul. Each proved to be – to redirect a phrase – a spiritual atom bomb of infinite power.

Almost each one. Let's not overstate it. Surely not the *Quotations from Chairman Mao Tse-Tung*.

ARTS AND LETTERS

AFTER 75 YEARS

Asyia Iftikhar
Photographs by Rehan Jamil

The decades since independence from colonial rule have seen Pakistanis settle in the UK and build communities that are now entering the fifth generation. As we celebrate 75 years since the creation of Pakistan, we ask people of Pakistani origin what this heritage means to them, and how they connect with their Pakistani roots.

Nehal Aamir

As a 24-year-old ceramic artist based in Manchester, Nehal Aamir has always had an affinity with sculpture, passed down through her maternal lineage.

Born in Gujranwala, Pakistan, Aamir moved to Manchester aged nine and as she straddled the chasm that opened up in her sense of identity, she turned to clay to express her Pakistani heritage.

'We moved to Manchester for a better education and lifestyle and to ultimately have a better future. Moving here was a big decision because no one in our family had done that before and it was a struggle. There was a different culture, language, new friends and new housing.

In our home growing up we had art pieces around the house that were made by family members, or my mother. So I started to explore my creativity through clay.'

Aamir eventually left Manchester and moved to London to study Ceramic Design at Central Saint Martins. It was here that she truly reconciled her two identities and embraced what it meant to be a British Pakistani Muslim.

'During that time, I felt like I was becoming my own person and at the
end of the course I wanted the pieces to reflect my personal journey.
People were curious about my past and connected with my work because
they are about my identity as a Pakistani Muslim living in Britain. It is great
to see South Asians can relate to my narratives - but also other immigrants
from different cultures. It was such a positive way to speak about
stereotypes and how Pakistani Muslim women are seen but celebrate us at
the same time. During those conversations I figured myself out and
discussed things I had never thought about before around my identity.'

Aamir regularly returns to Pakistan to visit her family and reflected on how her relationship with her motherland has developed over the years.

'My memories of Pakistan are fond because I was a child. My family is still in Pakistan and when I connect with my aunties, uncles and cousins my past comes alive and I feel like I am that Nehal again and it is so refreshing to return to the UK reminded of who you are and where your roots are. It was a journey settling in here trying to figure out where I was and where I belonged. Nine-year-old Nehal would be so proud to see how far I have come. I don't know if I could ever return to Pakistan permanently because of the opportunities I have been provided in the UK.'

When thinking about Pakistan, Aamir grasps onto certain moments and feelings which together shape her experience of the country.

'Pakistan is the feeling of home and knowing I can be there and have people who love me and understand my experiences. Having a midnight walk, going to the market, going out with cousins to get street food.'

However, similar to many Pakistanis living in diaspora communities, ultimately, her true connection is through her extended family.

'If I had my family here, would I feel the same way about Pakistan? No, I only go back because of them. Beyond them there is no reason for me to go back. It's not the food or any other aspect, you can get the same on Wilmslow Road. In Manchester, when it is Eid, you see a glimpse of Pakistan, you don't feel like you are still in the UK. The people, the smells, the dress, it genuinely transports you.'

Looking to the future, Aamir urgently believes that language is what will tether Pakistani diaspora to their motherland.

'When Pakistanis live and are brought up here the first thing they lose is their language. Urdu, Punjabi, Pashto, whatever your language, it becomes so difficult to speak it. Through language comes culture. For example, in Urdu you have a different language speaking to your elders and those younger to you. If British Pakistanis feel disconnected from their heritage then they should interact with the language, watch TV, films, and speak with their parents.'

Kamran Khan

Kamran Khan reflects on his disconnection from conventional notions of a Pakistani diaspora.

'I was never really immersed in my Pakistani identity during childhood. My dad didn't teach me Urdu or Pashto or spoke to me much about family. We never went to Pakistan and I still haven't been. I can't really define what it means to me to be Pakistani, but then again I don't have that feeling with any of my identities.

If anyone asks me about my background, I will tell them I am half-Pakistani and half Chinese-Malaysian without hesitation, but I don't meet the expectations they may have of all that entails, so I've always felt quite removed from the shared experience of my Pakistani friends. Pakistani cultural and social references were absent in my upbringing but my dad loved to cook Pakistani dishes so my connection was through food.

This all meant my Pakistani identity was not conventional and has been a journey of discovery, more so since my dad passed away. He was my only link to my Pakistani identity. Now he's gone, I'm facing up to the fact that it is now up to me to explore that side of me.

My brother went by himself in 2008 and would show me pictures and I remember thinking I had no idea how beautiful Pakistan was. Seeing his photos of my family changed my perspective of them too.

In 2008 I was in my final year at university, and a little later my mum and dad also went, so I didn't accompany them. It was the first time my dad visited Pakistan, since he left in 1968. He fled to escape a forced marriage, to the anger and shame of his family. But this same family were so happy to meet my mum, so I decided I would like to go one day too, but I never acted upon it. I always felt that I couldn't go by myself, I needed to go with my brother or my dad. When my dad travelled there, I thought that would start a cycle of him going back frequently and I thought I would go with him in the future, but when he returned he decided he would never go back again.

My dad's relationship with Pakistan was tinged by his experience with his family and that was the lens through which I perceived Pakistan. His relationship with Pakistan became quite abstract, he would send money back, was a passionate observer of Pakistani politics, but in terms of language and culture and family, I learned nothing. My dad even hated cricket!

One memory that fills me with nostalgia because it was a rare glimpse of my dad celebrating his heritage, was when Channel 4 aired a series of Qawwali performances and I remember my dad video-taped them and loved watching them. To this day I am moved when I hear Qawwali singers such as Nusrat Fateh Ali Khan because that was the only aspect of Pakistani culture my dad exposed me to.

My mum, on the other hand, would take me to Malaysia almost every year and I was close to my Malaysian family, some of whom also lived in London, so in terms of cultural identity that part of me was given life, while the Pakistani side wasn't at all. Yet I still consider myself half Pakistani and half Chinese-Malaysian, there is no question of that.

Unfortunately, my relationship with my dad's family is a continuation of the financial dependency that he fostered during his lifetime as that became the way they related to each other. As much as I love them and I know they are a part of me, it is a mostly transactional relationship, probably reflecting my dad's own complex reasons that speak to both his anger and his guilt at their estrangement. Since his death I just carried that on, although I'm trying now to gradually cease their financial dependence because I can see it has enabled a pattern that isn't healthy or empowering at all.

I'm hoping in time, perhaps by meeting them, by going there, I can change the dynamics of how we relate to each other. But I'm also aware that this financial arrangement isn't the link to my identity. I'm reading about where my dad comes from and appreciating it and that's been a great joy for me.

I'm also looking through the lens of colonialism, learning about history, and hearing people's stories about their lives there. But the reality is that I'm conflicted about my identity. I feel quite removed from the Pakistani diaspora, perhaps because of the other identities that exist within me - being queer, being half Chinese-Malysian and Bahai. But perhaps that's my internal battle; internalised biases and prejudices in my head that make me assume I would automatically be excluded from these spaces, when perhaps in reality I wouldn't.'

Tabassum Awan

Tabassum Awan is sitting in Pink Tea café in Mayfair. Her business which was once a dream is now a reality in the walls, seats, sofas and most importantly, chai.

The menu is home to baklava, artisan parathas, homemade cake and the signature drink, Pink Tea aka Kashmiri chai.

After spending 12 years in investment banking, a cup of chai changed Awan's perspective and she decided she wanted somewhere people could go to buy authentic Kashmiri chai.

'When I first discovered authentic Kashmiri chai I was madly in love. It was almost a feeling of escapism. I also really missed speaking with people in simple and sincere ways and I knew a cafe could do both.'

Awan reflected on how putting together the recipe connected her with her family and history in a way she never had before. Her discoveries taught her about British colonial history and its influence on the creation

of chai, the planting of indigenous tea, the transportation of the leaves across the world and how it ties together an entire land.

'There was so much research to put together this recipe. I spoke with people who make authentic pink tea, collecting recipes from family in Pakistan, looking into the history and source of the chai.

For the first two years of the business, I tried and tested so many different recipes trying to perfect the colouring and spices. I noticed the difference between how Pakistanis and Indians make chai. For example, Indians tend to use ginger whereas we stick with cloves, cardamom and spices. In Kashmir they prefer to drink the chai as a salty drink whereas in Pakistan we prefer everything slightly sweeter.

In this whole journey I have realised how much we have a rich cultural history and the importance of tea in the foundation of our lives. It is not just "oh I am going to make myself a cup of tea" but forms part of our society, it is integral to our culture.

In 2020 I started looking into how I was going to set up this cafe. Then COVID happened and I started online but it was never my dream to stay online so I started doing pop-ups around London. I realised people loved the drink from all backgrounds, all demographics.

My vision was not just about our products but to have a place for people to have tea over deep and meaningful conversations. We currently run monthly chai and poetry nights but soon I want to start Qawali nights and expand the community.'

Outside of chai, it is the creativity and artistry of Pakistani culture that Awan is most drawn to.

'For me poetry and Qawwali are the most beautiful parts of Pakistani culture to me. They are very creative and spiritual and they touch your soul and connect you with other people. I write my own poetry in Urdu.

It is such an incredible language and so expressive and in translation loses its context and meaning. The essence of it can't be translated. Urdu poetry really helps me contemplate where I come from.'

Zia Chaudhry

Growing up, Zia Chaudhry's relationship with Pakistan was shaped through the eyes of his father and decades later he reflects on how close he is with his motherland.

Author of *Just Your Average Muslim*, Chaudhry is a strong advocate for strong inter-faith relations and believes in dispelling myths around Islam.

'I was born in Burnley, Lancashire, which was home to the traditional Windrush generation who came in the 60s and eventually called their

families over. It was a very close-knit community, with the same villagers in Pakistan moving together over here.

My father came to England with an education and after becoming a teacher, got a job in Liverpool. It was such a different community to many of the Pakistani communities around the country. There we didn't have Pakistani neighbours and you would ring before going round to someone's house which was completely bizarre.

In my year at school there was one Pakistani, one Indian and one Bangladeshi and it meant you had to navigate through a school that was pretty much all white. In the '80s people's sensibilities were very different and what today is abhorrent was seen as playground banter.'

Growing up in such a white environment Chaudhry's main engagement with Pakistan came from his father's regular cultural evenings.

'My father was a very literary person and sought the poetry of Iqbal and the history of Quaid-i-Azam. He joined an organisation in Liverpool called "the circle of literary friends".

The people who organised this believed in educating the youth about Pakistani culture and history to stop it from being lost. So my father would write me speeches to read out and looking back I am so grateful that he did. I had pride in the achievement of these Pakistani poets and thinkers which established a connection with Pakistan.

However, my father also took the view that England was now home and going back to Pakistan was never on the cards at all. For a long time I was convinced of that. I believed I was British with a Pakistani background and this would be home forever. Now I do see changes in this country and wonder if the people who stay linked with Pakistan got it right.'

Chaudhry visited Pakistan for the first time in his life in his early 40s, a decade after his father's death. His family came from Jehlum, a place nestled in the middle of Islamabad and Lahore.

'I didn't go to Pakistan until I was around 40 years old and the first time I went was with my brother-in-law who is involved in politics. He showed me around Islamabad and Lahore and at one point we were in the Prime Minister's helicopter flying over Swat valley. So I came back thinking Pakistan was amazing.'

With a life so disconnected from Pakistan, a country riddled with political upheaval and corruption, Chaudry reflected on how there is a fundamental disconnect between his values and what Pakistan stands for.

'I'm at odds with members of my own family about how to preserve our heritage. On the one hand I have a real affinity with Pakistan, it is where my parents came from and there is a sense of pride when they play cricket. But when asked if I would go to Pakistan if I was thrown out of the UK I say no.

In that way I'm following the trajectory of my father but my 16-year-old son has got this complete fascination with Pakistan, with the culture, the music, and clothes. They are searching for belonging, maybe? Children now don't feel particularly British, especially since Brexit and think "maybe there is another place we would be welcomed".'

For Chaudhry his last thoughts remain bittersweet. 'I think the theory of Pakistan as an inclusive and enlightened place for Muslims is worth preserving but that all dissolved on day one of its creation. If you could recapture that then the country could thrive and be somewhere really worth learning about.'

Shahida Parveen

As Shahida Parveen's family enters its fifth generation of diaspora, the many decades that stretch between her and Pakistan have shaped what being British Pakistani means to her.

Now 54, Parveen and her extended family have lived between here and Pakistan over the years since coming in the 1960s but have always found themselves back in Bradford, England.

'My grandad came here to work and called his sons over and after my father got married to my mum she also came over to England. I myself was born in Pakistan and came over when I was 10 months old. Originally, we came to London and then moved to Nottingham but after my parent's divorce we moved to Bradford.

We are from Mirpur, Kashmir and in my adulthood have realised that if you do not go back regularly it is a culture shock at first. I was in my early 30s when I first visited Pakistan, and largely went to see family and sightsee.'

For Parveen the divide between British and Pakistani culture is huge, whether it is the traffic system, property or people. 'I could never drive a car in Pakistan and here we have a small house and a small garden but there they have massive houses, freedom and space.'

Parveen has worked as a professional interpreter speaking multiple South Asian languages for many years but acknowledges how difficult it is to embrace this part of British Pakistani identity.

'We know our languages less and less as the generations have gone on. Growing up you would feel embarrassed to speak it because people would

look at you funny so you would just stick to English. If your parents spoke it, you would feel embarrassed.

I always felt a bit apprehensive when I tried to speak my language or wear Asian clothes, I just felt like I didn't fit in.'

As a working South Asian mum, Parveen has had her life shaped by responsibility to her family and building a home for her children.

'I've worked since before I got married and I used to go to work, come home, cook and get the children ready for the next day. I have done interpreting, working with children with disabilities. I did a part-time cleaning job, and worked at reception. In the last ten years I have volunteered for local community projects and events just to keep the children occupied.'

As the years passed Parveen has noticed how the Pakistani community in Bradford has expanded. "Growing up there were not a lot of local Asian shops but now there are whole streets and areas that are home to Pakistani populations. When I first moved to the street I am on, there were about five Asian households and now there is only one white household left."

Reflecting on how we can move forward as a British Asian community, Parveen believes there are key problems the community needs to face up to.

'As the community expands people are marrying into families from different parts of Pakistan, who have been in the UK for a different amount of time or who might not be Pakistani at all which all makes it harder for the next generations to stay connected with the motherland.'

Tawseef Khan

Over the past 35 years Tawseef Khan has built a complex relationship with Pakistan, through the lens of his mother's East African roots, his father's childhood, and his own experiences visiting the country throughout his life.

'My idea of identity as a Pakistani person is already quite broad because my mum is brown, speaks Urdu and Punjabi but was born in Nairobi and has a completely different upbringing whereas my dad's side are mostly in Pakistan.

I have been travelling to Pakistan since I was a baby. The first time I went I was a week old and my dad was very keen for us to go a lot so we went every year all the way up to my GCSEs.

I have a really special fondness because I have had a lot of opportunities to see this place evolve over the 35 years I have been alive.

My relationship with Pakistan has always been slightly complicated because when you are young you feel a split within yourself in terms of where you belong.

People on the streets could always tell I was not born or raised in Pakistan because of the way you dress or handle yourself. You're constantly reminded that you don't belong fully anywhere.

You live on the margins of society in Britain because you are not white and are constantly reminded that you are not really from here even if you speak the language or do well in school.

In Pakistan you are reminded this is not completely your place either because maybe your language skills are not great, you hold your body differently, you dress differently. Even to this day my uncles insist on holding my hand when we cross a street.'

Khan's father was born in Faisalabad but when Khan was two his entire extended family moved to Lahore, which he considers his city.

'Eventually you grow a relationship with the streets and the buildings and the businesses and the shopping malls etc, that feels really amazing.

You begin to understand that actually this is a place where I might stick out because I am dressed differently but physically I look the same as everyone else and there is something quite beautiful about that.

For me, being connected with Pakistan enables me to come here and say I know who I am, who my family is, who my ancestors were and their story.'

Khan uses his South Asian roots and the traditions of respect and welcoming to inform his work as a solicitor working with immigrants and these values have shaped how he interacts with the world.

He believes diaspora communities need to understand Pakistan and its values better if we hope to keep a hold of our culture through the generations.

'There is always going to be a complexity within the diaspora community because we are all different generations, have different language levels, and go to Pakistan more or less often.

But Pakistan is much more complicated and expensive than we as diaspora give it credit for. It is really important for us to have a bigger understanding of our history, for example, Lahore used to be the cultural capital of the Mughal Empire.

Historically we come from one of the most advanced civilisations and I would love for young people to connect with our great heritage.'

VALLEY WITHIN THE VALLEY

Nafeesa Syeed

September 1966

Fresh from shaving, Bashir buttoned up his crisp shirt and straightened his collar. He'd have chai and then be off to Sopore's Government Degree Boys College. After spending the past few years as an English lecturer at the new college in Udhampur down in Jammu, a treacherous day's drive from Kashmir, he'd hoped for a transfer to Srinagar. Instead, he landed in his hometown. Today, they'd review Tennyson's "The Lady of Shalott," the boys reciting it aloud. Some mumbled, a few passionate students cried the verses. He explained the imagery, phrases, meter, until their confused looks turned into awe. The class laughed when one boy remarked: "Lancelot has 'coal-black curls,' just like Sir!" Bashir had memorised the poem years ago, at their age, delighting in the rhyme, even before he comprehended the meaning. "Whirls / churls" and "daffodilly / chilly" and "fear / near / ear / clear."

It was these boys' future they were trying to change. Bashir retrieved a packet from under his bed. He'd attend a secret meeting with a few Liberation Front recruits later in the day. He couldn't believe it was in his hands. He wondered how he'd get through classes, impatient to show off his work. For weeks, he'd been drafting it. On the first page, was his bold, block lettering, "KASHMIR: A MANIFESTO FOR LIBERATION." The movement, the revolution was leaping from his heart, from the page. Since his old friend Mansur had returned that spring from Pakistan, with a few other comrades, they'd spent the summer building cells. Mansur, who tasked Bashir with writing the English manifesto, called it Phase I. Like their brothers in Algeria, Vietnam, Cuba, Palestine, Congo, South Africa.

They were next. Bashir concealed the papers in a copy of *Astana*, his mother's Urdu magazine, and stuffed it into his bag. He couldn't wait.

His father's voice, calling his name, filtered from the *namazkot*. Bashir went upstairs. Taeth Sahib sat against the wall, his frail body drowning in his pheron cloak. With Bashir's salary shouldering many household expenses, Taeth Sahib had relented in his requests for Bashir to perform pir duties. Their own silent agreement. For three generations, since moving from the capital, the scholar-healer family served followers in Sopore and pockets of northern Kashmir. Though among the literate few, their finances had fallen with Taeth Sahib's illnesses, and they lost some murids over the years. They figured if his spiritual powers couldn't cure himself, then they should look elsewhere. Some of Sopore's wealthy apple-growers moved to pirs they believed would keep them prosperous.

"Son, I need a favour."

Bashir stood at the doorway, surprised yet pleased to hear his father use the word *favour*. It wasn't an order, which he'd been accustomed to receiving from his father.

"Mukhtar Kaak is gravely ill."

"I'm so sorry." Bashir remembered the big-armed man from his childhood who helped his father with errands and repairs.

"His family has requested that I visit for prayers and healing."

"When will you go?"

"That's the matter—I cannot go, in this state. But you know what service their family has given us; they've been devoted murids to us. We're interwoven."

Bashir didn't want to hear what his father was going to say.

"I need you to go."

Bashir was irritated. He had the recruits to meet and was expecting a telegram from Mansur, always sent in coded language, on where to meet next. Or sometimes, Mansur would suddenly pull up on his Enfield motorcycle, unannounced, to the house. And Bashir just had his shoes shined. He didn't want to go so far away. Yet, he thought of how his father had spared him the past nine months. This was the first time Taeth Sahib had asked for his help. Lolab, the smaller vale inside the larger valley, remained a stronghold of Taeth Sahib's following. Mukhtar Kaak was also special to Bashir, one of the men who showed him affection in childhood, when Taeth Sahib would not. Bashir took a deep breath.

"Of course, I'll send messages to the college and to—" he caught himself before mentioning his comrades, "and go at once."

Bashir asked a servant boy to run notes to the college and Ghulam Rasool, his oldest friend and fellow comrade, telling them he had a family emergency. Ghulam Rasool would be disappointed. Bashir had been raving about the Manifesto he'd unveil tonight. Bashir deliberated his course: he could take the bus to Kupwara and then a shared vehicle into Lolab. But there was no schedule for the vehicles into Lolab and the terrain into the village was rough. That gave him an excuse to opt for the means his family had relied upon for generations to minister to their murids: horseback.

Bashir popped his head into his father's room to take leave.

"Wait, take these,"Taeth Sahib handed him a string of black prayer beads, a small square prayer book, and scraps scrawled with entreaties of healing and diagrams with numbers. Bashir put them into his bag, after restoring the Manifesto under his bed. He pulled a pheron over his shirt and slacks.

Bashir hired a neighbour's horse and galloped from the narrow alleys of Nowhamam to the mountains. He came to the familiar range. It had been one of his favorite outings in his youth. This was his first time making the trip alone.

"*Hai*," he pulled the reins and started up the mountain.

The first few hours were an easy trot. Bashir stopped about a quarter of the way, dismounting to eat bread and drink from a canteen. The horse sipped from a stream and ate carrots from Bashir's hand, as he rested on a rock. The sun was strong, but the air cooled at this elevation. His brown skin shone coppery in the light. He rubbed sweat from his mustache. Tennyson's line about Lancelot came to him. Bashir told the mare, "His broad clear brow in sunlight glow'd; / On burnish'd hooves his war-horse trode…"

As the mountain became scragglier, Bashir turned the horse sideways, scaling at an angle. A few times, the horse nearly slipped, when the earth gave way. Bashir was an excellent rider, but much time had passed. He kept his balance, a few times cursing himself and the horse. Eventually, he reached the summit. He found a hut with a Gujjar family. The nomads, soon to settle for the winter, served him chai.

"You must stay the night," the man heading the house said.

"I need to get to Tsandigam right away, it may be our murid's final days," Bashir felt sombre once he said that aloud.

It took six hours to reach the top. He could make it to the bottom by maghrib time, at sunset, and then to the village by isha.

The descent was trying. Halfway, the horse again treading the mountain aslant, slid. Bashir tumbled onto his left side. She kicked and whinnied.

"Be more careful!" he chided her. He rubbed soil from his arms. When she stopped flailing, he brushed her off.

Bashir continued on foot for a period, holding her reins, until he tired and swung himself into the saddle. As the sun flattened to its final streak of yellow, the mare hit flat ground. Bashir paused her and took out a flashlight from his bag. He recalled the general direction, but began questioning his memory. There was a figure ahead.

"Excuse me, Tsandigam is this way?"

The shadow turned.

"I'm trying to find Tsandigam." Bashir clicked on the light; glad he'd checked the batteries before leaving. He flared the light off and on to get the person's attention. Then he stopped. It looked like a woman. Her hair was a long, tangled nest. The nose was long. Her face hideous. Bashir cringed.

"Is this the way to Tsandigam?"

The woman raised an arm pointing west.

He turned the horse in that direction, then thought to check on her.

"Do you need any help? Are you okay?" When he flashed the torch back, she was gone.

Bashir kicked the horse with his heel and raced away. His father always told him stories about the Rantas—the witches living in the mountains. But he assumed those were just myths to scare children. Though, on occasion, people returning from remote villages claimed sightings of a Rantas. Was that a Rantas? He couldn't confirm without the chance to see the telltale signs his father always described: breasts sagging to their knees and backward feet. He made a nervous chuckle as he entered Tsandigam. Being tired and hungry, he probably imagined it. Just in case, he recited some Qur'anic verses under his breath to ward off any potential spells. He wouldn't tell the murids about the sighting—they'd take it as a bad omen.

"Moulvi Sahib has come, Moulvi Sahib has come!" a boy shouted outside Mukhtar's home, using Bashir's childhood nickname. It was the same two-story wood house with a thatched roof over an exposed attic, for storing supplies. The family fed him, then he slept.

Early the next morning, Bashir took a walk in the village. He went along the brook that ran between the houses, under the canopy of massive trees. Children gathered water in tubs and splashed, as he'd done on visits here. Men squeezed him in for hugs, congratulated him on his engagement, and asked for prayers.

At the house, Bashir wrapped white cloth around his head, securing a turban. He picked up his father's items and went to Mukhtar. The shrunken old man was lying on a blanket, breathing audibly, almost a whistle at times. Bashir took his hand. When he was young, Bashir was in awe of Mukhtar—the legend being that Mukhtar had wrestled and killed a bear with his own bare fists.

"Mukhtar Kaak, it's me, Bashir," he whispered, rubbing the man's hand.

Mukhtar's wife, three sons, two daughters, and several grandchildren filled the room.

"Has he seen a doctor?"

"The medicine isn't helping. We need your ancestors to help," the wife said.

Bashir considered his audience, knowing he had to perform. He started reciting some Quran out loud, the same passages he'd heard his father quote. Mukhtar's wife sobbed, clearing her tears with the edges of the large white chadar wrapped around her. Bashir put one hand on Mukhtar's forehead, and began to read from his father's prayer book. It was a long, melodious supplication. He rocked back and forth, much like he'd been trained to do as a child. When he completed, Bashir pursed his lips and moved his head in circles, blowing onto Mukhtar's face, as though cooling hot tea.

Bashir tried not to reveal his dismay over some of the rituals, including asking certain saints, some of his famous forefathers, for intercession. From the onlookers, he could sense the hope in their eyes, that he might cure this sick man. They believed he had forces they didn't possess. He was a *syed*, after all, a descendent of the Prophet. His blood and body, they hoped, would pass some unseen grace to Mukhtar. Their father, grandfather, and great-grandfather had put that same faith in Bashir's own father, grandfather, and great-grandfathers. It was an arrangement neither side questioned, instead perpetuating the institution for centuries. He hoped his future wife, Feyruza, didn't believe in this hocus-pocus. If only they knew how rational faith could be, using their own intellect, not these beliefs that only held them back, left them ignorant.

Bashir felt ridiculous but had to do something that would seal the ceremony, bringing them satisfaction that what he'd done was significant.

"Can you bring some nuts and dry fruit?" Bashir asked. One of the daughters stepped out and returned with a tray of almonds, apricots, and raisins.

Bashir read a prayer over the assortment. "Eat these, please."

Mukhtar's wife held up a raisin, put it in her mouth, and belted: "*Ameen!*"

Bashir made up this final rite, to give the family a sense of relief. Once Bashir had seen his father bless some almonds and give them to a boy, whose mother asked for prayers that he do well on exams. Bashir added his own theatrics and clapped his hands together three times and put his palms on Mukhtar's eyes. The family gasped.

What Bashir yearned to tell Mukhtar and the family was that a great future awaited them. *If only you knew what and who you could be.* Just like Mansur had told him months ago. They would do away with blind faith in these old systems. Shedding and stripping away the past, brick by brick. Bashir could see it for himself, he always had. He would be great. Everyone had always expected him to be. So would their country. Free of sellouts and elites like Sher Shah, the Lion of Kashmir, rotting in jail somewhere in the south. Bashir would be one of the renowned leaders of the new nation they'd build.

"Let's do some *zikr.*" Bashir placed the black prayer beads between his forefingers, and used his thumb as the counter, moving on to the next bead after the chanting of each praise word. He pulled some rock candy from his pheron pocket and passed it to everyone, telling them his father had prayed upon the *shirini.* They said *bismillah* and sucked the sweetness.

After lunch, Bashir thought he might leave, but the family insisted he remain.

"Just the *baraka* of you being here, bringing blessings, I can tell Mukthar Sahib is feeling better," the wife said.

Bashir brandished the *taweez*, papers with his father's writing folded like the drawn-out bellows of a harmonium, instructing the family to keep one under Mukhtar's pillow. Mukhtar's wife handled the paper with utmost care, as though it were a piece of glass. Bashir knew she was illiterate and had no idea what was penned on the paper, but she had faith in it. Another sheet contained a list of prayers and acts for the family to perform. Mukhtar's children couldn't read, but a few of the youngsters attended a new primary school in a nearby village. Bashir reviewed the list of chants, verses, and rituals with one of the boys, and also went down the list verbally with one of the older sons.

Bashir agreed to stay in Mukhtar's room that night. Alone with Mukhtar, Bashir held the old man's hand. Bashir was moved, seeing the strong, playful man reduced so.

"Kaak, please, feel better," Bashir pleaded.

The old man squirmed. Then sighed.

"Moulvi? Moulvi Sahibo?"

"Yes, yes, it's me," Bashir almost teared up.

"How's your father?"

"He sends his prayers."

"How did you come?"

"By horse, over the pass."

"Ho, like we used to do."

"Like the old days."

Mukhtar coughed.

"Did you see any bears?" Mukhtar strained a half-smile.

After fajr, Bashir guided the horse to the edge of the village. They passed from under the shaded tree coves into the open, azure sky. Bashir remembered this view. He halted the horse. When he was young, the world seemed infinite here. Back then, this place was utterly secluded, with no road. He wondered about the Ghar-i-Rus, the legendary cave in Lolab that would take you to Russia. He'd never seen it, but it fascinated him in childhood.

In front of him, meadows stretched like green carpets filling a palace hall, dotted with purple wildflowers. Blue and green mountains curved to the right and left around the meadows, greeting one another in a point ahead, like the front hull of Noah's ark. Bashir remembered his father's

Kashmiri poetry about Lolab, this secret valley inside the larger valley. *In Lolab, I have seen clearly the flowers bloom, surrounded by thorns / How many of these shall I have to pick in Tsandigam / Oh my beloved, you are an orchard of flowers.* Valley within a valley, rich with water—the sustenance of life—springs and streams abounded, but would one day run dry. Above, another line of grey and white mountains towered overhead, then yet another range of pikes whispered above. Layers upon layers of serration.

Over the passes, slightly to the west, was Pakistan. The control line was a few miles away. An invisible line, made real with fences, wires, and soldiers. Thousands of troops from India and Pakistan peeping at each other through lenses above their guns, their hands on triggers; the Line of Control, the line they killed each other to control. These poor, illiterate people have had no choice, Bashir thought. No one asked them where, across these fields and mountains, they wanted this manmade border to be drawn. They don't want to be beholden to these two states. He could tell, they wanted change, even if they did not say it.

Petting the horse's mane, he thought of how different his life could've been. Slogging through the mountains like his ancestors on horseback, giving hope to devoted yet uneducated followers, and receiving them in Sopore. These vistas made Kashmir seem expansive. The enclosure of the mountains was also a reminder of being constricted, though, and of what he wanted to touch lying beyond. He wanted Kashmiris to have access to the whole world, to decide their own future. He had helped one family here. There was more he could do, more people who needed him. Out there, he'd show the world who they were, who he was. Bashir inhaled deeply, the bracing autumn air.

On the road toward Sopore, after the mountain crossing, Bashir stepped aside, allowing a military convoy to pass. Three large trucks, bearing the Indian flag, scuttled along. He'd seen a few of these this year, since moving back home. He was spared scenes of the war last year, holed up in Udhampur, outside Kashmir. This contingent was likely rolling in to replace another battalion that had served its border stint. Bashir thought of Tsandigam. He'd discuss recruitment with Mansur in these remote areas, among the unschooled classes. All he saw among the peasants was potential. They'd lift themselves up, they just didn't know it yet. They needed revolution, as Mansur often put it. It's our job to develop their awareness, to convince them of the struggle, he'd say. Phase I was the intellectuals, city-dwellers, merchants. But as Bashir had written in the Manifesto, next they needed the masses. They could even help those across the line. Think of all they could do with the natural resources to benefit everyone. Imagine, Bashir thought, his Manifesto being printed and distributed. His ideas, floating in the world. Shaping a new nation, their own borders.

At sunset, Bashir returned the mare to the neighbour.

"Ghulam Rasool is waiting for you in the *diwankhana*," his mother said, when she let him in.

What would he want at this hour? Bashir rushed to the living room.

Ghulam Rasool lunged toward Bashir, and started shaking him.

"Where have you been, idiot?" the vein in Ghulam Rasool's right temple bulged.

"Didn't you get my message? I was in Lolab."

"Mansur! He got arrested," perspiration dripped from Ghulam Rasool's forehead. "They say he killed someone."

"What? That's impossible. He's coming to see the Manifesto this week."

"I think it was a mistake. He'd become paranoid that some Pandit was following him in Baramulla. And they got into a fight and he shot him."

Bashir felt like he'd been struck by a loose mountain boulder. This wasn't a scenario they'd discussed in their meetings. Mansur had always been clear: This was to be an armed, guerrilla struggle. But it was only Phase I. Bashir perceived himself as the ideologue, mapping the group's philosophy. The guns had become abstracted in his mind. It was too early for all this.

"We have to go find him, now!"

Lolab had felt comforting, full of possibility. They couldn't carry on without their friend. Bashir made for the door.

"No, Basha, we shouldn't do anything crazy," Ghulam Rasool embraced Bashir.

A CONVERSATION IN MAYFAIR

Steve Noyes

London, 1904

Yusuf Ali, on furlough from the India Civil Service, now called to the bar in London, dressed and made his way on foot to Hutchinson and Sons. After years of passing judgment on mundane matters in the villages near Saharanpur, he was eager to prove what he could do. His last case in India – why, the court amounted to a charpoy dragged out of the chaukadar's bungalow and set in the dusty village square, his audience a crowd of kneeling peasants who chewed paan and spat liberally. Each of the appellants had bought off several witnesses, and as he had patiently listened, the witnesses in their turbans and dhotis had seemed like silkworm cocoons, and the lies they spun as gossamer-light as the finest katin silk.

All behind him now. To summon statute and precedent, to orate, to get to the pith, the arguable meat of the matter, and be acknowledged as a fellow sophisticate before the Court, to *litigate*. He could hardly wait.

He arrived at Hutchinson and Sons, queued behind the other young lawyers. McNulty, the senior clerk, wearing a banker's visor, scampered from one end to the other of a long table, checking the grey boxes, tying them with ribbons: the briefs. He enjoyed making the young rafes wait. His assistant, young Tommy Grey, sorted papers beside him with his fingerless mitts – the two had been working since the cold dawn.

When they got to Yusuf, he imagined that a moue of rare mirth passed between the two.

'Here ye be. Best of blooming luck, guv'nor,' said Tommy.

Yusuf repaired to the library where his counterparts in their black court-robes were busily reading their briefs and scrawling notes on foolscap, or reaching for a volume where there might be a helpful precedent.

Yusuf's brief disappointed him. The Marquis of Netherthorpe intended to sue Lord Northcliffe, publisher of several scurrilous newspapers, for libel. *Tit-bits* had reported that the Marquis was charged with frequenting a common bawdyhouse. There was a charge sheet, and a photograph of the receipt for the fine. It fell to Yusuf to tell the Marquis that Hutchinson and Sons declined to represent him. Why, it was a task for a solicitor -- or a clerk. He brought the brief back to McNulty, who wryly watched him approach.

'Master McNulty,' Yusuf said, 'surely there is some kind of mistake.'

McNulty with a practiced yank undid the ribbon and laid out the materials.

'Nowt mistake, Master Yusuf, none at all. You see this 'ere? Tell me what this is, pray tell?'

'It is Lord Cherwick's signature,' said Yusuf, regretting his objection already.

'And what we have 'ere? Mister Yusuf? What's this 'ere word?' pinning it with a finger.

'"Spurious,"' said Yusuf. 'But -- '

'Plain as day,' McNulty said. 'Now pay good notice to the good Lord's reasoning, 'ere, and 'ere,' his finger jabbing, 'and go tell the Marquis that his suit is spurious, just like his last few that all got scarpered. So.'

Tommy Gray had on his impudent gob a wide grin.

'If you hurry, Master Yusuf, you can catch the Marquis at his club. The Junior Carlton Club in Mayfair. We 'ave it on good authority he don't stir from there till past elevenses.'

'This is likely to result in a vigorous objection,' Yusuf, frowning, said.

'An that's why Hizzoner chose you, with all your Inja experience. You better get on it.'

'But, I rather think,' said Yusuf, his mind now whirling in a frictionless way, 'if I might ... '

'You mean you might disturb the partners, who are meeting even now, to tell them you had rather not?'

'No.'

'Capital decision.'

Yusuf re-tied the brief, tucked it under his arm, and went to gather his robe.

When Yusuf had gone, Tommy Greye said, 'He dint have to take his court rags.'

'Won't help him nowt,' said McNulty.

'There is those what's above themselves,' Tommy said.

'Aye,' said McNulty.

Yusuf took his calling-card out of his breast-pocket and rapped on the door of the Junior Carlton Club.

A metal grille shot back and a pair of eyes regarded him for a second. 'Trade entrance,' this person said, and shot the grille back in place.

Yusuf was nonplussed. Fighting a lurking sense of injury, he rapped again, held up the calling-card. When the grille banged open, he said, 'Abdullah Yusuf Ali, Esquire, Barrister, for the Marquis of Netherthorpe.'

'Trade entrance, off the alley.'

Seeing there was no recourse, Yusuf sought the trade entrance. The unhappy man who met him and took his card was slight in the shoulders and portly in the middle, with a black cummerbund that made him resemble a bowling-pin. 'Follow me,' he said, and took off at such a pace that Ali's rehearsed remonstrations – '... have you know that I represented Her Majesty ...' – were ignored as they trotted through the kitchen – '... fully registered barrister!' – where a white-smocked yob was slowly turning the handle of a meat-grinder and, at its other end, another man was forming sausage links – up a narrow stone servants' stairway – '... profession, not a trade!' – that released them into a high-ceilinged foyer. Yusuf barely registered a palm tree in a Qing planter and an African shield with spears before the butler sprang up the grand stairway and Yusuf trailed him into a hall lined with dark oil-paintings and glass display-cases. He thought he saw a stuffed anteater. They whisked through gilded-panel doors into a vast, burgundy-curtained hall of plush red chairs and end-tables with softly glowing lamps.

There were only two men in this room, widely spaced. One was reading *The Times* out-folded, the broadsheet entirely eclipsing him. It wasn't hard for Yusuf to guess which was the Marquis.

The Marquis of Netherthorpe's face, his youth subsiding, was curdled and incurious. He cradled a half-full snifter and wore a striped silk morning-coat over pyjamas. From one foot he dandled a fuzzy slipper.

The butler handed the Marquis the calling card. 'Master Yusuf Ali, Barrister.' He beetled off.

The Marquis flipped the card onto the end-table. He took a good glug from his snifter.

'Your Lordship,' said Yusuf.

'It's "my Lord,"' said the Marquis, fishing a crumb out of the snifter. 'Bloody sign of the times, I suppose. Well, out with it, man. How soon can I expect a date for this scurrilous brouhaha?'

'Well, you see, my Lord, it seems that there are some insuperable factors which we at Hutchinson and Partners must apprise you of in order to continue our long association.'

'Oh, a well-spoken poppet,' said the Marquis. 'Don't pussyfoot around, *babu*.'

Yusuf blinked. 'Though we can well imagine that your feelings, my Lord, have been affected by this smirching of your reputation, the plain fact of it is that, after due deliberation, the firm believes that it is not in your best interest to pursue this matter.'

'Bloody hell.' The Marquis gulped his brandy. 'This is nothing better than another of that vile pooter Northcliffe's ploys to hawk his papers at the expense of his betters, and you know it.'

'Quite, my Lord.' But Yusuf said this with little resolve.

There was a rustle as the reader of *The Times* opposite them turned the pages.

The Marquis studied Yusuf, took another healthy slug, belched, and said, 'People cannot and will not respect the way that things have been done, and bloody well ought to continue to be done.'

'And I quite agree with you that we ought –'

'Oh, bottle it.' The Marquis lolled in the pleasure of his brandy until a bilious gust arose in him, and he said: 'Monstrous. Horrid. That a shameless blackamoor ...' He raised his chin. 'So I can expect no help from Hutchinson's, then, even at the handsome rates I pay?'

'Oh, you can, my Lord, you surely can. In most matters. But this particular affair. Well, you see, ever since the whole Cleveland Street affair ... '

'Cleveland Street.'

'Why, yes, my Lord. The hunger of the press for – '

'Somerset rogered boys. I do not roger boys. It offends me that you should even mention that.'

'I apologise, my Lord. My main point is that journalists have rather taken it upon themselves to report indiscriminately on moral matters. As distasteful as it may be, it is unlikely to stop.'

'Very well. I might as well get a taste of this new century. Go on.'

Yusuf undid the brief and placed the charge sheet and the receipt for the fine on the end-table.

'These have been sworn to by the constable and his superior, my Lord, and clearly acknowledge the charge and the fine duly paid, so ... '

'Time was ...' said the Marquis, and his eyes rolled back. He slumped.

Yusuf looked around. Across the room, *The Times* had been discreetly lowered and a moustached man was sympathetically staring directly at him.

The Marquis whiplashed awake. 'Shall I spell it out, then? Time was that a good romp was forgotten, merely a pleasurable evening out between gentlemen. Gentlemen who support orphanages and the like. Why, I'm virtually propping up the whole parish back home. Anyway, the ladies involved were well-compensated. Time was, we just got slapped on the hand and paid our guineas. The papers busied themselves with the windy-shindy of the politicians. They didn't skulk around bordellos, cameras ready. They didn't cry foul when one of King Bertie's friends cheated on a hand of baccarat. And Somerset ... why, Somerset ... '

'I don't quite follow ... '

'"I don't quite follow, *my Lord*," for the umpteenth time. You brought up Somerset yourself. The Constabulary practically insured, as safely as Lloyd's, that blackguard's flight from the law to the Costa de Sol! But now, now, I tell you, any misstep is fodder for the gutter press, the bloody punters.' The Marquis lit a cigarillo and just as quickly stubbed it out. 'So you say your firm will not represent me?'

'Your Excellency, this was not my decision. I am in this matter merely the amanuensis.'

'Then kindly tell me why Old Julian has abandoned me.'

Yusuf breathed. There was no avoiding it. 'My Lord, it is a long-standing tenet of the Common Law that truth is an insuperable defence in matters of libel. It is the defence *par excellence*.'

'Truth.'

'Yes, my Lord. *Tit-bits* simply reported the facts, facts sworn to by a peace officer and countersigned by you. It did not speculate further. If I might be so bold, your peccadillo appears alongside other indiscretions of your Peers, so it would be futile to claim you have been singled out.'

'Incredible...insufferable.'

Yusuf twitched and shifted, but pressed on. 'The courts, you see, have lately taken a dim view of such suits, which have acquired the not altogether fair sobriquet of "spurious actions". If Hutchinson and Sons is to be effective in acting for you in the future ... '

'Well, we'll have to see about that,' said the Marquis.

'I know you are disappointed by this, but ... '

'But what?'

'Have you considered consequences should you proceed with another barrister? With all due respect, my Lord, you would redouble your misery by furnishing Northcliffe – and the prurient press in general – the opportunity to drag all this out again in Court, with even more salacious details. Supposing you won, it would be a victory you would be a long time in recovering from, my Lord.'

The Marquis snatched up his cigarillos, tried to do up his morning-jacket, fumbled and failed, sucked a drop of brandy from his thumb, and stalked out of the lounge, fuming all the way,

Persnickety n***ers ... blasted gutter-press ... Modern times!

Yusuf crumpled some and wiped his brow.

Across the room, the gentleman lowered and folded his *Times*, and said, 'It appears the Marquis is upset. But, I say, you handled yourself well. You'll come join me, won't you?'

Yusuf looked at his watch. 'I don't know, I must be – '

'Nonsense!'

Yusuf, after a hesitation, gathered up the brief and joined the man.

'This is terribly kind of you. I suppose I will have to give a good accounting of myself to my employers,' Yusuf said. 'I'm guessing that they anticipated his negative response.'

'Ah, the Marquis. Old Netherwhoop. Young Netherwhoop, I should say. Obstinate he was, wasn't he? Which caused you no end of sticky difficulty, having to outline *l'esprit de loi.*'

Yusuf regarded this man. He seemed hale and respectable. He was about Yusuf's age. He wore a waistcoat, the chains of a pocket-watch protruding. He hefted an unlit meerschaum pipe.

'Which caused you, I don't doubt, to hear for your establishment's future prospects. I heard the whole shebang. Marmaduke Pickthall,' he said, extending his hand.

'Abdullah Yusuf Ali,' said Yusuf.

They shook.

Marmaduke Pickthall picked up Yusuf's calling card. 'What do you make of this sudden rage for everyone to be photographed?' he said. 'They say in Africa there are those who fear it because they worry about the taking of their souls.'

'Mere superstition,' said Yusuf. 'There is only One who can take a soul.'

'Ah, you must be a Muslim. Very well put, sir, and yet it seems that Kodak has conquered this city. Myself, I rather miss the work of the portraitists whose sketches used to decorate the papers. Now all of London is chopped up into these horrid little exact pictures. I like to think of the un-photographed village, its greenswards and thatched roofs, as the centre of our national life.'

'I'm afraid that's passed -- for a truer estimate of England we must repair to the mill, the factory, the mine,' said Yusuf. 'The new wealth that materializes here in motor-cars and tarmacadam.'

'I say let them tarmacadam the lot,' said Marmaduke. 'Progress is a mixed bag, I daresay. I should be grateful not to be further jostled over cobblestones. A fitting epitaph – "he was jostled overmuch by cobbles."'

'How about, "Replicated to ribbons by the photograph?"' said Yusuf.

'Oversold by advertisements.'

'Tortured by tinctures.'

'*Da-dit, da-da'd, da-dit da-da'd* by Marconi's little lever.'

'Sterilised by Lister's strictures.'

'By God, man, you can joust!' said Marmaduke, and Yusuf smiled. 'Yes, the City. The Great Wen! Such ruckus, such tumultuousness, and it is amply reflected every day in Parliament. The sparring of men with only the most abstract acquaintance with the hard facts of the nation. Men with diverse interests and motivations ... well, I fear it will produce the same result as de Tocqueville warned of in America, a constant churning of trivial grievances. Endless, fruitless agitation ... a quagmire that even the sovereign ventures to wade into.'

'Oh, His Majesty would hardly step beyond his constitutional role.'

'I wouldn't be so sure. Bertie likes to dabble in politics.'

'I do agree that that is unseemly for a monarch, but I am sure his advisers will restrain him.'

'You know,' said Marmaduke, 'the decline of the ruling class in quality of character has been much remarked upon lately. Why, the whole Somerset affair you mentioned.'

'I was surprised the Marquis remembered that. It was nearly fifteen years ago, and he clearly considered such matters far beneath him.'

'And I daresay Somerset, the poor bugger, is still running. Eventually he shall reach Cape Town — then Antarctica, where he shall descry the paucity of whorehouses and the dearth of good port.'

Yusuf frowned. He was thinking about what the Marquis might say to Hutchinson and Sons.

Marmaduke picked up on Yusuf's concern. 'Rest easy, my friend. I wouldn't worry about the Marquis. He has a long and convivial amity linked to the grape. One might say he has worshipped Bacchus in every press and vintage, so much so that he makes old Chaucer's Pardoner look like an oenophilic simpleton. He certainly has lost no opportunity, how does it go? "To burst joy's grape upon his strenuous tongue." He's steaming now, but later today his head will clear, and he will be lightly troubled by the memory of something vaguely unpleasant, a trifling bitter taste, like mould on white bloomer — and he will not remember you at all in some two weeks' time. He will decamp to his Yorkshire pile for the autumn shooting and bask in the good opinion of his hounds.'

Marmaduke gave his little service-bell a shake.

'You'll have coffee then?' he said.

'I really should ...' said Yusuf.

'One cup,' said Marmaduke. 'They do a proper coffee here — none of this chicory rot.'

'But I really do have to get back,' said Yusuf.

'Ah, you don't want to go out in that.' He pointed. The far window was lashed with rain.

'I suppose...'

'Good then, it's settled. Here he is.'

The butler cast a worried eye on Yusuf. 'If Master's business is concluded,' he began.

'Some coffee, my good man,' said Marmaduke, 'my legal friend here is thirsty.'

The butler looked more dubious, considering the stretching of guest privileges so that cobblers, connected by horses to the member-list, might overflow the premises. But he nodded, and tootled off.

'Are you a member here?' said Yusuf.

'No, no. I had an early meeting with my literary agent. I'm actually living in Maida Vale.'

'You are a writer then?'

'I am,' said Marmaduke. 'A humble purveyor of tales both long and short.'

'Marvellous,' said Yusuf. 'What have you published?'

'My dear man, have you not heard of my novel *Sa'id the Fisherman?*'

'I haven't had the pleasure,' said Yusuf. 'What is it about?'

'It follows the misadventures of a Muslim mountebank named Sa'id, and explores the most alluring theme, that of fortune and fate, those illusions that blind all men, come what may.'

The butler returned with cups and carafe, poured, and left.

Yusuf had read some novels written about Muslims by foreigners that piled on the sumptuous luxuries – *Haji Baba of Isfahan* and Pierre Loti came to mind – but he was more curious than censorious. 'And how might you come to write, if I may ask, about Muslims?'

'Why, by travelling and living among Arab Muslims in the Levant some years ago, and by studying Arabic, that most eloquent of tongues. As-salaam 'alaykum!'

'Are you? A Muslim, then?' said Yusuf. 'Wa 'alaykum as-salaam.'

'No, I am not. But I have great respect for Islam. I must confess that I have a certain aversion to religious conversion, for I believe that faith ... Well, you see, I've always thought ... that is ... '

Marmaduke paused to sip his coffee. Ten years ago he'd met with the sheikh in the Damascus mosque, eager to learn more about Islam. The sheikh had lit a candle and said, 'Observe this fire. There is a shapely flame, the light that shines around us, and when I put my hand out, heat. I blow, and all is gone. How many things? You answer three; I answer one. We are both right.'

Marmaduke put his cup down, and focused again on Yusuf. 'Excuse me, I drifted off there. As I was saying, I've always believed that faith is absorbed when we are children, like mother's milk.'

'And yet you are knowledgeable about Islam, far more so than your countrymen.'

Marmaduke shrugged. 'I am waiting.'

'Waiting for what?'

'Why – I don't know,' said Marmaduke.

'Allah guides those whom he wills,' said Yusuf. 'None of my business. As the Qur'an says, "*La ikri fii ad-diin.*" There should be no compulsion in religion. You ought to write about your travels.'

'I might. What a sweet life it was – days on end on horseback, with the best of companions.'

'You must come up to St. Albans. I have horses and a paddock. I meet few Englishmen who know about Islam, even in the Royal Asiatic Society, where I recently lectured on Muslim India.'

'Oh, how did that go?' said Marmaduke. He could picture the sleepy harrumphing gentlemen.

'They made me a Fellow,' said Yusuf. 'But when my speech appeared in their journal, I was dismayed to see they'd printed one member's comments alongside, to wit, that my talk was confined to the past greatness of the Muslims, and not the present. I was disappointed.'

Marmaduke twirled his moustache. 'Some people ought to have more respect. I suppose ... let me put it this way. "There is no God but God" – this is a proposition I find impossible to refute.'

'I look forward to reading your novel about this Sa'id. You say it has been a success.'

'It has survived many impressions, true. Perhaps you've read my pieces in the *New Age?*'

'Sorry.'

'*The Temple Bar? The Athenaeum?*'

'Again, I confess I've never heard of your work. I'll look for it.'

Marmaduke gestured as though this were neither here nor there. 'Ah, now, where were we? Oh yes, the insufferable Marquis. You know, the, er, decline of the ruling class. Not so much their decline *per se*, but it's the rise of others that's more pertinent. The middling folk, who make things and sell them, they are gaining in strength. And then there's a much more vigorous and courageous press.' Marmaduke leaned closer to Yusuf. 'Say, you're not the same Abdullah Yusuf Ali who upbraided the Archbishop of Canterbury in *The Times*?'

'Please, I would have hardly upbraided him. I pride myself on my tact.'

'Fair enough. Shall I say "greatly remonstrated with?"'

'That sounds more like me.'

'It was a remarkable letter. I seem to recall that it took His Worship to task for his claim that all Muslims believe that women have no souls. A ridiculous notion.'

'I did indeed write that letter. I summoned up the pluck because that calumny could not go unchallenged. The Archbishop's comments were so shocking that I felt I could risk whatever opprobrium there was attached to the dropping of an indignant gauntlet, as it were.'

Marmaduke took this in with plain amusement. 'And I'm glad you did!' he said. 'For the Archbishop's opinion was a perfect trifecta of ignorance, prejudice and cant. One wonders where he got such an idea. It's well known that the Prophet, peace and prayers be upon him, insisted on the highest standards of treatment of women in his farewell sermon. And in the Qur'an, it would make no sense for Allah to say, "indeed we have made partners for you from among yourselves for you to live together in joy," if one of the partners had no soul, like a marionette, or a tea-caddy.'

'This is astonishing. You know the Qur'an well, too.'

'Oh, bits and bobs. In those lands, it is all around one. One can hardly avoid it.'

'Yet you seem to know a great deal. *Mashallah.*'

'*Astafarghallah*, may God forgive me; I only know a little,' said Marmaduke.

Yusuf, sipping, recalled some overheard remarks by the Asiatic Society members in their klatches, as he'd circulated and gathered handshakes: 'Altogether an articulate young man, considering,' 'Yes, very well-spoken, I should say,' 'And was it Cambridge he is down from?' Well, what had they expected? Oaths and curses delivered in a pidgin?

The butler had drifted nearby, again vexed by club-guests sponsoring in other guests, until a whole illegitimate membership obtained, like a pyramid of Brighton Beach acrobats. He frowned, and tapped his watch.

'I have heard,' Yusuf said, 'there have been some recent English converts to Islam.'

'I have heard that, too. There's a gentleman in Liverpool called Quilliam.'

'Anyway,' said Yusuf. 'I wrote that letter to refute an obvious slur, just as you would wield your pen, I dare say, should some imam announce that Englishmen's souls are like Swift's houyhnhnms.'

'Well, that took some mettle. Bully for you. Though I can't think why the Archbishop had that particular bee in his bonnet.'

'Quite. Why he would squander the occasion of speaking *ex cathedra* on such a silly notion is beyond me. But that was some time ago. Why would you remember it?'

'I was back home in Surrey, visiting my parents, and my father — he's a minister — actually put down the paper and expounded on the sin of prejudice, though normally an equitable view of Muslims was not a steady feature of his character. But soon his commentary, knocked off its tramway, degenerated into a black screed about Popish encyclicals and bulls and all things Romish and infallible, that became, as he hollered, more and more richly ironic. I had to remind him that his whipping boy was, in this case, Church of England.'

'And what did your dear Mother say, I wonder?'

'She said that she was glad to hear that she had a soul, as there would be someone to help her with the washing-up.'

Yusuf laughed. '*Wallahi*, that's good.'

'I nearly dropped my toast,' said Marmaduke. 'I see you wear a ring yourself. I wonder what your good wife would make of the Archbishop's notion that she's soulless, and all her sisters.'

'Well, you see, she's English,' said Yusuf. 'And she — '

'Of course she is! By virtue of the marriage bond!'

'I mean she's English. She was born in England.'

'Now there's a proper good story, I daresay, how you courted the daughter of a *memsahib*.'

Yusuf didn't respond. There wasn't any point in saying 'She's English,' again.

Marmaduke continued to elaborate. 'Well, of course she's English. Aren't we all, these times? All our far-flung friends across the Empire are English. Take Canada, and Australia, and your birthplace, India. All, all English, in name and deed.'

Yusuf said, 'She was born in England, and the farthest she'd been when I met her was Brighton.'

'Oh. How silly of me! I made an assumption. How is she, your wife? In good health I hope.'

'At present she is rather busy with our two children, but in good spirits.'

'Ah. I thought you looked a bit short of sleep. Wearied by the weans, are you?'

'Absolutely. But I have my legal duties; I have my bolt-hole in King's Cross.' Yusuf brightened. 'When at home, I *am* rather knackered by the nippers, the nippers and their nappies.'

'Dumbfounded by their diapers.'

'Crazed by all the nightly caterwauling. Poor Theresa! I don't know how she does it.'

Marmaduke thought, Unless this Yusuf is never at home, why, the man must surely have some inkling of how she did it. Saint Theresa of Saint Albans, swaddling and coddling her brood.

Ali thought, I must get Theresa some help: a nurse-maid, an *ayah*.

A memory of an angry man, an awkward moment in Syria, vexed Marmaduke, and he said, 'I say, I should apologise. Out of politeness, I should never have asked about your wife.'

'Oh, pshaw. Rubbish, man. I may be a Muslim, but I am not a Wahhabi. There was nothing prurient about your question; it was a polite inquiry. Are you married?'

'Indeed, I am, to my excellent wife Muriel, for some ten years.'

'And do you have children?'

'No, Allah has not seen fit to bless us with a child.'

Marmaduke suspected that Yusuf was thinking of the Qur'anic *ayat* that said Allah well knew the numbers of children borne by every woman's womb.

Ali was not thinking this at all; he was trying to imagine this Marmaduke's wife. She must be slight, quiet and would have to have a sense of humour, as though he were fitting her out with a necessary accessory, like a pair of gloves.

The men became sensible to the bustle around them. The elder members of the Carlton Club had crept from their chambers into the surrounding chairs, clutching canes as they waited for their mid-day chops. A whole partition was now folded back, revealing white islands of dining-tables. Waiters in their penguin best were being punctilious about the placement of cutlery; a boy with a napkin draped over his forearm and a jug was going around filling water glasses.

'I suspect we'd better...' said Marmaduke. 'Come.'

Marmaduke led, and Yusuf followed, clutching his brief, out of the parlour and into the Great Hall, but before Marmaduke could say anything, Yusuf stopped at a photograph in a glass case: the Nizam of Hyderabad and his retinue crowded in front of the white columns of his residence.

'You really should visit India,' Yusuf said. 'Hyderabad is lovely -- and the nizamlik is nearly as big as Britain.'

'Really? I suppose I should. But come, man.' He led Yusuf by the arm one case over and stopped before a shelf of trophies.

As Yusuf, puzzled, politely inspected the trophies, the golden statuettes of cavalrymen and horses rearing above the brass-plate names on their bases, Marmaduke thought, I must be the wrong sort of Englishman, for I have never wanted to kill anything.

'What do you think of these artefacts of the Afghanistan campaign?' said Marmaduke.

When Yusuf didn't say anything, Marmaduke realised that he had been virtually *curating* his aversion to these sorts of displays all these years. He was disappointed by Yusuf's somewhat neutral face; possibly Marmaduke was quite alone in his distaste. 'You do realise,' he said, 'that each of these represents some scores, nay, hundreds of your fellow Muslims?'

Yusuf blinked.

'Is this all worth it?' said Marmaduke. 'The Great Game and all that?'

Yusuf's response was measured, for he sensed this mattered to Marmaduke. 'It is human enough for these soldiers to memorialise their fallen comrades,' Yusuf began, 'I hardly think …' but Marmaduke cut in. 'Do you suppose these unfortunate Afghanis are fashioning their own miniature monuments back in their villages?'

'My friend,' said Yusuf, 'you are attempting to ascribe a much deeper significance than reason would permit for these minor skirmishes.'

'Skirmishes? Well, what about the Mutiny? What about the Mahdi's followers at Omdurman?'

'These Afghan tribesmen lost their lives, it's true, but such losses, I'm afraid, are necessary to shore up a bulwark against the Russian bear.'

'For how much longer though? And at what cost?'

'I'm simply saying that there are greater forces at play.'

'And time is the greatest force of them all. In time, why, all the red-daubed portions of the map will change their colours, and these baubles will lose their meaning. They will be like the sad factory of First Republic statuettes in Flaubert's *A Sentimental Education*.'

Yusuf, his hands clasped behind his back, muttered, mostly to himself:

'*Ghulibati ar-ruum fii adna al-arDi wa hum min ba'di*

ghalabihim sayaghlibuun / fii biD'i siniina lillah al-amuur'

'I'm sorry,' said Marmaduke. 'What verse was that?'

'"The Roman Empire has been defeated in another land, but in a few years they will be the victors. With Allah is the decision."'

'*Hadha al-Haqq!* That is the truth,' said Marmaduke.

'I don't deny that worldly dominion is transient,' said Yusuf. 'There *are* forces that can crumple Empires. But I have seen our Empire's salubrious effects in my India.'

'And yet we rule India by military force alone. I tell you, my man, the East is waking up!'

'I agree. The East *is* waking up. But it is doing so in concert with Europe, and under the influence of Western laws and institutions. Legal codes more in step with modernity. Advances in education.'

'There is something in what you say,' said Marmaduke, 'Many of the Arabs I met said they admired our sense of fair play and "the word of an Englishman". That meant something. Or it used to mean something.'

The word of an Englishman, thought Yusuf, it was often slippery in the East India Company.

'I gather,' said Yusuf, 'that you deplore violence. I too refuse the simple pieties of the jingoistic music-hall, the tired figures of Tommy-in-Khaki and Jack Tar. Yet I believe that Britain must lead, especially since Ottoman strength is waning.'

'It seems madness, though,' said Marmaduke, 'to abandon Disraeli's former policy of support to the Ottomans, regardless of the odious newspaper clamour about the Sick Man of Europe. If he be afflicted, why, then let us bring to him our physic, and not let him shrivel until he is but a name.'

'We shall see how it all plays out,' said Yusuf. 'You mentioned military rule.'

'Why yes, the Turks.' Marmaduke said. 'In Syria. The French in Lebanon.'

'There were always two soldiers who escorted me to the villages as I made my circuit as the Collector. They were hardy sorts, and as able as any within their métiers. And yet – they seemed more than a little smug concerning the people they had come to rule. They certainly thought they were above the peasants, viewing them as unfortunate, erratic nuisances one had to contend with, rather than get to know. They were determined to keep their distance. It seems to me that being in a position of power necessarily narrows one's vision in accordance with one's interests.'

'You've put your finger on it. It can blind a man, power. It may prevent him from seeing that his interests have changed, or are changing. I can provide you with an illustration. Look at our policy with Ireland. Surely you've seen the futility of our attempts to quash Home Rule by a Parliamentary decree? The Irish are waking up, and the East is waking up. I said it again! And a condition of this awakened state is choice. What should happen, I ask you, if India should press for independence with the same fiery determination of the Irish? How long would our stolid refusal last?'

'They would be immoderately irrational to do so,' said Yusuf. 'They would be at once relinquishing the rule of law to creep out from under the benevolent bosom of Empire, only then to confront the most unruly forms of sectarian anarchy. I am afraid I am all with Lord Curzon: "Our work there shall continue." Your high regard for the Ottomans and your scepticism about the Raj is analogous to preferring the gentleman amateur over the professional at cricket. The amateur has all the tradition and history of his class behind him, but it is only tradition, whereas the professional is more geared for success, and has much more at stake. But to return to the Ottomans, you predict —'

'Hardly. I worry.'

'You worry that the Ottoman Empire might become merely nominal, but isn't that the very looseness of all civilising states? A certain largesse granted to the local and the regional?'

'To be sure, the Sultan and his court, whatever he may intend, is ultimately at the far end of an unimaginable journey for many. Much closer to hand are the tax-farmers and their depredations. But when government does not progress, and becomes an overextended machine for tribute ... well ... '

'But this is not the case in India at all: Railways. Schools. Roads. Hospitals and proper courts. The telegraph. All beneficial. All British.'

'Forts. Prisons. Clubs. Gymkhanas. Hill-stations. Missions. Casks of opium in Bengali warehouses. For whom is the real benefit?'

'This is quite a battle of substantives,' said Yusuf. 'These are large topics. Nonetheless, I hold with Sayyid Khan, that – '

'Who?'

'Sayyid Ahmed Khan.'

'I've never heard of him.'

'He wrote in Urdu.'

'Well, there you have it. What about him?'

'Simply that Indian Muslims can best develop their institutions and progress through education within the British framework. No empire lasts forever, but ours has been the longest-lived and most benevolent. What can the Turks put forward to match it, with their slavish imitation of the West's laws and styles, which the Ottoman heartlands ignore?'

'Four centuries of peace, that's what,' said Marmaduke. 'The Sultan's reign and reach was sufficient and but faintly exercised among the *millets*, and then only to quell mere factions.'

'Aha. You have come full circle in your perorations, sir. Where I saw trifling skirmishes in Afghanistan, you saw the bloody hand of Empire, and where I might see the arbitrary Turkish use of force, you call the mere quelling of factions. A perfect circle, and I think that my adamancy compelled it. It is as the poet wrote: "Your firmness makes my circle just / And makes me end, where I begun.'"

Marmaduke chuckled, pleased. By God, the man knew his Donne. He thought, but did not say, that Donne also wrote 'Reason, your viceroy in me, me should defend, / But is captive, and proves weak or untrue.' Instead, he laughed, and said, 'Well, we've really gotten into it, haven't we? Come.' He clapped Yusuf on the back.

Outside the Carlton Club, they faced each other amid the fresh smell of puddles.

'A pleasure,' said Marmaduke. 'I do hope we'll meet again.'

'Inshallah,' said Yusuf.

Marmaduke had gone a block before the figments of this entirely likeable Yusuf Ali – the stirrings of a minor character down the road, perhaps? – dissipated and were replaced by his recent preoccupations: a dingy suburb, Brendle, and the eccentrics he was peopling it with as he nudged them towards print.

Yusuf picked up his pace. He was late, he knew, due in court that afternoon, and had to cobble together a report about the Marquis. But that did not seem so dire or consequential now. He was pleased to have met this extraordinary gentleman.

What was his name again? Mandrake Beckinsall? Marmalade ... no, that couldn't be it.

Malamute?

FOUR POEMS

Halimah Adisa

A Glossary of Time

Heavy but soft was the heart and hand
that birthed you to the world.

When they asked them for your form of
identity, they said,

'you are now into the world to find yourself'
You were born nameless. Your identity lie in every

border you'll journey. To seek a name, they'll call you Asiah — a path that
opens to livelihood

So, you'll watch in admonition, and be lived with joy of what enriches
your journey.

Once, you'll grow apart your aliveness, you'll begin to wonder the
existence of life — the pain and

struggle that eat deep into the skin. You'll drink portion of steadfastness
that holds onto the notion

to be chosen. In line for the cause to search for yourself, you'll seek a
name. They'll call you,

Hamila, the one/girl who travels. You'll tour the world of acceptance. You'll fall in your skin, your

words — seeking no validation. You'll recognise in your words and body, your faults. You'll wake up to

a transition of accepting a new form. And when you look around for a name, you'll see yourself

everywhere, Aniyah, God's Favour — a recognition of your freedom.

Dawn

I have read the books of faith.
I have travelled every page and conveyed every word that lies beneath the truth.

In my country, we believe in faith
You may only walk half a mile of no journey to be washed with half battered lies.

When the sun sets, you may see them examining their sheds — their truth beneath the night is withered away.

In my country, I have watched survivors tell their stories — the truth that still linger in their throats.

I have watched them write history, in faith and honour of the one's they've lost.

And then, a spread force of silence is pressed against history. Lost in fate, their faith, my people denounce.

Whisperer of the Dark

Isn't it funny how I was left with
the things that stayed in the days of the dark when light was feared most.

To escape through the dark,
I carried three things with me: a lantern, a mind and a face.
How do you tell people about light they never touched?
How do they see through the path that has only caused them to wait a
generation.

So, with fear in my heart,
I carried a stone for it;
a lantern in my right hand while I ate my mind.
To put into work, my identity, in the later days of my confidence,
I'd speak fully with illumination blinding my eyes to their minds.
Singing songs of joy, dancing to the rhythm of the aftermath, and telling
tales of my fathers
welcoming a little girl home to herself.

Metamorphosis of the Mind

The mind…

Fickle and old.

Focusing, reasoning.

Sometimes, a powerful tool that

Changes.

REVIEWS

SPORT TRANSFERS

Adama Juldeh Munu

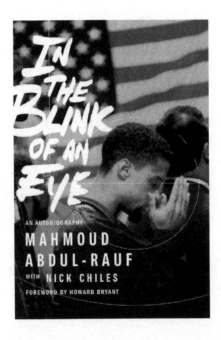

Time is the capsule through which we interact with great sporting moments. One of these was when NFL San Francisco 49ers quarterback, Colin Kaepernick, began kneeling as the US national anthem played, before playoffs during the 2016 season. A bold move that echoed the pulse of the Black Lives Matter movement at the time and a homage to the Black Power Fist raised by Tommie Smith and John Carlos at the 1968 Olympic Games in Mexico City. 'I am not going to stand up to show pride in a flag for a country that oppresses Black people and people of colour. To me, this is bigger than football,' Kaepernick commented at the time. Other players would soon follow in his example. The protests made national headlines and drew strong reactions from both supporters and critics alike, all the way up to the echelons of political power. Then US President Barack Obama heralded Kaepernick's 'constitutional right to make a statement,' while then-Republican presidential nominee Donald Trump postured: 'I think it's a terrible thing, and you know, maybe he should find a country that works better for him. Let him try, it won't happen.' It came with a hefty price though for Kaepernick, who went unsigned the following offseason, and by the time this has gone to print, has been unable to land a place on another team since.

For millennials like myself, this may have appeared as an unprecedented moment for our generation, ground-breaking even. But Kaepernick's protest is not the only more recent example of political protest in the sporting arena. Through his publishing house, founded two years later, Kaepernick has chosen to showcase the story of a co-athlete who walked a similar trajectory just over two decades ago.

In the Blink of an Eye is a powerful testimony from former Denver Nuggets and Sacramento Kings basketball player, Mahmoud Abdul-Rauf (formerly Chris Jackson). From the late 1980s through to the mid-1990s, he was one of the most recognisable people in American basketball, with some record-breaking plays at the high school, collegiate and professional levels.

Mahmoud Abdul-Rauf with Nick Chiles, *In the Blink of An Eye: An Autobiography*, Kaepernick Publishing, 2022

While the memoir charts his life's twists, turns, trials and triumphs, he is most well known for being exiled from the NBA for praying - instead of saluting the US flag – during the national anthem before games for the 1995-6 season, just as Kaepernick did in football just over a decade later. He took the position that the US flag and national anthem were symbols of the country's longstanding history of racial oppression. He received a one-game ban, afterwards reaching a compromise to stand for the anthem, by bowing his head in silent prayer. Abdul-Rauf's actions generated great deal of criticism and personal turmoil which included an unoccupied house of his getting burned down. *In a Blink of an Eye* is a comprehensive but brutally honest and candid narrative that gives the reader a good seat, front and centre, of his story, as he intends. The book is his arena, and we, the readers, are the spectators. For the first time, we hear in his own words a full treatment of how his world was turned upside down from his decision to 'act in conscience', bringing to light the realities of America's dark past and present. But it is also an important read for anyone who wants greater insight into the idiosyncrasies of how American sport and race perversely coalesce for the Black athlete.

History shows us that sportsmanship can be a political act and that it should not be taken for granted. We are made to believe spaces that platform the very best of professional athleticism and competitive sport represent neutrality and equal advantage for those who perform and those who spectate. That is to say, all game players are equal, with none given an 'unfair' advantage over their competitor. But there are nuances to this. For instance, what does 'equal advantage' mean during games like the Olympics when countries whose infrastructures have been blighted and impacted by colonialism or warfare compete against countries who have in time been the orchestrators of those same atrocities? If these spaces are to be considered 'politically neutral', what are we supposed to make of authoritarian regimes that have used sporting events to bolster their country's image or power? If the recent detainment of Women's National Basketball Association Star Brittney Griner in Russia for alleged drug use is anything to go by, realpolitik even has the power to implicate sports with 'Cold War' effect.

And yet those same spaces have also given way to special moments, created by people who've moved hearts or minds on issues of inequality while traversing the field, track, or tennis court. Others have done this just by their presence alone. The United States has a litany of examples from within the African-American community who form an important cornerstone for the discourse. Jesse Owens, an African-American track and field athlete, who won four gold medals during the 1936 Olympic Games in Berlin was the most successful of any athlete at the games. German Nazi leader, Adolf Hitler, chose to snub, rather than meet and congratulate Owens, as his performance trumped the idea of Aryan superiority, which was used to legitimise the Nazi regime at the time.

US tennis great, Serena Williams, may have retired to much acclaim and accolade in 2022, (having won more Grand Slam singles titles – 23 – than any other person during the open era), but she (and her sister Venus) faced a barrage of misogynoir, on and off the court during the length and breadth of her career. British writer and broadcaster, Afua Hirsch poignantly describes William's unexpected meteoric rise in the sport' (which was largely white and middle class) as the part that she has played in 'problematising' the 'American Dream'.

US boxing legend, Muhammad Ali who 'stung like a butterfly' in the ring, found his career interrupted after he refused military conscription for the Vietnam War. Ali attended the compulsory induction in 1967 but refused to answer to his name or take the oath. This led to his arrest and conviction, which the US Supreme Court later overturned in 1971. He said priorly, 'I will not disgrace my religion, my people or myself by becoming a tool to enslave those who are fighting for their own justice, freedom and equality'.

The controversy surrounding Abdul-Rauf's protest is therefore a fitting opening to the book: 'Of course, white American politicians can speak all day long about America's wrongs. But, as I quickly learned, if a Black athlete making millions of dollars claims that America is corrupt, the sky will come crashing down on his head.' I must admit that I had some initial reservations about whether I wanted to dig into his protest right away. I thought it would ruin the anticipation that often comes with chronological storytelling, especially of the biographical kind. In other words, I wanted the crescendo. But as I would come to find out during the course of reading the memoir, this most contentious and prolific part of his life was a minuscule part of a larger whole. One could fully appreciate the other parts of his life – particularly the difficult moments – that made his career in the NBA and subsequent life both possible and remarkable. He was and is more than a dissenter.

Born in Gulfport, Mississippi, five years after the 1964 Civil Rights Act was passed, and almost one year after the assassination of Civil Rights Leader, Dr Martin Luther King, we learn Abdul-Rauf grapples with a Tourette condition, which was not diagnosed until his later years. It was the first of many trials to come his way and one that remains with him until this day. Sports, and especially basketball, became his saving grace from 'ridicule' from his classmates. He began nurturing an insatiable drive to fulfil his dream of one day playing professionally. He takes us through the strict regime he pledged to commit to, waking up as early as 5 am to 'work on his game', even leveraging his love for basketball against his first girlfriend, which I found comedic.

Abdul-Rauf faced struggles one would expect of any young man, from the complex relationship with his mother to his dealing with community members, some of whom appear to have taken advantage of his success as a rising star, including as he says, his basketball coach. And yet one cannot help but admire his commitment to his craft, which naturally pays off for him after he plays at Louisiana State University. During the 1988–89 season, he was hailed a 'sport wonder', averaging 30 points per game and scoring a total of 965 points, both of which were records for a freshman player at the NCAA Division I level. He earned numerous awards such as the South-eastern Conference Player of the Year and *Sports Illustrated* did a cover story of him for its February 1989 issue.

But it's the lack of academic support for him that stood out the most to me, and his perspective offers a window into the precarious nature of being a Black male student-athlete.

There is a litany of literature revealing how money-generating collegiate athletics is not free from the politicisation of identity, and as such, the infrastructures continuously disfavour the Black student-athlete. College GPA scores, college persistence rate, and college graduation rates tend to be significantly lower for Black men, who are reported to have the lowest graduation rates of any group. That's 55% to 70% for student-athletes in total while making up half of all NCAA Division 1 football and basketball teams, according to a study devised by the University of Southern California. Abdul Rauf's candid narrative is an important addition to the canon of research that exists on the subject, but it's an important backdrop to how promising he was, to begin with, ahead of the problem that would follow at the height of his NBA career, when he played for the Sacramento Kings, after his first draft with the Denver Nuggets.

His immersion in history, world events and social commentary grew, matched only by his love for his sport. It would eventually lead him to read Alex Haley's critically-acclaimed Autobiography of Malcolm X. He says, 'NBA basketball wasn't enough...I needed a more profound way to make sense of it all...The words of Malcolm X were still bouncing around in my head...I wanted to be more like Malcolm'. He wanted to understand more of what was being to me and my people.' He wanted to learn more about Islam, and after reading two to three pages of the Qur'an, he decided he wanted to become Muslim. He was given the name Mahmoud Abdul-Rauf by the Muslim community in Denver. This was in 1991.

The memoir is an important testament to the power the autobiography of Malcolm X has wielded in the public imagination of Islam in the US since its release in 1965. More specifically, the candid, intellectual approach Malcolm X used to tell his life story lays bare the systemic failings of the country towards its Black citizens, and its social conditioning which made possible his criminal past. As such, Abdul-Rauf is notably following the same literary tradition as his hero and that of another NBA legend Kareem Abdul Jabbar, formerly Lew Alcindor. An Al-Jazeera article cites him as saying he found a similar path to Islam through Malcolm X's story and subsequently the Qur'an.

But their conversion to Islam and decision to adopt new names are also reflective of a wider discourse that has, and continues, to take place among African Americans. This includes how one identifies as a person or peoples of African descent, with a history of a disruption in their ties to their ancestral home of West and Central Africa. This process of 'reclaiming' their identities is made up of various phases, from formerly enslaved peoples taking on the names of their ex-captors to the use of African and Arabic names during the Black Cultural Movement of the 1960s and 1970s. The relationship between Islamic heritage and the Black Power Movement meant many Black Americans embraced names such as Aaliyah, Fatima, Assata and Afeni. Malcolm X and Muhammad Ali are prominent examples of this, as the Netflix film 'Blood Brothers' shows. In Ali's case, this included the difficulty some American media commentators had in accepting his new 'unchristian' and 'non-European' names; and who questioned if he was still 'American' and 'patriotic'. When such a narrow depiction of patriotism is so easily heralded in professional sports against those who are not of Anglo-European descent or Christian practice, it's easy to understand why, as Abdul-Rauf explains, there was an unwarranted uneasiness and difficulty some had with his new identity and spiritual practice. Paradoxically, he, like Ali, was a celebrity Muslim, who was expected to provide commentary on US domestic and foreign policies, where it concerned 'his community'. Similarly to Ali's critique on US foreign policy during the Vietnam War, Abdul-Rauf's critique of US foreign policy in the aftermath of the 9/11 attacks in New York led, by his own admission, to the curtailment of his career.

Following his ailing career in the US, Abdul-Rauf launched his international basketball career (which included short stints in Japan and Saudi Arabia). As a 'Black Istanbulian', I was surprised and thrilled to learn that he played for a team in Turkey. However, it is clear by this point in the memoir, that Abdul-Rauf is falling out of love with basketball. He slowly makes room for his newfound faith and a greater involvement with world politics that takes him on another unexpected journey in mentoring and public speaking.

In the Blink of an Eye is an eye-opening memoir. It is a stark reminder of the importance of how Black Muslim sports personalities have historically driven forward conversations that have tested the conscience of their countries.

CLASH OF CIVILISATIONS?

Liam McKenna

In an article published in *Foreign Affairs* magazine in 1993, the American political scientist, Samuel Huntington, suggested that world politics was entering a new phase. In that new phase, ideological disputes and economic interests would no longer be the primary source of global conflict. Instead, 'the principal conflicts of global politics will occur between nations and groups of different civilizations.' Huntington identified a list of 'major civilizations' whose interactions would shape the global order: 'Western, Confucian, Japanese, Islamic, Hindu, Slavic-Orthodox, Latin American and possibly African civilization.' These civilisations, claimed Huntington, were marked by real and fundamental differences of 'history, language, culture, tradition and, most important, religion.' Out of such differences, 'the most prolonged and the most violent conflicts' had arisen. While such conflicts were not inevitable in the future, if they came it would be out of the clash between civilisations.

Peter Oborne, *The Fate of Abraham*, Simon and Schuster, London, 2022

Huntington also quoted passages from other authors characterising Islamic nations as those most fundamentally and immediately opposed to Western interests and values. The historian Bernard Lewis was quoted as saying:

> We are facing a mood and a movement far transcending the level of issues and policies and the governments that pursue them. This is no less than a clash of civilizations—the perhaps irrational but surely historic reaction of an ancient rival against our Judeo-Christian heritage, our secular present, and the world-wide expansion of both.

While he refrained from outright approving those sentiments, Huntington claimed that they represented how Western and Islamic countries themselves perceived one another. But in 1996, in a book-length exposition of his 'clash of civilisations' theory, he went further:

> The underlying problem for the West is not Islamic fundamentalism. It is Islam, a different civilization whose people are convinced of the superiority of their culture and obsessed with the inferiority of their power. The problem for Islam is not the CIA or the U.S. Department of Defense. It is the West, a different civilization whose people are convinced of the universality of their culture and believe that their superior, if declining, power imposes on them the obligation to extend that culture throughout the world. These are the basic ingredients that fuel conflict between Islam and the West.

Huntington thus rejected the assertions of Western politicians that they held no quarrel with or distaste for Islam itself, only 'Islamism' or 'extremist Islam'. It is Islam itself that the West takes issue with; and the West itself with which Islamic countries find themselves in conflict.

For a long time, except at the fringes, politicians at least in the US and the UK denied Huntington's framing, insisting on the great respect in which they held the Islamic faith. President George W. Bush, for example, declared:

> Some of the comments that have been uttered about Islam do not reflect the sentiments of my government or the sentiments of most Americans. Islam, as practiced by the vast majority of people, is a peaceful religion, a religion that respects others. Ours is a country based upon tolerance and we welcome people of all faiths in America.

In a speech on extremism in July 2015, the then Prime Minister, David Cameron, announced:

> Every one of the communities that has come to call our country home has made Britain a better place. And because the focus of my remarks today is on tackling Islamist extremism – not Islam the religion – let me say this.

> I know what a profound contribution Muslims from all backgrounds and denominations are making in every sphere of our society, proud to be both British and Muslim, without conflict or contradiction.

> And I know something else: I know too how much you hate the extremists who are seeking to divide our communities and how you loathe that damage they do.

It might be said that these protestations of tolerance were only that – protestations attempting to obscure that Western countries' treatment of Muslims both domestically and geopolitically were actually characterised by tacit acceptance of Huntington's thesis of Islam itself as fundamentally opposed to Western values and interests. Donald Trump's open antipathy towards Islam and Muslims themselves, while deplorable, might at least be commended for dropping the pretence, and laying bare a perception of Islam that, whilst taken to extremes in Trump's presidency, has permeated Western policy throughout the last decades:

> Donald J. Trump is calling for a total and complete shutdown of Muslims entering the United States until our country's representatives can figure out what is going on. [...] Mr. Trump stated, 'Without looking at the various polling data, it is obvious to anybody the hatred is beyond comprehension. Where this hatred comes from and why we will have to determine. Until we are able to determine and understand this problem and the dangerous threat it poses, our country cannot be the victims of horrendous attacks by people that believe only in Jihad, and have no sense of reason or respect for human life. If I win the election for President, we are going to Make America Great Again.'

In *The Fate of Abraham: Why the West is Wrong about Islam*, Peter Oborne, the highly respected conservative journalist and broadcaster, sets himself against Huntington's thesis and its prevailing influence on US and UK domestic and foreign policy. Western politicians and governments, Oborne sets out to prove, have misrepresented, misunderstood and mistreated Islam and Muslims for as long as they have interacted with Islamic countries or had Muslim populations. There is no 'clash' between Islam and Western culture and values. By proceeding on the false basis that Islam is fundamentally incompatible with Western society, the West has wronged Muslims both in their countries and worldwide.

Oborne approaches his task in three stages. First, in Parts One to Three of the book, he addresses each of the US, the UK and France, in turn, giving a narrative of each country's interaction with Islam across its history. These chapters are comprehensive in breadth, ranging from the Venerable Bede's description in the eighth century of 'Saracens' as 'shiftless, hateful and violent' to up to date (at the time of writing) comment on the nascent Biden administration's restoration of 'normality' to US-Muslim relations.

The chapters addressing the UK, however, end around the middle of the twentieth century with discussion of Winston Churchill's attitudes towards Islam. Recent UK politics are then the subject of the second stage of Oborne's analysis, filling Part Four of the book. Oborne's discussion here focuses on the role of right-wing think tanks, in particular Policy Exchange's influence on leading Conservative party lights, and on two of the most notable recent incidents of hysteria directed against Muslims, namely the Trojan Horse affair in Birmingham's schools and the narrative of Muslim 'grooming gangs' operating across the country unburdened by police forces which are themselves too frightful of accusations of racism to intervene. Oborne then, in Part Five, gives a more personal narrative, describing his interactions with Muslim communities at the 'bloody borders', quoting Huntington's language, over the last fifteen years – amongst them Darfur in 2006, Syria in 2014 and Myanmar in 2017.

The book concludes by emphasising the fundamental similarities between Islamic, Christian and Jewish traditions as descended from the faith of Abraham. As Oborne puts it, when describing his visit to Hebron and the site of the 1994 killings by Baruch Goldstein:

> Surely it [the Tomb of the Patriarchs, also called the Sanctuary of Abraham or the Cave of Machpelah] belongs to Abraham alone, patriarch to three great religions and a man of peace. We are all his descendants: the people of the book. We all worship his God. I fell to my knees and I prayed.

With this shared heritage in mind, Oborne implores us to reclaim our common humanity by 'thinking again about Islam and the West', setting aside recent analysis 'beset by intellectual and moral error' and rejecting the hypothesis that Islam and the West represent two incompatible and clashing civilisations. The results of that false hypothesis have been catastrophic, including 'illegal wars, torture and a general repudiation of democracy, human rights and decency' which have 'awarded a legitimacy to movements such as al-Qaeda and Islamic State' which 'had always argued that Western support for liberal democracy was a sham.'

It does not take much persuading to accept Oborne's basic point that policymakers and the commentariat in the US and UK by and large agree with Huntington's characterisation of Islam as the 'other', contrasted against what they would label their countries' Judeo-Christian traditions.

Some commentators have accepted this clearly and without demur, as did Douglas Murray when he said in 2006 that conditions 'for Muslims in Europe must be made harder across the board', or in 2017 that what the UK needs is 'a bit less Islam'. Others, such as George Bush or David Cameron, at least make the pretence of tolerance and understanding. Perhaps the best recent indicator that this is just pretence, though post-dating Oborne's book, can be seen by comparing reactions to the Ukrainian refugee crisis with reactions to the plight of Syrian or Afghan refugees. Ukrainian refugees – admittedly after some reluctance in the case of the UK – have been granted an open door to seek safety throughout Europe. That same door is firmly shut to Afghans and Syrians. In France, 79% of the public favoured accepting Ukrainian refugees while at the same time 51% opposed welcoming Afghan refugees. Said one commentator in France: 'They [Ukrainians] are culturally European'. Said another: 'there is a difference between Ukrainians who take part in our civilisational space and other populations who belong to other civilisations.'

Despite its sub-title, 'Why the West is Wrong about Islam', Oborne's book is not an apologia for Islam against such attitudes. The reader looking for an account of the diversity of Islamic thought and cultures, and their relations to Western norms, should look elsewhere – for instance, Christopher de Bellaigue's excellent *The Islamic Enlightenment* – though they could do worse than starting with Oborne's suggested list of further reading. Oborne's concern is instead to take the West's treatment of Islam and Muslims on its own terms, exposing the ignorance and arrogance at the heart of that treatment. One does not need a detailed account of Islamic cultures and thought across history to see just how far the West has gone wrong in this respect.

Here, the book perhaps suffers in its attempt to do too much. Oborne compresses a little over a thousand years of history of three countries – the US, the UK and France – and their colonies into around two hundred and fifty pages. Inevitably some detail falls by the wayside, though within that constraint these chapters are an impressive history and worthwhile to the general reader. Even when Oborne turns to discuss the UK in the modern day – chapters fifteen to twenty covering about the last twenty years – there is so much to cover that Oborne lacks the space to fully justify his analysis and conclusions. In chapter 18, for instance, Oborne deals with the 'Trojan Horse affair', which purported to expose a conspiracy to infiltrate and 'Islamise' a series of schools in Birmingham. Oborne does his best in the space available to pull apart the alleged conspiracy – the treatment, for instance, of ordinary Muslim practices such as the call to prayer or Arabic tuition as evidence of extremism when the equivalent Christian practices, such as singing of hymns in assembly, are considered unexceptional. But the network of allegations and evidence involved is simply too vast for a convincing rebuttal to be contained in the few pages Oborne allots to the topic.

Notwithstanding those limitations, Oborne's basic analysis is compelling. Nobody is helped by the Western insistence on treating Islam as a policy problem to be solved. We would all benefit if politicians and commentators were willing to acknowledge the prejudices that continue to underlie their treatment of Muslim individuals and nations. As Oborne argues, though the West denies Huntington's analysis, disavowing that it sees any clash of civilisations, its actions belie that denial. So the West gives succour to retrogressive forces both within itself, and to those in Islamic societies which rely on that same 'clash of civilisations' narrative to bolster their support. Oborne gives the example of al-Qaeda, who claim the actions of the US and its allies as a 'twisted moral sanction'.

Oborne ends his book with an appeal for unity, comparing Christ's injunction to love thy neighbour as thyself to the Prophet Muhammad's similar words on being asked by a Bedouin for something to take him to heaven. Coming as it does at the end of a catalogue of mistreatment and misunderstanding, the prospects of this appeal being taken up might feel remote. As Oborne notes just a few paragraphs previously, the 'American, British and French media don't report on Muslims. It targets them, fabricating stories and fomenting at best distrust and at worst hatred.' While this continues, Oborne's call for understanding seems likely to go unanswered, at least by those politicians and journalists who most need to hear it.

There seems then a danger that the reader of Oborne's book will come away with a message not quite intended. While there need not have been a 'clash of civilisations' between Islam and the West, ultimately one has been created, by avoidable and regrettable, but now long-established, policy choices and a culture of distrust and misunderstanding.

Such a gloomy attitude should be resisted. As a corrective, one need only turn to one of the countless accounts of positive interchange and understanding between Muslims and non-Muslims. One such account, all the more compelling for taking place during a period of intense conflict between Christian and Islamic societies, can be found in the writings of Usama Ibn Munqidh. Usama was a poet and diplomat, born in northern Syria in July 1095, shortly before Pope Urban II began preaching for the First Crusade. He travelled widely over the ninety years of his life, including in the lands conquered and ruled by the European crusaders. In his autobiography, the *Kitab al-I'tibar*, Usama spoke in some detail about his interactions with Europeans ('Franks'). As one would expect, given the era and that Usama was dealing with Franks as invaders, precursors of modern colonialists, the work is not a marvel of tolerance or cross-cultural understanding. Usama describes the Franks as 'mere beasts possessing no other virtues but courage and fighting'. But underneath this invective one can see real affection by Usama for the people he meets. In one passage, he describes a Christian knight as his 'constant companion' who called him 'my brother', adding that 'Between us there were ties of amity and sociability'. While he records, and mocks, examples of barbaric attempts at medicine by certain Franks, equally he acknowledges the good when he sees it. In one passage, he relates a 'wondrous example' of Frankish medicine, saying that he later adopted the technique he observed for his own use as a physician. Most telling is the following passage, in which Usama describes praying at the al-Aqsa mosque in Jerusalem, at that time controlled by the Franks:

> Whenever I went to visit the holy sites in Jerusalem, I would go in and make my way up to the al-Aqsa mosque, beside which stood a small mosque that the Franks had converted into a church. When I went into the al-Aqsa mosque – where the Templars, who are my friends, were – they would clear out that little mosque so that I could pray in it. One day, I went into the little mosque, recited the opening formula 'God is Great!' and stood up in prayer.

It was possible a thousand years ago for Usama ibn Munqidh to describe the Templars, today the stereotypical symbol of Christian intolerance and violence, as his friends. *The Fate of Abraham* rightly focuses on the divisions that have been fostered by the West, and the harm that has been done, and is still taking place, as a result. But we would be justified in believing that where we are is not inevitable or unchangeable. Oborne's book is to be welcomed as a contribution to the more mature and informed conversation that will be necessary to encourage that change.

THE OTHER HOME

Khaldoon Ahmed

My mother came to an alien London in 1972 when she married my father who was already here. They didn't have any relatives in the UK, and I remember my mother saying she would approach women in the street wearing *shalwar kameez*, and befriend them. Before long, we had our own Pakistani network in London.

The California of Sabaa Tahir's *All My Rage*, sounds more like a sparse desert than the London my mother encountered. Teenagers Sal and Noor are the only Pakistanis in their school. The town is indifferent to their background. Their Muslimness, or Asian identity becomes a shared bond. The Urdu and Punjabi they speak with the older generation, with all the cultural references, become a private code between them. My mother was again on my mind when I picked up Aamina Ahmad's novel *The Return of Faraz Ali*. My eyes were drawn to the date I saw written on the first page: 'Lahore, February 1943'. By coincidence the place, year, and exact month of my mother's birth.

Both Sabaa Tahir's *All My Rage* and Aamina Ahmad's *The Return of Faraz Ali* are written by second generation Pakistanis, like me. One from the USA, and one from Britain. Aamina recreates scenes from Pakistan's history, while Sabaa constructs a microcosm of an immigrant world in California. As I read the novels, questions swirled around in my mind. How does the 'immigrant self' come into being? It is not the first time I have wondered this or reflected on my experience of being born in Britain to parents from Pakistan. Your difference, and the fact that you are seen as different, become part of your identity. From an early age in interactions with the white world, you are aware, and made aware, that you are not the same. A process that generates difference, in addition to the difference that is already there.

All My Rage is the love story between Sal and Noor. The youngsters carry with them the failed dreams of their parents. And yearn for an empowered future beyond the small desert town of Juniper, away from main cities and main centres. But the voraciously open minds of our protagonists source a wealth of ideas and inspiration from a few dedicated teachers at school, and in particular, from English literature. Worlds of imagination are vital if your daily reality is running a motel or liquor store. For these adolescents, the ability to imagine another world is about survival itself. Daily life is precarious, weighed down by debt. Their elders have given up, and in an

Sabaa Tahir, *All My Rage*, Atom, London 2022
Aamina Ahmad, *The Return of Faraz Ali*, Riverhead Books, Hull, 2022

indifferent world, they turn to the few adults who care, their idealistic and principled teachers.

Education is a way out, and for this second generation going to university becomes imbued with multiple meanings. Escape from the small town, and escape from parents who did their best but who found their spirit inevitably broken by survival in the New World.

The aspirations Noor and Sal carry are not just their own. They are inherited ambitions, sometimes forgotten or unconscious, of parents and grandparents. 'He will be a neurosurgeon, your father said. He will be a writer. He will be an architect.' The parents and children, albeit in different ways, share this will to build something. It is a will to life, they cannot rest. There is an inner and external turmoil that drives them. I recognise this completely. Both my parents were teachers, and our environment at home was about education. We were expected to become doctors or engineers. I found some old home videos of myself at the time of applying for university aged 17. I see my brother coaching me on interviews, and what to put on application forms. And there is a scene in which I get offers from various colleges, and my entire family is discussing my future. I can see the existential pressure written on my face at that pivotal time.

Juniper, California, is a world away from London where I grew up. I zoomed into this small town on google maps and found a dusty landscape. A few listings close by are the Alturas Gun Range (temporarily closed), the Modoc National Wildlife Refuge, and the Desert Rose Casino. But despite this contrast of location, Sabaa Tahir captures well the culture of immigrants from Pakistan that I am familiar with. And also, the way this culture goes down a blind alley. When Sal's mother dies, they 'scrape together 19 Muslims from Juniper' to have an Islamic funeral. Sal depends on a religious man to guide them through the process. He feels acutely at this point that culture and religion are something he is dislocated from, and he yearns for a guide to make things intelligible in the Californian landscape.

My mother died last year. She was more embedded in a Muslim Pakistani community in London than Sabaa Tahir describes of her life in the USA. But after her death there was a gap in ritual and cultural practice that I continue to feel like a constant ache. My link to Pakistani culture was my mother. When she died I lost the person I would have asked what to do. So instead of 40 days of mourning, and 'Quran khatams', gatherings of aunties and uncles, there was a painful void. This does pertain to my very specific family circumstances, but it is says something more - about beached cultures on alien shores.

In the novel, Sal's full name, Salahuddin, is pronounced and mispronounced in various ways. A daily reminder of his other-ness. This has a reinforcing effect of feeling like an outsider. And surely this must be one of the many origins of unstable cultural identities we see in the children of immigrants. In my own fragmented self I look for a mirror but find vague approximations. I grew up feeling my bicultural British-Pakistani situation was unique, although of course it's not. I have always looked for glimpses of myself in others' stories. It is in this comparative mode that I approached *All My Rage*.

If being second generation means existing in fragments, what must follow is a search for wholeness. You seek it in a number of places, one of which is literature. By comparing my fragmentation with the fiction in *All my Rage*, I could see the active sorting, shifting and processing happening in my mind. All of it in the end to assemble a more complete image of who I am. An elusive end of course.

It is curious and interesting why out of all the books Sabaa Tahir has written; this is the first in which she refers to her own cultural background. She is a renowned writer in the fantasy book world and has had a number of bestsellers. In interviews she speaks about taking 15 years to write *All*

My Rage. This book then, is something in a different category to her other writing. Much closer to home, and also something I imagine she wanted to 'get right'. It is the work of an accomplished, clear and confident writer. I think Sabaa wanted to do justice to this story, so she was patient with herself to arrive as a writer (and a writer with an established audience) to finish it.

The Return of Faraz Ali, in contrast to *All My Rage*, is set in Pakistan's past. Aamina Ahmed constructs an elaborate interlocking world of the lives of a policeman – Faraz, and politicians and bureaucrats, set in the red-light district of the *androon shaher* (walled city) of Lahore. In doing so, she creates a vivid picture of the first decades of a new nation. Where regardless of class and privilege, individuals enact their desperate existential struggles.

A girl from a prostitute's family is killed. And this sets up the story. Faraz the policeman lives the life of a state functionary. His ability to act is bounded by his superiors. Secretly, he carries inside the stigma of being born into the red-light district himself. The tensions of his loyalty to his superiors, and to his origins, is what propels the narrative.

Like Aamina I was born and brought up in London. Via my mother and her family I have a deep connection to the city of Lahore. We went there every few years and it is barely possible to capture the essence of the city and what makes the place what it is in all its beauty and imperfections. But Aamina manages this, conveying Pakistan's Lahore in a way that is neither romantic nor objectified. My own relationship to the country of my parents is complex, and I realise how unthinkingly it tends towards a romantic lens. But Aamina's Pakistan is brutal. Where an ageing film star rises from the red-light district to the cinema screens of Lollywood to a different social circle. But is in constant danger of slipping back to the world she emerged from

The book moves through pivotal moments in Pakistan's history. From protests against Ayub Khan, the first military dictator, to mass support for Zulfiqar Ali Bhutto, his rise to power, and then the breakup of the country and the creation of Bangladesh. The characters are participants and witnesses to what happened. So, this book is in effect, a fictional political and social history from 1942–1968. In a short but poignant episode, Faraz finds himself stranded in Dhaka on the eve of its independence. There is a strange liminal moment when he realises he is considered a foreigner and occupier, and not a fellow countryman. This reminded me of a memory I have of speaking with my *mamoon* (uncle) in Lahore. My uncle was an engineering intern in Chittagong in 1969, and insisted that Bengalis were 'lovely and hospitable'. He had no idea at that point they wanted to be free of West Pakistan.

As children, we went to see the usual sights during our summer trips to Lahore: Badshahi masjid, Shalimar gardens, and Jahangir's *maqbara*. But I had to insist to be taken inside the walled city itself. My relatives with their Victorian, middle-class sensibilities failed to mention the *heera mandi* (red light) bazaar there. Walking through you heard snippets of music and *tabla*. And the occasional flash of a woman in a red dress in a window. I heard about a time before partition when some of those streets were known as the 'Chelsea of Lahore'. Muhammad Iqbal, the famous poet and philosopher, lived there. This was the forgotten time of the 1920s and 30s when Lahore was on a par with Bombay and Calcutta as a centre of creativity, boasting publishing houses, the cinema industry and a vibrant intellectual life. I was told that some of our relatives had a whole street in the *adroon shahar* called '*kakazai gully*', named after the Pashtoon-Punjabi tribe they belonged to. Some of them were also involved in the publishing industry before partition.

The conservative attitudes of my own family did not permit any interest in the trashy 'cheap' world of Lollywood in Punjabi films. Growing up in London, we only knew about it through Pakistani TV comedies like '50/50' that spoofed giant moustaches, *dhotis* and guns. This was considered low culture, in contrast to the elevated world of Urdu poetry and ghazals sung by the likes of Iqbal Bano and Munni Begum. For me the strength of Aamina's novel is to blow apart these binaries of low and high culture. It is fiction yes, but a way into seeing how power intersected with entertainment in Pakistan's history. There is no Islamic purity in the land of pure. There is nothing elegant in a world of prostitutes and murder. But there is still dignity in how the characters try and keep their heads and lives above water.

The Lahore of my childhood visits was of the narrow streets of Mughalpura, the colonial bungalows of Mayo Gardens, and the crumbling plaster of the British-era Mall road. In my most recent visits the rooftops of the Heera Mandi, the red light district, are now fancy cafes overlooking the grandiose Mughal expanse of Badshahi Masjid. And the historic street beneath has been given the unromantic name of 'Food Street'.

I recently learned that the word 'nostalgia' is a combination of the Greek for 'homecoming' and 'sorrow'. I connect to Pakistan through this emotion, even though it's a place I've never lived in. Perhaps the pain is related to this displacement, or an alienation that goes alongside. My mother would have been intrigued by these two novels. The world of *The Return of Faraz Ali* would have been intimately familiar to her – a world of horse drawn tongas, Zulfiqar Ali Bhutto and Indo-Pak wars. But she would have been equally intrigued by *All My Rage*. A book that captures so well this year zero of the arrival of an immigrant, and the birth of a new hybrid generation that inhabits multiple identities.

ET CETERA

ON DEATH

Hina Khalid

The English word 'transition' enters into our lexicon through the Latin *transitio*, which denotes a going across or over, a traversing of boundaries, a passage into the new. Indeed, any 'transition' is always already infused with an existential dynamism of liminality: to tread across a boundary, physical or otherwise, is to take leave of the familiar terrain on which one stands and to implant oneself in fresh soil. There is perhaps no ground as solidly felt, as unshakeably inhabited, as the ground of our existence itself: that existence which is not an attribute among attributes but constitutes rather the ontological context, the fertile seedbed, for *all* attributes. When listing a person's many qualities, let's call him John, we do not *also* affirm that John 'exists', for the actuality of John's being is enfolded in our very naming of him. Life is, in other words, that stable resting place in which our quirks and quiddities are intimately nestled; to *be* is not a state among states but is the condition of possibility for every state. The cessation of our life, then, is the most 'radical' transition woven into our finite fabrics: 'radical' in the sense that it strikes at the primordial *root* of our-selves. To die is not merely to lose one of the petals that abundantly adorns our personhood, but it is to be shorn of the very *possibility* of future flowering: no-thing shall flourish here anymore, for this wayfarer has passed on.

The Qur'an is replete with sonorous insistences on the ineluctability of death: that firm bedrock of vitality on which we repose will ineludibly erode, and all our varying ventures bear the indelible imprint of mortality. In limning the human person's finitude, the Qur'an relates death to the embodied experience of 'tasting', thus conveying something of death's tangible reality and material immediacy: 'Every soul shall taste death. Then unto Us shall you be returned' (29:57). Since all human beings will taste death, it is futile to try and evade it, as it will have the last word: 'Say, "Truly the death from which you flee will meet you; then you shall be returned to the Knower of the unseen and the seen, and He will inform you of that which you used to do"' (62:8). Significantly, both of these verses body forth the notion of death as a 'return'. Indeed, Sufi cosmology elaborates this scriptural motif of 'being brought back' to the divine presence by conceiving of our material existence as a terrestrial 'interim', a dynamic 'interlude', between our pre- and post- earthly states of complete union with God. As the Qur'an affirms in 7:172, all human beings joyously testified to the divine unicity in the 'Primordial Covenant' with God, and while we may veer away from this intimate God-consciousness through our heedless absorption in the world, death marks an emphatic re-cognition of this pre-cosmic witnessing. It is perhaps this promise of a spiritual homecoming that undergirds the Prophetic declaration, 'death is a precious gift to the believer'. In his reflective gloss on this Hadith, the celebrated theologian al-Ghazali (d. 1111) affirms that death relieves us of the continual clamour of lower desires and ignoble impulses with which we wrestle in this life, thus laying final rest to the torments and turbulences of our souls.

If death is that ultimate transition that awaits each of us, it is also, crucially, that which pertains universally to all living beings: every creature, in virtue of its very *creatureliness*, will succumb to death. Indeed, the Qur'an repeatedly directs its listeners' attention to the rhythmic cyclicality of life and death: the changing seasons, the coursing winds, and the cultivable earth are all signs of an elemental fragility which stands in cosmic contradistinction to the ever-living, eternal God. As 45:5 asserts, 'in the variation of the night and the day, and in that which God sends down from the sky as provision whereby He revives the earth after its death, and in the shifting of the winds are signs for a people who understand'. We are to reflect on these 'signs' of fluctuation and finitude not as distant observers of an external fact but as creatures who constitutively *share in* this vulnerability to temporality: as the day fades into night, so too will the 'day' of our youth pass into the darkness of death; as the earth is rendered arid in times of drought, so too will our mortal frames disintegrate when the water of life is exhausted; and as the breeze gently wafts across distant landscapes, so too will our breath slowly depart from us as we transition into the ultimate unknown. The fact of our finitude bears witness to our ontological kinship with all of material creation: that which is born must die, and in this fundamental sense, despite our pretensions to permanence, we are no different from the humble honeybee, the majestic mammoth, and the delicate dandelion. All must cross the threshold, and return to that divine origin from which they came.

And yet, while death confirms our corporeal, creaturely commonality with all lifeforms, it is also a state to which we can relate in a *distinctively* human way, acting as a portal into those lofty stations of virtue of which only human beings are capable. While all creatures do indeed *die* (and some even appear to mourn in ways that suggest intense grief), only human beings can reflectively 'confront' the actuality of their finitude, render it an ever-present epistemic horizon, and live their lives with the abiding awareness that they, and all whom they love, will one day breathe their last. This uniquely human capacity to contemplate a future in which one no longer *is*, is crystallised in the hadith literature and Sufi discourse, which repeatedly enjoin the believer to recall the fact of death – indeed, *dhikr al-maut* (the remembrance of death) constitutes an integral pillar of the spiritual path. As the Prophet instructed, 'remember death abundantly, for to recall it wipes away sins and makes one abstemious in the world'.

This remembrance of death is, crucially, not a matter of static mentation but is intended to inspire an actively God-centred mode of being *in* and *with* the world. In other words, we recall *death* in order to *live* better; and several reflections by the Prophet and his companions suggest that the buds of moral beauty and piety effloresce where the reality of death is deeply and devotedly dwelt upon. A companion of the Prophet, Ibn 'Umar, relates that he once heard a man from the Helpers (*Al-Ansar*) inquire, 'Who is the most intelligent and generous of men, O emissary of God?' The Prophet replied, 'the most diligent in recalling death, and the one who is best prepared for it. Such are the intelligent ones, who have gained the honour of this world and the dignity of the next'. Echoing this spiritual synergy between rigorous remembrance of *death* and virtuous sagacity in *life*, the grandson of the Prophet, Hassan, affirmed, 'never have I seen an intelligent man without finding him to be wary of death and saddened by it'. Indeed, the recollection of death is conducive to a receptive tenderness of heart;

to attend to the fleeting fragility of life is to awaken to the enduring urgency of love. Thus, the Prophet's wife Safiya narrates that an old woman once complained to Aisha of the hardness of her heart, and Aisha advised her, 'remember death frequently, and your heart will be softened'. She undertook this *memento mori*, and her heart was indeed softened.

This ethos of meditatively 'interiorizing' the reality of impermanence is perhaps most vividly encoded in the Prophetic injunction, so beloved to Sufis, to 'die before you die'. This hadith issues a resonant call to the believer to dissolve their self-serving proclivities (to 'die' to their lower selves) so as to be 'reborn' into the depths of divine intimacy. This dynamic process of de-centering the ego and becoming stably re-centred in the divine is otherwise expressed through the modalities of *fana'* (annihilation) and *baqa'* (subsistence): to 'annihilate' the base qualities of the self is to subsist in the luminous divine attributes, which marks the summit of spiritual transmutation. Through this exhortation to overcome one's egocentric dispersion, we have a subtle reconfiguration of the categories of 'life' and 'death': no longer do they stand as two diametrically opposed states, for within the matrix of embodied life, a kind of death is (already) possible (and indeed encouraged). One might be spiritually 'dead' to the self even as one is physically 'alive', and inasmuch as the purgative undertaking of *fana'* betokens a diaphanous openness to the divine, such an annihilation constitutes *true* life. To live whilst one is 'dead' to the vices and vicissitudes of the ego is to uphold that resplendent Qur'anic invitation to 'tread on the earth gently' (25:63) — no longer do we appropriate the world to our-selves, circumscribing things as 'mine', for we know that all things live, move, and have their finite being in God alone.

One thus moves through the world with a lightness of being, aware of the radical precarity of our lives that rest like a feather on the divine breath. We might otherwise term this mode of active repose in God as the sensibility of 'wayfaring' — as the Prophet instructed us, we dwell in this world 'as a stranger or traveller', surrendering all affairs to the ever-living and ever-loving God. This intricate entwinement of living and dying is enfolded in the formula that is uttered when one hears the news of someone's death: 'Verily, to God we belong and to Him we return'. As the American Muslim scholar, Omid Safi, has pointed out, the verbal form of 'return' in this sentence, *raji'un*, corresponds to the active participle, which denotes an ongoing process; in this sense, a more accurate translation would be, 'Verily, to God we belong and to Him we are *perpetually returning*'. As we saw above, death is conceived of in the Qur'an as a 'return' to the divine, and insofar as our existence is always already bathed in the divine presence, this 'return' is not an unreachable, shadowed horizon but is an ontological habitat in which we abide at each moment: with each inhalation and exhalation, we are environed by the God who is 'closer to us than our jugular vein' (50:16). Reinforcing this notion that our creaturely lives insistently gesture towards death, the companion Abu'l-Darda', who died in 652, instructed, 'when you recall the departed, count yourself as one of them'. We are always inhabiting that existential point of 'return' to God, for there is no step we take which is not in-spirited by the unshakeable divine reality. Thus, when it was said to the early Sufi al-Junayd, as he lay on his deathbed in 910, 'affirm: "There is no deity but God!", he replied, "I have not forgotten it that I might thus recall it"'.

Al-Junayd had so utterly 'died' to him-self that the possibility of remembering God never arose: one cannot recall that from which one is never distant, just as one cannot return to a place from which one has never left. In this annihilation, or death, to his egoic identity, and in his firm anchorage in the divine reality, al-Junayd dynamically embodies the spiritual telos of the human person, which is to move through the routes of the world with a steadfast rootedness in God. Crucially, if the Islamic vision thus elaborates a certain form of death as a possibility in *life*, it also sets forth the promise of a renewed life *after* death. In other words, one can die whilst one is still alive, and one will live even after one has died. Again, then, our understanding of life as the antitype of death is decisively disrupted: if the meaning of our physical life is in our spiritual death to the self, the finality of our physical death is eclipsed by a spiritual life to come. Indeed, the Qur'an resonantly directs its hearers to the reality of the resurrection, wherein all will stand before God to testify to their earthly deeds.

If, as we saw above, the cosmic patterns of change and finitude provide irrefragable insight into death, the Qur'an also adduces these very patterns to point forward to the horizon of eschatological life. In response to those who denied that dead matter could ever be re-inspirited, the Qur'an appeals to the variegated cycles of birth, decay, and regeneration in the plant and animal kingdoms as evidence of God's boundless creative power. Something of the resurrection is thus intimated here below through the rhythmic oscillations between life and death that colour the cosmos: 'And God is He Who sends the winds; then they cause clouds to rise. Then We drive them to a land that is dead, and thereby revive the earth after its death. Thus shall be the Resurrection!' (Q35:9). Human beings are subject to the same cosmic cycles that re-animate our terrestrial terrains; just as surely as seeds sprout in the spring, so too will we be restored to new life with God.

How then are we to confront the actuality of this ultimate transition, which is not a domain of existential closure but marks rather an opening outward into a life beyond? One response, based on our discussion above, might be: with the humble equanimity that typifies the true servant of the divine. Al-Junayd narrates that he went to visit the saint Sari al-Saqati whilst the latter lay on his sickbed, and asked him how he was faring. Al-*Saqati* gave a rather poetic response: 'how may I complain to my physician of what ails me, when what ails me from my physician comes?' This is the consummate God-orientation that is proper to the saints and the prophets: they rest firmly and contentedly in the divine will, secure in the knowledge that in life and in death, they belong wholly to God. And yet, there is a space within this contentment, paradoxically, for the authentically human emotions of sorrow and pain; for a kind of poignant longing that attends our intimate awareness of life's fragility.

It is said that when the Prophet's son took his last breath, the Prophet held him, tears flowing, and one of his companions expressed his surprise for he thought that the Prophet had spoken against 'excessive' displays of grief. Muhammad affirmed that his tears were 'signs of tenderness and mercy' and then uttered what became a foundational ethical and spiritual teaching in the Islamic tradition: 'He who is not merciful will not be shown mercy'. The expression of grief, as a testament to one's love and a 'bearing witness' to the finitude of human life, brings one ever closer to the all-encompassing mercy (*rahma*) of God. Perhaps it is not coincidental that the Arabic term for 'passage' or 'transition', '*abr* shares a trilateral root with the word for 'tear' ('*ibar*) — the final transition of death is to be met with a fortitude that encompasses a tearful softness of heart. On this delicate interlacing of contentment and sorrow in the tapestry of human finitude, I will let the celebrated poet Rabindranath Tagore, who here addresses God with a poignant synthesis of strength and surrender, have the last word:

Death, your servant, is at my door.

He has crossed the unknown sea and brought your call to my home.

The night is dark and my heart is fearful---yet I will take up the lamp, open my gates and bow to him my welcome. It is your messenger who stands at my door.

I will worship him placing at his feet the treasure of my heart.

He will go back with his errand done, leaving a dark shadow on my morning; and in my desolate home only my forlorn self will remain as my last offering to you.

THE LIST: TEN SHAPESHIFTERS

Transitions. The word conjures images of changes that are or are hoped to be smooth and orderly –childhood to maturity, day to night and night to day, the four seasons. Some transitions are sudden, some are irreversible, some are cyclical or reversible – think about the freezing of water and the melting of ice. If we're unprepared, we can be deeply unsettled by the changing of physical forms or the crossing of boundaries that are too abrupt, or that seem to flout logical rules.

We don't pretend to be psychoanalytical experts at *Critical Muslim* – not publicly anyway – but there is therefore something intriguing about humankind's fascination with shapeshifters, especially the mythical variety. We mean creatures that can undergo drastic transitions that defy normal explanation. So not just, say, the changing of colours displayed by chameleons.

Supernatural shapeshifters are not merely the stuff of spooky stories or playful pranks. Tales of shapeshifters often contain clues about the ways that social anxieties or political upheavals are expressed during certain moments in time. And who is to say they're simply objects of superstition? Many of them have endured alongside the advancement of scientific knowledge and reason – some have simply transitioned into new manifestations in the aftermath of particular social transformations.

Take the vampire which, according to cultural historian Christopher Frayling, is 'as old as the world'. From a contemporary perspective, we might associate vampires largely with Eastern Europe or the Balkans, where they emerged amidst epidemics that struck in the eighteenth century. But vampirism and accounts of vampire-like shapeshifters were present long before this and could be found even in Mongolia and Nepal. Most famously, however, modern conceptions of the vampire have been shaped by Bram Stoker's *Dracula*.

It is widely known that the character of Count Dracula was loosely based upon the fifteenth century Romanian ruler, Vlad III, or Vlad the Impaler.

Stoker transformed this national hero into a supernatural villain due not so much to meticulous historical research than to his own recurring dreams. Whilst the transition of Dracula from medieval ruler to bloodthirsty vampire has not-so-subtle Orientalist and even anti-Semitic connotations, what is more interesting is the rest of Stoker's social context. The man was fascinated by the products of the nineteenth century's technological transition – typewriters, phonographs, blood transfusions, Kodak cameras, weaponry.

Somewhere in the middle of all of this, Stoker managed to create a character that inverted a core Christian ritual – the Eucharist – and beliefs about Jesus Christ. In the Gospel according to John, Jesus says, 'Unless you eat my flesh and drink my blood, you have no life in you. He who eats my flesh and drinks my blood has eternal life and I will raise him up on the last day.' Bram Stoker's Dracula drinks *human* blood, and lots of it. But then instead of being raised in eternal life, he remains eternally undead. And the way to repel him is through the ritual of a *proper* Eucharist.

We won't wander into theorising about the themes of race, gender, sexuality, colonialism, disease and the myriad analytical directions pursued by academics interested in *Dracula*. Instead, we'll use this vignette as a transition into our list of ten examples of shapeshifting and their social significance.

1. Jesus Christ

What the devil? No, we're not calling Jesus Christ a shapeshifter. But the transition of Christianity from persecuted sect into an imperial religion in the fourth century was marked by an explosive theological dispute about the exact nature of Jesus's divine status.

To cut a long story short, Arius (c. 250–336) believed that Jesus the Son proceeded from God the Father, but was not Eternal – Father and Son were not of the same essence. In other words, Jesus was the Son of God but was not fully divine. Athanasius (c. 293–373), on the other hand, held that Jesus's divine nature was identical to that of the Father – Father and Son have the same substance, and therefore Jesus Christ *is* God. This disagreement, known as the Arian controversy, bitterly divided early

Christians and almost destabilised the Roman Empire. In the end, the Athanasian position was adopted through subsequent councils, and Arianism was condemned as heresy.

The evolution of this controversy laid the groundwork for the development of the Roman Catholic doctrine of transubstantiation. This is the change by which the substance (though not the appearance) of the bread and wine in the Eucharist becomes Christ's real presence – that is, his body and blood. Now *that's* a transition. But let's not get started on how this compares with *con*substantiation – we've reached the end of our theological tether.

Although the Councils of Nicaea and Chalcedon were milestones in the history of Christology, they could not fully resolve the disputes about the divine nature of Jesus Christ. The key contested terms were *homoousios* ('of the same substance' or 'of the same essence') and *homoiousios* ('of like essence'). Their close resemblance prompted the British historian and writer Thomas Carlyle to surmise that Christendom was split by strife over a diphthong.

2. Apes in the Quran

The Qur'an contains brief and intriguing references to an instance of shapeshifting, albeit as divine punishment, which has itself transmogrified into a modern anti-Semitic motif. According to verse 65 of the second chapter, Al-Baqarah (The Cow), 'You are already aware of those of you who broke the Sabbath. We said to them, "Be disgraced apes!"' This episode is elaborated at slightly greater length in the seventh chapter, Al-A'raf (The Heights), in verses 163-166.

These passages might be referring to the accounts in the Hebrew Scriptures in which the Israelites whinge repeatedly to Moses about not having a variety of foods to eat after escaping Pharaoh's Egypt. God replies, fine, 'for a whole month' you will get meat 'until it comes out of your nostrils and becomes loathsome to you—because you have rejected the Lord who is among you, and have wailed before him, saying, "Why did we ever leave Egypt?"' (Numbers 11: 20).

In the Book of Numbers, this is followed by an exchange in which Moses questions God's ability to provide enough meat to satisfy the complaining Israelites for an entire month. Moses asks: 'Are there enough flocks and herds to slaughter for them? Are there enough fish in the sea to catch for them?' To which God responds by bringing the Israelites 'quails from the sea' which they gather, day and night. But, 'while the meat was still between their teeth, before it was consumed, the anger of the Lord was kindled against the people, and the Lord struck the people with a very great plague' (Numbers 11: 33).

The Qur'an recounts this story in abridged form, with some key terms experiencing a metamorphosis: the Biblical references to 'Israelites' being brought 'quails from the sea' become the 'People of the Book' (often glossed as 'the Jews' by many modern Muslim preachers) being given fish. The nature of their sin also changes. In Numbers, the Israelites are punished for being ungrateful and greedy, while the Qur'an introduces an additional idea that they are also punished for breaking the Sabbath. And, whilst the Israelites are cursed by a 'great plague' in Numbers, the Qur'an tells us that they were turned into apes.

While many a fiery Muslim preacher in contemporary times has therefore denounced Jews as apes (and pigs), there was historically more ambivalence about the kind of shapeshifting that occurred and the reasons for it. As Muhammad Asad explains:

> As for the substance of God's decree, 'Be as apes despicable', the famous *tabi'i* Mujahid explains it thus: '[Only] their hearts were transformed, that is, they were not [really] transformed into apes: this is but a metaphor (*mathal*) coined by God with regard to them, similar to the metaphor of 'the ass carrying the books' [62:5]'.... It should be borne in mind that the expression 'like an ape' is often used in classical Arabic to describe a person who is unable to restrain his gross appetites or passions.

3. Jinn

In *Critical Muslim 43: Ignorance*, Alireza Doostdar recalled an episode in which his research assistant, Mehdi, encountered a jinn in Tehran. The story is creepy enough, but for the purposes of this list, Doostdar's description of jinn is what we're interested in:

> These are invisible, intelligent beings whose intentions and actions are opaque to us, and yet whose doings sometimes intersect with the world of humans in ways that tend to produce anxiety, discomfort, and terror. Jinn are said to displace or steal valuables, cause nightmares, and sometimes possess their victims and drive them to madness. But on rare occasions they may initiate friendly contact with humans and even offer their service.

This description accords with widespread Muslim understandings of jinn as capricious beings which, according to the Qur'an, can be malevolent as well as pious. For example, in 72:1, we are told that the Prophet Muhammad knew of 'a group of jinn [that] listened to the Quran, and said to their fellow jinn: Indeed, we have heard a wondrous recitation'.

Jinn are not always invisible. According to Brother Abdur Rahman, a 'spiritual practitioner and healer' with '35+ years experience', some 'can fly and move at great speeds' and 'can change their appearance to almost anything they choose'. But often, people who encounter jinn do not even know that what they have encountered are jinn. And so, 'even if a jinn decides to take the form of an animal and come into our physical world, it…involves a very well-activated third eye and strong spiritual sense to see the jinn…'.

Doostdar instead suggests that we think of jinn:

> …not as unknowable beings but as a name for unknowability itself, or in other words, the terrifying encounter with a world that has withdrawn from sense. In this way, jinn are not so much presences as absences…. Jinn are the name that some people give to those occasions when the world slinks away from familiar sense.

4. Pontianak

Where Doostdar's analysis of jinn leads us into the realm of ineffability, the *pontianak* in the pantheon of Malay monsters is anything but abstract. The *pontianak* is a female vampire obsessed with childbirth and the blood from labour. She often appears young and beautiful in order to attract male victims. In this guise, she haunts deserted stretches of motorways and quiet spots, usually in the dead of night, asking passing male motorists for a lift. Occasionally, she might appear to be carrying a baby – which usually turns out to be a gravestone. One tell-tale sign she gives off is the scent of fragrant frangipani. Woe betide the man who does not pay attention to these details and still gives her a lift. If he is lucky enough to escape, he will usually fall ill with fever for several days afterwards.

Blokes who are not so lucky will see her transform into an old, hideous being who will then feed on their intestines and blood, and perhaps castrate them, too. The *pontianak* also eats babies, preferably ripped out fresh from a mother's womb.

Yet this monstrous shapeshifter does not actually symbolise patriarchal fears about female empowerment.

Are you kidding us? Of course the *pontianak* is all about gendered anxieties! Just look at what is needed to subdue her. If you drive an iron nail into a hole at the back of her neck, she will become docile and obedient and might even marry and have children. She will die a normal death and can be buried according to the usual rites. But if the nail is ever removed....

5. Beauty and the Beast

Much digital ink has been spilt over whether *Beauty and the Beast* – specifically, the 2017 Hollywood film version starring Emma Watson – can be considered feminist. To summarise – Watson said yes, every other *Guardian* columnist said no. Yet their arguments centred quite strangely on whether the invention of the washing machine by Belle, i.e., Beauty, qualified as feminist. Again, yes for Watson, no for the *Guardian* columnists.

Much more disturbing is the moral of the story – that if you are kidnapped by a monster and forced to marry him, all you need to do is love him (and all the housework) *and he will change.*

6. Shakespeare in the Bush

A classic introductory text in social anthropology – cultural anthropology for you Americans – is Laura Bohannan's delightful 'Shakespeare in the Bush'. The article starts with a sort of literary wager. Before setting off to do ethnographic fieldwork in West Africa, Bohannan, an American, is told by an English friend that Americans struggle with Shakespeare because he is just too quintessentially English. One can therefore 'easily misinterpret the universal by misunderstanding the particular'.

What follows is such a gem that we've actually referred to it already in *Critical Muslim 20: PostWest*. In his introduction, Shanon Shah wrote:

> Bohannan was stunned and things continued going downhill. The Tiv quibbled about almost every element of the story. They were especially stumped by 'ghost' as a concept. Surely Bohannan meant that what Hamlet saw was an omen sent by a witch? No, Bohannan explained, it was a ghost – 'someone who is dead but who walks around and can talk, and people can hear him and see him but not touch him'.
>
> The Tiv objected. 'One can touch zombies.'
>
> Bohannan tried again. 'A "ghost" is the dead man's shadow.'
>
> Again the Tiv objected. 'Dead man cast no shadows.'
>
> 'They do in my country,' Bohannan snapped. Despite their incredulous smirks the Tiv villagers begged Bohannan to continue.

So a ghost is a ghost and a zombie is a zombie, and never the twain shall meet. Some shapeshifters are just not meant to transition across cultural boundaries.

Or are they? In Bohannan's telling of the story, the Tiv elders seem to be tricksters who have distorted the meaning of a Shakespearean tragedy beyond all recognition. But perhaps the reason why this text remains so popular is that, to make a larger point about cultural bias, Bohannan expertly opened with this variation of a comedy of errors, a very Shakespearean device. Sometimes the slyest shapeshifters are the ones that deceptively stay the same.

7. Tricksters

There's a difference between being a shapeshifter and being a trickster, another archetype that can be found in many cultures. Tricksters are masters of disguise who achieve their goals through wit and cunning rather than strength and aggression. They might use magic and are sometimes morally suspect, but they are almost always loveable rogues. They're also usually men – Norse mythology has Loki, the Greeks have Hermes, the Chinese have the Monkey King, West Africans have Anansi and for Native Americans, there's Coyote. In Muslim contexts, the enormously popular *Maqamat* of Al-Hariri (the twelfth century Arab poet and linguist), showcased the exploits of Abu Zayd, a wanderer and con artist who survived by his wiles and eloquence. The ninth century poet, Abu Nuwas, also became a fixture in numerous collections and oral traditions as a trickster-like libertine.

On the surface, it might seem that tricksters just want to have fun. But it can be argued that they serve as role models for the downtrodden or the marginalised. Tricksters, after all, very often undermine authority or break rigid social rules and regulations. They provide models for latent social reformers. Yet at the same time, trickster figures also foil the hero in pursuit of a noble goal. They might distract the hero and lead him – and it's usually a male hero – astray, steal a crucial object, or pretend to be the hero's friend whilst secretly undermining him.

8. Aliens

Sometimes shapeshifting is in the eye of the beholder. In the 1950s, just after the end of the Second World War, people who reported encounters with aliens often described them as angelic, blond-haired, blue-eyed creatures. This is actually a discernible type in ufology – the Nordic alien. They were largely benign, sent to warn us Earthlings about the dangers of nuclear warfare and to exalt the virtues of spiritual growth.

In the 1960s, contactees started describing different aliens – sinister, grey-skinned, diminutive humanoids with large heads. These aliens abducted humans and performed disturbing experiments on them. Think Roswell and *The X-Files* rather than *E.T.* and *Close Encounters of the Third Kind*. Grey aliens have since inspired conspiracy theorists who believe they represent a government cover-up, or that they are a product of mind-control experiments.

This narrative shift between encounters with Nordic aliens and Greys roughly corresponds with the transition from altruistic post-War reconstruction ideals in the West to the more troubling developments in the Cold War. There have, however, been memorable attempts to reconcile the two archetypes, for example, in the quirky 1976 rock ballad 'Calling Occupants of Interplanetary Craft' by Klaatu, remade by the Carpenters in 1977.

9. Reptilians

Our whole discussion about Grey and Nordic aliens could be complete rubbish, though. According to British conspiracy theorist David Icke, it is the tall, blood-drinking, shape-shifting reptilian humanoids from the Alpha Draconis star system that are out to destroy humanity. Many of us have not met them because they are hiding in underground bases. According to Icke, most of the world's ancient and modern leaders are related to these reptilians, including the Frankish Merovingian dynasty, the Rothschilds, the Bush family and the British Royal family.

Variations of this reptilian conspiracy are part and parcel of a disturbing trend of violence. On Christmas Day in 2020, Anthony Quinn Warner, who referred to a conspiracy of lizard people taking over the planet, detonated a bomb in Nashville that damaged 41 buildings and injured three people. In August 2021, Matthew Taylor Coleman, a Californian surfing school owner, stabbed his two-year-old son and 10-month-old daughter to death with a spearfishing gun because he believed that his wife had passed her 'serpent DNA' to them and that they 'were going to grow into monsters'.

10. The Exorcist

The Exorcist — the 1971 novel by William Peter Blatty and its 1973 film adaptation — is not a story of shapeshifting. It is, rather, a story of demonic possession of an adolescent girl and its religious, specifically Roman Catholic, antidote. But it is the cultural transition that the book and film marked that makes it a fitting item to close our list.

In contemporary Western culture, the possession archetype draws heavily from the New Testament — possession is virtually absent from the Hebrew Scriptures. And given the infamous inquisitions that marked Western Christendom from the Middle Ages to the sixteenth century, you would be forgiven for thinking this was the period when possession was rife. But the 'Golden Age' of demonic possession was actually during the two centuries *after* the Protestant Reformation. And in the modern US, exorcism was previously rare — Catholics were ashamed by it and Protestants thought it was superstitious Catholic heresy.

The Exorcist changed everything. The surge in popularity of exorcisms it augured was followed by the Catholic Church's increasing assertiveness within American public life — and the Church began embracing exorcism openly. There are now courses at the Vatican to train more exorcists, who are needed more urgently to combat newer demonic cultural trends such as yoga and Harry Potter.

Meanwhile, Evangelicals and Pentecostals still could not quite label their activities 'exorcism', which they continued to regard as a Catholic heresy. But they soon had their own post-*Exorcist* flourishing of 'deliverance ministries'. This brand of spiritual warfare swiftly spread throughout Asia, Africa, South America and the Caribbean.

Whatever it is called, the prevalence of exorcism is *not* correlated with a culture's level of scientific advancement, or alleged lack of it. It is, rather, more of an indicator of religious, social, and political upheaval. The most prominent cases of exorcism are almost always political. Accounts of successful exorcisms are usually about identifying the correct religious belief or authoritative religious institution or figure, or they aim to target a rival religion or controversial group or practice as demonic.

But then this raises a chicken-and-egg question: Is it a world in transition that influences exorcism, or is it exorcism that shifts our experience of the world?

CITATIONS

Introduction: Alterations and Convulsions
by Samia Rahman

David Graeber posthumous book, written with David Wengrow, *The Dawn of Everything: A New History of Humanity* is published by Penguin (2022); his anthropological works can be accessed at https://davidgraeber.org/. To find out more about a just transition to a green economy, visit https://climatejusticealliance.org/just-transition/ and to learn more about Seyyed Hossein Nasr's views see Tarik M Quadir, *Traditional Islamic Environmentalism, The Vision of Seyyed Hossein Nasr* (University Press of America, 2013). To read Ankur Barua's discussion of the synthesis of bhakti and tasawwuf see https://jhiblog.org/2022/12/07/bhakti-beyond-borders-sufi-serenades-in-loves-laboratory/ and for more on Ras Khan go to https://en.wikipedia.org/wiki/Raskhan.

Other works cited or referenced include Ziauddin Sardar, editor, *CM10: Sects* (Hurst, 2014), *CM43: Ignorance* (Hurst 2021). See also: Mustafa Akyol, *Reopening Muslim Minds: A Return to Reason, Freedom and Tolerance* (Forum, 2022).

Epistemologies of the South
by Boaventura de Sousa Santos

This essay builds upon a body of previous work that includes Boaventura de Sousa Santos, 1998: 'The Fall of the Angelus Novus: Beyond the Modern Game of Roots and Options', *Current Sociology*, 46, 2, 81-118; 2002: *Toward a New Legal Common Sense: Law, Globalization, and Emancipation.* London: Butterworths; 2009: 'A Non-Occidentalist West?: Learned Ignorance and Ecology of Knowledge', *Theory, Culture & Society*, 26, 7-8, 103-125; 2014: *Epistemologies of the South: justice against epistemicide.* Boulder, London: Paradigm Publishers; 2017: 'The Resilience of Abyssal Exclusions in Our Societies: Toward a Post-Abyssal Law', *Tilburg Law*

Review, 22, 1-2, 237-258; 2018: *The End of the Cognitive Empire. The Coming of Age of Epistemologies of the South*. Durham and London: Duke University Press; 2020a: '*A New Vision of Europe: Learning from the Global South*', in Santos, Boaventura de Sousa; Mendes, José Manuel (eds.), *Demodiversity: Toward Post-Abyssal Democracies*. New York: Routledge, 31-53; 2020b: *Toward a New Legal Common Sense. Law, Globalization, and Emancipation - 3rd Edition*. Cambridge: Cambridge University Press; 2020c: 'The Alternative to Utopia Is Myopia', *Politics & Society*, 48, 4, 567-584; 2021: 'Postcolonialism, Decoloniality, and Epistemologies of the South', *Oxford Research Encyclopedia of Literature;* and the edited volume (with Maria Paula Meneses) from 2019: *Knowledges Born in the Struggle. Constructing the Epistemologies of the Global South*. New York / London: Routledge.

The discussion on Nicholas of Cusa relied upon the following works: the work of João Maria André, 1993: 'O problema da linguagem no pensamento filosófico-teológico de Nicolau de Cusa', *Revista Filosófica de Coimbra*, 4 (2), 369-402; 1995; 'La dimensión simbólica del arte en Nicolás de Cusa', *Anuário Filosófico*, (28), 547-582; 2006: 'Nicolau de Cusa e a Força da Palavra', *Revista Filosófica de Coimbra*, 29 3-32; 2016: 'Relire Descartes à partir de Nicolas de Cues', *Noesis*, 26-27, 135-153; 2019: *Douta ignorância linguagem e diálogo: o poder e os limites da palavra em Nicolau de Cusa*. Coimbra: Coimbra University Press; Nicholas Cusa (1985), *On Learned Ignorance (De Docta Ignorantia)*. Minneapolis: Arthur J. Banning Press. URL: http://cla.umn.edu/sites/jhopkins/DI-I-12–2000.pdf; Jasper Hopkins's 1988 book *Nicholas of Cusa's debate with John Wenck. A Translation and an Appraisal of De Ignota Litteratura and Apologia Doctae Ignorantiae*. Minneapolis: The Arthur J. Banning Press, 3rd Edition and his 1996 publication *Nicolas of Cusa on Wisdom and Knowledge*. Minneapolis: The Arthur J. Banning Press.

Other works referred to were: Abdul Halim Abdul Karim & Muhammad Ibnur (2008), 'The Nature and Concept of Light in Islam: Insights from Al-Ghazali's Mishkat al-Anwar and Scientific Theories Pertaining to Light', *Paper presented at the 1st ISTAC International Conference On Islamic Science and the Contemporary World: 'Islamic Science In Contemporary Education'*. Kuala

Lumpur, January 2008; Abu Hamid Al-Ghazali (1980), *Deliverance from Error*. Translated by Richard J. Mccarthy, S. J., as Freedom and Fulfillment. Boston: Twayne; Giordano Bruno (2009 [1582]), *Las sombras de las ideas (De umbris idearum)*. Translation from the Latim by Jordi Raventós. Madrid: Ediciones Siruela; John Climacus (1959), *The Ladder of Divine Ascent*. Translated by Archimandrite Lazarus Moore. New York, Harper & Brothers; Orlando Fals Borda (2009), *Una sociología sentipensante para América Latina*. Bogotá: Siglo del Hombre Editores and CLACSO; Franz Fanon (1952), *Peau noire, masques blancs*. Paris: Seuil; Antonio Gramsci (1971), *Selections from the Prison Notebooks of Antonio Gramsci*. Ed. and trans. Quintin Hoare and Geoffrey Nowell-Smith. London: Lawrence & Wishart; Patricio Guerrero Arias (2016), *Colonialidad del Saber e Insurgencia de las Sabidurías Otras: Corazonar las Epistemologías Hegemónicas, Como Respuesta de Insurgencia (de)colonial*. Quito: Universidad Andina Simón Bolívar Sede Ecuador; Carl Gustav Jung (1973), *Memories, Dreams, Reflections*. New York: Pantheon Books; Ibn Khaldun (1980), *The Muqaddimah*. Translated from the Arabic by Franz Rosenthal, vol. 3. Princeton, Princeton University Press; Rudyard Kipling (1899), 'The White Man's Burden: The United States and the Philippine Islands', *The Times* (London), February 4, 1899; Nur Kirabaev & Olga Chistyakova (2020), 'Knowing God in Eastern Christianity and Islamic Tradition: A Comparative Study', *Religions*, 11 (675), 1-16; Albert Memmi (1965), *The Colonizer and the Colonized*. New York: Orion Press; Fernando Ortiz (1973), *Contrapunteo cubano del tabaco y el azucar*. Barcelona: Ariel.

Eternity's Sunrise by Naomi Foyle

The Guardian summarised the results of COP27 here: https://www.theguardian.com/environment/2022/nov/20/deal-on-loss-and-damage-fund-at-cop27-marks-climbdown-by-rich-countries

The Transition Network can be explored at their website, including a downloaded guide to the movement: https://transitionnetwork.org/wp-content/uploads/2018/08/The-Essential-Guide-to-Doing-Transition-English-V1.2.pdf?pdf=essential-guide-to-transition-v-1

Shaun Chamberlain can be found at www.darkoptimism.org. His *book The Transition Timeline for a local, resilient future* (Green Books, 2009) remains a useful introduction to the Transition movement. The Reboot Food website www.rebootfood.org, contains a video with George Monbiot introducing the movement. *Tribe: Homecoming and Belonging* by Sebastian Junger (Fourth Estate, 2017) largely concerns the experiences of war veterans.

In a radio programme entitled 'Is Free Speech Under Attack?', the BBC framed the stabbing of Salman Rushdie as a freedom of expression issue; panellists discussed the persecution of writers by states, but no dissenting nuanced view on the offensive content of *The Satanic Verses* was aired: https://www.bbc.co.uk/programmes/w3ct37rt

The demands of Extinction Rebellion US and UK can be compared at their respective websites: https://extinctionrebellion.us/demands-principles and https://extinctionrebellion.uk/.

The world of ASTRA can be explored at www.astratheatre.earth. I read a library copy of *The Perennial Philosophy* by Aldous Huxley (London: Chatto and Windus, 1972) [1946].

The Gaps of History by Saeed Khan

Works mentioned include: Akbar Ahmed, *Discovering Islam: Making Sense of Muslim History and Society 2nd Edition*, (London: Routledge, 2002)'; Gayatari Spivak, 'Can the Subaltern Speak,' in Cary Nelson & Lawrence Grossberg, eds., *Marxism and the Interpretation of Culture*, (Urbana: University of Illinois Press, 1988), pp.271–313; Miguel de Cervantes, *Don Quixote* (New York: Ecco, 2003).

Thomas Kuhn's most famous book arguably is *The Structure of Scientific Revolutions,* (Chicago: University of Chicago Press, 1962). Neil DeGrasse Tyson offers commentary on the decline of the Islamic intellectual tradition in a lecture that is available at https://www.youtube.com/watch?v=_BJW2lX4TPA.

Crying Trees by Leyla Jagiella

For further reading see Reinhold Loeffler, *Islam in Practice: Religious Beliefs in a Persian Village* (Albany: State University of New York Press, 1988); Patricia Crone, *The Nativist Prophets of Early Islamic Iran: Rural Revolt and Local Zoroastrianism* (Cambridge University Press 2012); Jonathan Parkes Allen's Thicket and Thorpe blog which can be accessed at https://thicketandthorp.com/; Mulla Sadra, *Transcendent Philosophy*, (Routledge, 2016); Sophie Strand, *My Body the Ancestor* (The Dark Mountain Project, 2022); Sarra Tlili, *Animals in the Qur'an* (Cambridge University Press, 2012): and Jalaluddin Rumi, *The Essential Rumi* (HarperCollins, New York, 1995).

Shiaphobia by Sarah Shah

For more on Shiaphobia, see Sarah Shah, "Voices that Matter: An Intersectional Analysis of Canadian Muslim Women," *Canadian Council of Muslim Women* (2022), www.ccmw.com/voices-that-matter-report; and Shereen Yousuf, 'Right to Offense, Right to Shiaphobia: A Rhetorical Analysis of Yasir Qadhi's Framings of Offense,' *Journal of Shi'a Islamic Studies* 9, no. 1 (2016): 39-62. DOI: 10.1353/isl.2016.0005. Pp. 39; 40-41

Tūqān and Autobiography as History
by Sameena Kausar

For more on Fadwā Tūqān's writing, see Fadwā Tūqān, *An autobiography: A Mountainous Journey*, Graywolf Press, Saint Paul, Minnesota, U.S.A (1990); Mohammed Sawaie (ed.) *The Tent Generations: Palestinian Poems*, Banipal Books, London, 2022; For more on alternative methods and sources for history, see Carolyn Steedman, *Landscape for a Good Woman: A Story of Two Lives*, Rutgers University Press, New Brunswick, 1987, E.H. Carr *What is History*, Penguin, London, 1961, and Gerda Lerner 'New approaches to the study of women in American History', *Journal of Social History*, Vol. 3, No. 1 (Autumn, 1969), 53-62.

Mum's the Word by Robert Hainault

The books and articles mentioned in the essay are as follows: Liam O'Brian, "Man threatens students at debate", *The Independent*, https://www.independent.co.uk/news/uk/crime/man-threatens-students-at-debate-6291022.html (accessed 6 December).

Joan Smith, "Joan Smith: Strong religious belief is no excuse for intimidation", *The Independent*, 22 January 2012 https://www.independent.co.uk/voices/commentators/joan-smith/joan-smith-strong-religious-belief-is-no-excuse-for-intimidation-6292815.html (accessed 6 December 202). Nick Cohen, "How freedom goes", *The Spectator*, 22 January 2012, https://www.spectator.co.uk/article/how-freedom-goes/ (accessed 6 December 2022). Anonymous, "Islamist stops university debate with threats of violence", National Secular Society website, 17 January 2012, https://www.secularism.org.uk/news/2012/01/islamist-stops-university-debate-with-threats-of-violence (accessed 6 December 2022). Nadia Sam-Daliri, "Sharia law debate attracts threat of violence at Queen Mary university", *East London Advertiser*, 19 January 2012, https://www.eastlondonadvertiser.co.uk/news/education/20972623.sharia-law-debate-attracts-threat-violence-queen-mary-university/ (accessed 6 December 2022). Niall Flynn, "Pegida member says there's still time for Ireland", *Irish Times*, 3 August 2013, https://www.irishtimes.com/news/ireland/irish-news/pegida-member-says-there-s-still-time-for-ireland-1.2744264 (accessed 6 December 2022). Paul Wright, "Who is Anne Marie Waters? Ukip leadership hopeful accused of stoking up anti-muslim hatred", *International Business Times*, 3 July 2017, https://www.ibtimes.co.uk/who-anne-marie-waters-ukip-leadership-hopeful-accused-stoking-anti-muslim-hatred-1628789 (accessed 6 December 2022). James Bloodworth, "Meet Anne Marie Waters – the Ukip politician too extreme for Nigel Farage", *New Statesman*, 18 August 2017, https://www.newstatesman.com/politics/2017/08/meet-anne-marie-waters-ukip-politician-too-extreme-nigel-farage (accessed 6 December 2022). Sean O'Driscoll, "Ukip reject Anne Marie Waters founds own far-right party", *The Times*, 10 October 2017, https://www.thetimes.co.uk/article/ukip-reject-anne-marie-waters-founds-own-far-right-party-95wmr6wrh (accessed 6 December 2022). For Britain National Manifesto 2022, https://www.forbritain.uk/wp-content/uploads/2021/12/Manifesto-2022-new-version-FINAL.pdf (accessed 6 December 2022). PEN American Center, 2005. "The PEN/Martha Albrand Award for First Nonfiction Archived 2006-05-21 at the Wayback Machine." Harris, Sam. *The End of Faith: Religion, Terror, and the Future of Reason*. W.W. Norton and Company. New York 2004. Dawkins, Richard. *The God Delusion*. Bantam Press. London 2006. Asfaruddin, Asma; Warraq, Ibn (2001). "The Quest for the Historical Muhammad". *Journal of the American Oriental Society*. American Oriental Society. 121 (4): 728–729. Donner, Fred. (2001) Review: The Quest for the Historical Muhammad Archived 11 June 2007 at the Wayback Machine. *Middle East Studies Association Bulletin*, University of Chicago. Blois, François de (2000). "Review of Ibn Warraq's *The Origins of the Koran: Classic Essays on Islam's Holy Book*". *Journal of the Royal Asiatic Society*. 10 (1): 88. Christopher Hitchens, "Holy Writ," *The Atlantic*, 1 April 2003, https://www.theatlantic.com/magazine/archive/2003/04/holy-writ/302701/(Accessed 7 December 2022). Douglas Murray, "I am not afraid to say the West's values are better," *The Spectator*, https://www.spectator.co.uk/article/i-am-not-afraid -to-say-the-west-s-values-are-better/3 October 2007 (accessed 7 December 2022). Elizabeth Bruenig, "Is the New Atheism dead?", The New Republic, 4 November 2015 https://newrepublic.com/article/123349/new-atheism-dead (accessed 7 December 2022). Centre for Social Cohesion website, 1 May 2007. https://web.archive.org/web/20070501021959/http://www.socialcohesion.co.uk/(accessed through Wayback Machine 8 December 2022). Centre for Social Cohesion website, 8th December 2022. https://socialcohesion.co.uk/(accessed on 8 December 2022). Parekh, Bhiku. 'Political theory and the multicultural society', Radical Philosophy 095, May/Jun 1999. *The Weekly Dish* (podcast with Andrew Sullivan) "Christopher Hitchens on Religion and Terrorism". https://andrewsullivan.substack.com/p/christopher-hitchens-on-religion (accessed 9 December 2022). The National Counterterrorism Centre, *Report on Terrorism*, 2011. Mona Saddiqui. "Isis: a contrived ideology justifying barbarism and sexual control". *The Guardian*, 24 August 2014. https://www.theguardian.com/commentisfree/2014/aug/24/isis-ideology-islamic-militants-british-appeal-iraq-syria (accessed 8

December). Hitchens, Christopher. *God Is Not Great: How Religion Poisons Everything*. McClelland & Stewart. Toronto 2007. Creath, Richard. "Logical Empiricism", The Stanford Encyclopedia of Philosophy (Winter 2022 Edition). Edward N. Zalta & Uri Nodelman (eds.), forthcoming URL = <https://plato.stanford.edu/archives/win2022/entries/logical-empiricism/>. (Accessed 8 December). Badiou, Alain. *Being and Event*, translated by Oliver Feltham. Continuum, London 2005. Kielinger, Vicky and Paterson, Susan. *Hate Crimes Against London's Muslim Communities: An analysis of incidents recorded by the Metropolitan Police Service 2005-2012*. Diversity and Citizen Focus Directorate, Metropolitan Police. London 2013. https://www.report-it.org.uk/files/hate_crime_against_london_highres_print_final.pdf (accessed 9 December 2022). Sandrin, Paula. "The Rise of Right-Wing Populism in Europe: A Psychoanalytical Contribution". *Financial Crisis Management and Democracy*, Edited by Bettina De Souza Guilherme, Christian Ghymers, Stephany Griffith-Jones, and Andrea Ribeiro Hoffmann. Springer. Switzerland 2021. https://doi.org/10.1007/978-3-030-54895-7 (accessed 9 December 2022).

Clash of Civilisations? by Liam McKenna

All the quotes by politicians can be easily accessed on the internet. Douglas Murray quotes can be found at: http://web.archive.org/web/20080201133647/; http://www.socialaffairsunit.org.uk/blog/archives/000809.php; https://www.lbc.co.uk/radio/presenters/nick-ferrari/douglas-murray-less-terrorism-the-uk-less-islam/

Those interested in the Trojan Horse affair should listen to the *New York Times'* podcast on the topic, 'The Trojan Horse Affair', which Oborne cites, as well as Policy Exchange's response maintaining that the allegations were well-founded, *The Trojan Horse Affair: A Documentary Record* (available online at https://policyexchange.org.uk/publication/the-trojan-horse-affair/), which postdates Oborne's book (and indeed directly responds to Oborne's treatment of the affair,). The Policy Exchange report was published only recently and I am not aware of any in-depth response, but Hamza Syed (who co-hosted the *New York Times* podcast) posted an initial reaction via his

Twitter account (online at https://twitter.com/hamzamsyed/status/160 3099426062417921?lang=en).

Kitab al-I'tibar by Usama Ibn Munqidh has been translated by Paul Michael Cobb and published by Penguin Books in 2008. See also, Christopher de Bellaigue, *The Islamic Enlightenment* (Vintage, London, 2018).

Last Word On Death by Hina Khalid

The Al Ghazali's reflection on death are from *The Remembrance of Death and the Afterlife: Kitab dhikr al-maut wa-ma ba 'dahu; Book* XL of the Revival of the Religious Sciences (*Ihya' 'Ulum al-Din*) translated with an introduction and notes by T.J. Winter (The Islamic Texts Society, Cambridge, 2015). The Tagore poem is from his English poetry collection, *Gitanjali* (full text available here: https://www.sacred-texts.com/hin/tagore/gitnjali.htm).

CONTRIBUTORS

Yassmin Abdel-Magied is a Sudanese-Australian writer, former engineer, social activist and award-winning author ● **Halimah Adisa**, Nigerian poet and writer, is the author of *In Light, Fears and Love* ● **Khaldoon Ahmed** is a psychiatrist working for the NHS in London ● **Naomi Foyle** is a celebrated science fiction writer ● **Robert Hainault**, writer, classical musician, choir conductor and organist, is the author of the novel *The Goldberg Variations* ● **Asyia Iftikhar** is a journalist covering socio-political issues, mental health, LGBTQ+ issues and identity ● **Leyla Jagiella**, a cultural anthropologist and scholar of religion, is currently project coordinator of the Jewish-Muslim Cultural Festival at the Muslimische Akademie Heidelberg, Germany ● **Rehan Jamil** is a social documentary photographer based in London ● **Saeed Khan** is Associate Professor of Teaching in Near East & Asian Studies and Global Studies at Wayne State University, Detroit, Michigan ● **Hina Khalid** is an AHRC Doctoral Scholar at Trinity College, Cambridge, and an Honorary PhD Scholar at the Woolf Institute ● **Sameena Kausar** is Assistant Professor, Department of Arabic, Maulana Azad National Urdu University, Hyderabad, India ● **Liam McKenna** is a paralegal and research assistant working in human rights ● **Adama Juldeh Munu** is a journalist and producer who has worked with TRT World, Al-Jazeera, the Huffington Post, the Middle East Eye and OkayAfrica ● **Steve Noyes** is a British (and Canadian) Muslim writer living in Sheffield ● **Raha Rafii** is a historian, writer, and independent scholar ● **Samia Rahman** is the Director of the Muslim Institute ● **Sarah Shah** is Assistant Professor, Department of Sociology, The University of Toronto Mississauga ● **Nafeesa Syeed** is an award-winning journalist, an opinion editor at the *LA Times,* and is working on her debut novel, from which this story was excerpted ● **Boaventura de Sousa Santos** is Emeritus Professor of Sociology, University of Coimbra (Portugal), and Distinguished Legal Scholar at the University of Wisconsin-Madison ● **amina wadud** is a feminist theologian ● **Robin Yassin-Kassab** is the author of *The Road from Damascus* and other books.